CONTRASTS & CONNECTIONS

18/98

THE SCHOOLS HISTORY PROJECT

This project was set up by the Schools Council in 1972. Its main aim was to suggest suitable objectives for History teachers, and to promote the use of appropriate materials and teaching methods for their realisation. This involved a reconsideration of the nature of History and its relevance in secondary schools, the design of a syllabus framework which shows the uses of History in the education of adolescents, and the setting up of appropriate examinations.

Since 1978 the project has been based at Trinity and All Saints' College, Leeds, where it is one of three curriculum development projects run and supported by the Centre for History Education. The project is now self funding and with the advent of the National Curriculum it has expanded its publications to provide courses throughout the Key Stages for pupils aged 5–16. The project provides INSET for all aspects of National Curriculum History.

Support materials are available for the *Medieval Realms* unit.
Medieval Realms Special Needs Support Material
    Picture Pack ISBN 0–7195–5382–2
    Picture Pack Workbook ISBN 0–7195–7056–5 (single)
                       ISBN 0–7195–7057–3 (pack of 5)
    Teachers' Resource Book ISBN 0–7195–5381–4

Note: The wording and sentence structure of some written sources have been adapted and simplified to make them accessible to all pupils, while faithfully preserving the sense of the original. A bibliography is provided in the Teachers' Resource Book.

© Colin Shephard, Mike Corbishley, Alan Large and Richard Tames, 1991
First published 1991
by John Murray (Publishers) Ltd
50 Albemarle Street, London W1X 4BD

Reprinted 1991 (twice), 1992, 1993, 1994, 1995, 1997

Typeset by Wearset, Boldon, Tyne and Wear
Printed and bound in Great Britain by
Butler & Tanner Ltd, Frome and London

A CIP catalogue record for this book is available from the British Library
ISBN 0–7195–4938–8

S·H·P
THE
SCHOOLS
HISTORY
PROJECT

DISCOVERING THE PAST Y7

CONTRASTS & CONNECTIONS

Colin Shephard (Director, SHP)
Mike Corbishley
Alan Large
Richard Tames

JOHN MURRAY

Contents

Acknowledgements

Illustrations by David Anstey; Peter Bull Art Studio; Art Construction; John Lupton/Linden Artists; Chris Rothero/Linden Artists.

Further illustrations reproduced by kind permission of: **p.2** *bottom* Editions Albert René/Editions Gallimard; **p.21** from *The Roman World* by Mike Corbishley, Kingfisher Books, © Grisewood and Dempsey Ltd, 1986 **p.49** from *Energy through Time* by Joe Scott, Oxford University Press; **p.85** Wharram Research Project; **p.145** from *A New Scottish History* by Melvin, Gould and Thompson, John Murray **p.161, 174** *top*, **182, 191, 212** *all* Richard Leacroft from The Buildings of Early Islam by Helen and Richard Leacroft, © Helen Leacroft.

Photographs reproduced by kind permission of:
cover: *top* British Library, London: *centre* Trustees of the British Museum; *bottom* Sonia Halliday Photographs; **p.1** Trustees of the British Museum; **p.2** *top left* C.M. Dixon; *top right* Grosvenor Museum, Chester; **p.3** *top left* Ronald Sheridan/Ancient Art and Architecture Collection; *top right* Rheinisches Landesmuseum, Trier; *centre* Musée du Louvre, Paris/Réunion des Musées Nationaux; *bottom left and right* Mary Evans Picture Library; **pp.4/5** C.M. Dixon; **p.6** Mansell Collection/Alinari; **p.8** *top* The Mansell Collection; *bottom* Peter Clayton; **p.13** Mary Evans Picture Library; **p.16** Ronald Sheridan/Ancient Art and Architecture Collection; **p.17** *top left* Werner Forman Archive; *top right* G.T. Garvey/Ancient Art and Architecture Collection; *bottom right* Mansell Collection/Alinari; **p.18** Alan Sorrell ©Mark Sorrell (photo: F.W. Wombwell–Robinson); **p.19** Ronald Sheridan/Ancient Art and Architecture Collection; **p.20** C.M. Dixon; **p.23** The Hulton Deutsch Collection; **p.24** *top* Ronald Sheridan/Ancient Art and Architecture Collection; *bottom* C.M. Dixon; **p.25** *top* Musée du Louvre, Paris/Réunion des Musées Nationaux; *centre left and right* Trustees of the British Museum; **p.26** The Museum of London; **p.27** *top, centre bottom, bottom left* Mansell Collection/Alinari; *centre top, bottom right* C.M. Dixon; **p.29** *top, bottom* C.M. Dixon; *centre* Sonia Halliday Photographs; **p.31** Peter Clayton; **p.32** *centre* C.M. Dixon; *bottom left* Rheinisches Landesmuseum, Trier; *bottom right* Dr P.J. Reynolds/Butser Ancient Farm; **p.35** *top* Alan Sorrell/English Heritage; *bottom* English Heritage; **p.36** Mansell Collection/Alinari; **p.37** Grosvenor Museum, Chester; **p.39** Ronald Sheridan/Ancient Art and Architecture Collection; **p.41** Ivan Lapper/English Heritage; **p.43** English Heritage; **p.45** English Heritage; **p.46** *top* Ronald Sheridan/Ancient Art and Architecture Collection; *bottom* Michael Holford; **p.49** C.M. Dixon; **p.50** *left* Mary Evans Picture Library; *centre* Peter Connolly; **p.52** C.M. Dixon; **p.53** Mary Evans Picture Library; **p.55** Sonia Halliday and Laura Lushington; **pp.56/7** Roger Wood; **p.59** Jason Wood; **p.61** Trustees of the British Museum; **p.63** British Library; **p.64** *top left* The Pierpont Morgan Library, New York; *top right* The Hulton Deutsch Collection; *bottom left* Bodleian Library, Oxford; *centre and bottom right* British Library; **p.65** *top left* The Hulton Deutsch Collection; *top right* British Library; *bottom left* Michael Holford; *centre right* The Master and Fellows of Trinity College, Cambridge; *bottom right* Bodleian Library, Oxford; **p.66** L. and R. Adkins; **pp.68–77** *all* Michael Holford; **p.79** Dean and Chapter of Durham Cathedral; **p.82** *top* Cambridge University Collection: Crown Copyright 1991 MoD; *bottom* Michael Holford; **p.83** *top left* English Heritage; *top right* Walter Rawlings/Robert Harding Picture Library; **p.84** Cambridge University Collection; **p.85** Peter Dunn/English Heritage; **p.86** British Library; **p.87** *top right* Bodleian Library, Oxford; *bottom right* British Library; **p.88** *top* The Hulton Deutsch Collection; *bottom* AA Picture Library; **p.89** *both* British Library; **p.91** *all* British Library; **p.93** *top, bottom centre, bottom left and right* British Library; *top centre* The Bridgeman Art Library; **p.95** *all* British Library; **p.98** Peter Dunn/English Heritage; **p.99** Bodleian Library, Oxford; **p.100** British Library; **p.101** *both* British Library; **p.105** *top* Scala; *bottom* British Library; **p.106** British Library; **p.107** *top* Michael Holford; *bottom* The Bridgeman Art Library; **p.108** Peter Bartlett/Ludlow Museum, Shropshire Museum Service; **p.109** AA Picture Library; **p.110** Ronald Sheridan/Ancient Art and Architecture Collection; **p.111** *top* Bibliothèque Arsenal, Paris/Photographie Bulloz; *bottom* British Library; **p.112** Michael Holford; **p.117** British Library; **p.118** Mary Evans Picture Library; **p.119** Public Record Office; **p.120** *top* British Library; *bottom* The Bridgeman Art Library; **p.122** Ronald Sheridan/Ancient Art and Architecture Collection; **p.123** Masters of the Bench of the Inner Temple/E.T. Archive; **pp.124/5** Scala; **pp.128/9** The President and Fellows of Corpus Christi College, Oxford/The Bodleian Library, Oxford; **pp.130–5** *all* British Library; **p.136** The Bridgeman Art Library; **p.138** *top* British Library; *centre* Windsor Castle, Royal Library, ©1991 H.M. the Queen; *bottom* House of Commons Public Information Office; **pp.141–2** *both* British Library; **p.145** The Master and Fellows of Corpus Christi College, Cambridge; **p.146** Windsor Castle, Royal Library, ©1991 H.M. the Queen; **p.147** Robert Harding Picture Library; **p.149** *top and bottom left* Michael Holford; *bottom right* Michael Jenner; **p.153** Sonia Halliday Photographs; **p.154** *top left* Screen Ventures; *top right, bottom left and right* James Green/Robert Harding Picture Library; **p.156** Peter Stephenson/Planet Earth Pictures; **p.163** *top* Bibliothèque Nationale, Paris; *bottom* Peter Sanders/Screen Ventures; **p.164** *both* Bibliothèque Nationale; **p.170** *top left* British Library; *bottom left* Trustees of the British Museum; *top right* Bodleian Library, Oxford; *bottom right* Musée du Louvre/Réunion des Musées Nationaux, Paris; **pp.172/3** Rijksmuseum, Amsterdam; **p.176** *left* Trustees of the Chester Beatty Library, Dublin; *right* Bildarchive Preussischer Kulturbesitz/D. Graf/Museum für Islamische Kunst; **p.177** *both* Bibliothèque Nationale; **p.178** *left* Kunsthistorische Museum, Vienna; *right* Bruno Barbey/Magnum; **p.179** *top* Werner Forman Archive; **p.180** Bibliothèque Nationale; **p.181** *top right* Bibliothèque Nationale; *bottom left* Landesbildstelle Rhineland/Hetjens Museum, Dusseldorf; **p.183** Bibliothèque Nationale; **p.184** Bodleian Library, Oxford; **p.186** Sonia Halliday Photographs; **pp.188/9** Freer Gallery of Art, Smithsonian Institution, Washington D.C.; **p.191** Edinburgh University Library; **p.194** Ronald Sheridan/Ancient Art and Architecture Collection; **p.195** Kunglingen Biblioteket, Stockholm; **p.197** *top right* Michael Holford; *bottom left* Bibliothèque Nationale; **p.199** British Library; **p.201** *top, bottom right* Bibliothèque Nationale; *bottom left* Escorial Library/Patrimonio Nacional, Madrid; **p.202** *left* The Mansell Collection; *right* Mary Evans Picture Library; **p.203** *top* British Library; *bottom* Bibliothèque Nationale; **p.204** Wellcome Institute Library, London; **p.205** *top* Michael Jenner/Robert Harding Picture Library; *bottom* Bibliothèque Nationale; **p.207** British Library; **p.209** *top* British Library; *bottom* Sonia Halliday Photographs; **p.210** *top* Edinburgh University Library; *bottom* Sonia Halliday Photographs; **p.211** *top left* Sonia Halliday Photographs; *top right* The Mansell Collection; *bottom left* M. and J. Lynch/Ancient Art and Architecture Collection; **p.214** Sonia Halliday Photographs; **p.215** Ole Woldbye/David Collection, Copenhagen.

THE ROMAN EMPIRE

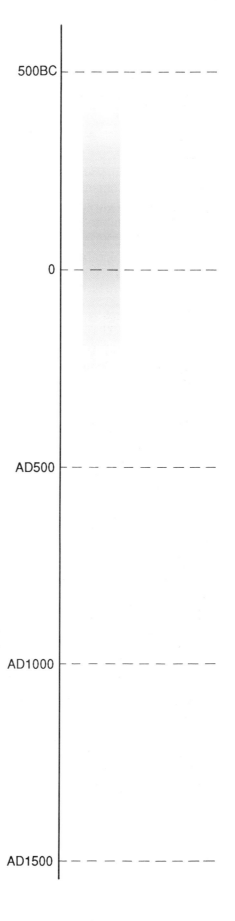

500BC

0

AD500

AD1000

AD1500

Who were the Romans?

1. What is your image of the Romans? Write down three words that sum up the Romans for you.

SOURCES 1–8 show various pictures of Roman people and of things that the Romans made. In this unit we will be using evidence like this to investigate life in the Roman EMPIRE, 2000 years ago. You'll need to look carefully at the evidence.

2. Look at Sources 1–8. Which ones best fit your ideas about the Romans?
3. Decide which of Sources 1–8 were made at the time of the Roman Empire – from the first to the fourth centuries AD.
4. Which of the sources were made more recently – in the last 150 years?
5. What do these sources tell us about the Romans – for example, how they dressed and what they did in their leisure time?
6. What else would you like to find out about the Romans?

▲ **SOURCE 1** The painting on the cover of a Roman man's coffin. He was buried in Egypt in the third century AD

▲ **SOURCE 2** A modern reconstruction of what a Roman soldier would have looked like in the first century AD, and the weapons he would have carried

▼ **SOURCE 3** A cartoon drawn in 1967 by a French artist. The cartoon is about life in Gaul (France) while it was occupied by the Romans

▲ **SOURCE 4** An aqueduct in Spain, built by the Romans in the second century AD to carry fresh water for the city of Segovia

▲ **SOURCE 5** A wall painting from the third century AD showing farmworkers in Roman-occupied Germany

▲ **SOURCE 6** A carving from the second century AD showing four stages in a boy's life

▲ **SOURCE 7** A picture of Roman women, painted about 100 years ago

▲ **SOURCE 8** A drawing of gladiators, who fought to the death to entertain Roman people. It was drawn about 100 years ago

From village to Empire

The beginnings of Rome

◄ **SOURCE 1**
Drawing of a Roman coin from AD120

JULIUS and Livia settled down happily at their mother's feet. She was going to tell them their favourite story. They had heard it many times before, but they still enjoyed being told how their city, Rome, had been founded many years ago. This is what she said.

'Long ago and in a faraway country lived Venus. She was the goddess of love and beauty. She had a son called Aeneas. She was very proud of him. He had fought bravely in defending his city, Troy, against its enemies.

'But when Troy was captured, Aeneas had to flee for his life. He made a long voyage by land and sea and eventually reached the beautiful plain of Latium in Italy. Here he married the King's daughter and founded a kingdom of his own.

'Many, many years passed, and the kingdom entered troubled times. Numitor, one of Aeneas' descendants, was now King. His daughter Rhea had just given birth to twin sons called Romulus and Remus. Their father was Mars, the mighty god of war. It should have been a happy time for Numitor. But his wicked brother Amulius wanted his kingdom and drove Numitor out of the country.

'Amulius ordered his soldiers to throw the babies Romulus and Remus into the River Tiber. But the babies didn't drown. They were washed ashore. A she-wolf heard them crying, took them away and cared for them alongside her cubs. Later they were discovered by a shepherd, who carried the boys home and looked after them as if they were his own children.

'The boys grew up strong and brave, and with their help their grandfather, King Numitor, won back his throne from his brother.

'Romulus then began to build a city of his own. He chose a place where the River Tiber could be crossed, surrounded by seven hills overlooking the river. But Remus made fun of him and the city he was building. The twins fought each other and Remus was killed. But Romulus carried on building. And when he finished his city he became its first King. The city was called Rome.

'After reigning as King for forty years, Romulus mysteriously disappeared in the darkness of a great storm and became a god.'

1. Which scene from the story do Sources 1 and 2 illustrate?
2. Find three things in the story that you think might be true.
3. Find three things in the story which you think are unlikely to be true.
4. Find out what things other people in the class have chosen. Then discuss whether Sources 1 and 2 prove that the story is true.
5. What does the fact that the Romans made the objects in Sources 1 and 2 tell us about the story?
6. Teachers and parents told this story to Roman children. What do you think they wanted them to learn from it? Here are some suggestions:
   ■ Romans are descended from gods. The gods like the Romans.
   ■ Good Romans should be loyal to their city and be prepared to kill for it.
   Now add your own ideas.

Activity

This story would make a good cartoon strip. Draw a strip with five frames. First of all choose what you think are the five most important scenes from the story. Then draw a picture and write a caption for each scene.

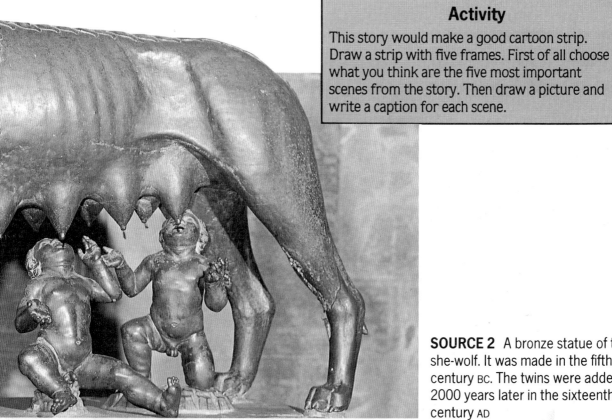

SOURCE 2 A bronze statue of the she-wolf. It was made in the fifth century BC. The twins were added 2000 years later in the sixteenth century AD

We do not know how much of the story of Romulus and Remus is true. We do know that around 753BC there were some villages on the seven hills overlooking the River Tiber. The people who lived there were called the Latins. The villages were gradually combined to form a city called Rome.

This city grew in importance until it controlled the whole of Italy, and later the whole of the land around the Mediterranean Sea.

We are going to look at two important moments (or turning points) in Rome's history – moments when Rome won decisive victories that allowed it to become more powerful.

Turning point 1 – the defeat of the Etruscans

The king of Rome in the sixth century was not Roman. He came from a TRIBE called the Etruscans and was called Tarquin the Proud. He was a harsh and unpopular ruler and the Romans drove him out. They were determined never to have a king again. Instead they set up a Republic, which meant that the citizens of Rome elected their rulers for just a year at a time.

It wasn't only the Etruscans who were troubling the Romans. Other neighbouring tribes, who wanted to capture the Romans' rich farming land, were always making raids.

To start with, the Romans only fought to defend themselves. But as they grew stronger and better at fighting they realised that attack was better than defence. They began to defeat the neighbouring tribes and take over their lands. Some tribes were wiped out, others surrendered and became allies. By 250BC, the Romans controlled the whole of Italy.

Turning point 2 – war with Carthage

Across the Mediterranean Sea, just a few hundred miles away, lay the great North African city of Carthage. You can see the CARTHAGINIAN EMPIRE marked on Source 4.

The Carthaginians traded all over the Mediterranean. The Romans were trying to expand their trade, but the Carthaginians treated the Roman traders as pirates and sank their ships. The Carthaginians also controlled much of Sicily – an

▼ **SOURCE 3** A Roman warship

island only a few miles off the coast of Italy – which was a fertile corn-growing area. It was only a matter of time before Rome went to war against Carthage.

The Romans had become skilful soldiers during their conquest of Italy. They had a large army of 100,000 soldiers. But they were faced with an enemy which had an excellent navy. To win the war, the Romans had to win control of the sea. They had no navy and little experience as sailors. However, they began building a huge battle fleet.

They also invented new tactics. On each ship they built a kind of drawbridge, called a *corvus*, with a huge iron spike on the end. The *corvus* stood upright by the mast. When an enemy ship was close it was lowered so that the spike sank into the enemy's deck. The Roman soldiers then charged across onto the enemy ship.

With the new navy, Rome managed to capture Sicily. The war with Carthage seemed to be over.

But peace did not last long. Hannibal, the leading Carthaginian general, intended to defeat the Romans once and for all. He planned a daring attack on Rome itself.

Hannibal was a determined and skilful general. When he was only nine years old his father had made him swear to be always an enemy of Rome. In 218BC Hannibal set out with an army of nearly 100,000 troops and 36 elephants.

---

1. Look at Source 3. Match up these captions with the numbers on the picture:
   - look-out tower
   - oars
   - a battering ram just out of sight below the surface of the water
   - soldiers with spears and shields
   - mascot – a crocodile, showing that this boat had fought successfully in the Nile.
2. How would each feature be useful in battle?
3. No drawing of a *corvus* has survived. Using the information given above, draw what you think it would have looked like.

Activity

You are a general in the Roman army. The government in Rome (called the Senate) has asked you to write a short report on Hannibal.

They want to know if you think he presents any danger to Rome.

Use the information in Source 4 to help you write your report. Mention:
- how Hannibal might try to get to Rome
- the obstacles in his way
- the size of his army compared with the Roman army
- whether you think he can succeed.

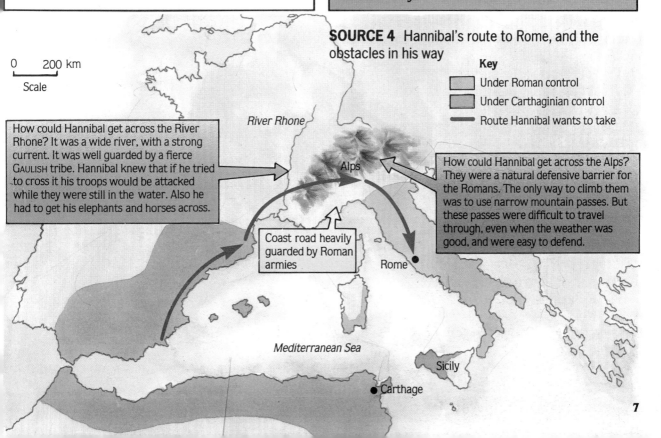

SOURCE 4 Hannibal's route to Rome, and the obstacles in his way

Key
- Under Roman control
- Under Carthaginian control
- Route Hannibal wants to take

0   200 km
Scale

River Rhone

Alps

How could Hannibal get across the River Rhone? It was a wide river, with a strong current. It was well guarded by a fierce GAULISH tribe. Hannibal knew that if he tried to cross it his troops would be attacked while they were still in the water. Also he had to get his elephants and horses across.

How could Hannibal get across the Alps? They were a natural defensive barrier for the Romans. The only way to climb them was to use narrow mountain passes. But these passes were difficult to travel through, even when the weather was good, and were easy to defend.

Coast road heavily guarded by Roman armies

Rome

Mediterranean Sea

Sicily

Carthage

The Romans were sure that they were safe from Hannibal. But they were wrong. The information on this page tells you how Hannibal dealt with the obstacles in his way(see Source 4 on the previous page).

The River Rhone

Hannibal first sent a small advance force of his best soldiers to cross the river secretly.

Hannibal then filled small boats and canoes with the light soldiers. The large boats were placed upstream of the light boats to protect them from the full force of the current.

Horses were towed behind the boats. One man on each side of the stern guided the horses.

As they crossed, the GAULISH tribesmen poured out of their camp — just as Hannibal had expected. But Hannibal's advance party rushed in to attack them and the tribesmen ran away.

The elephants then crossed, on huge rafts covered with earth and grass.

The Alps and the Allobrogians

Hannibal could not march along the well guarded coast road to Italy. So he took the only possible route, over the Alps, even though it was winter.

The Allobrogian tribe, who were friends of the Romans, had a large army in a strong position overlooking the Carthaginians' route down from the mountains.

Hannibal ordered the fires to be lit in his camp. He left most of his army there. He led his best soldiers to ambush the Allobrogians.

Up on the Alps the snow was already falling heavily. Hannibal saw that his men were in low spirits, because they had suffered much. To cheer them up, he called them together and pointed out Italy, which lay close beneath the mountains. The path down was very narrow and steep.

It was a treacherous path. Neither the soldiers nor the animals could tell where they were treading in the deep snow. Those that stepped wide of the path fell down the cliff to certain death.

Hannibal got his soldiers to cut a path out of the snow. After a day the path was wide enough for the packhorses and animals. It took three days to get the elephants through.

SOURCE 5 Hannibal's army crossing the Alps, drawn in the nineteenth century

SOURCE 6 Roman coin showing a war elephant

SOURCE 7 Written by the historian Polybius, about 60 years after the events

The elephants were of great use to the Carthaginians. The enemy were too terrified of their appearance to come anywhere near them. 99

Look at Sources 5, 6 and 7.
1. Why was Hannibal so keen to take war elephants with him?
2. What problems did the elephants cause for Hannibal?

Hannibal had started his campaign with 100,000 soldiers; 60,000 climbed the Alps with him, but only 23,000 reached Italy. Hannibal knew his army might not be strong enough to attack Rome, and he had no siege engines. He marched south until he was within three days' march of Rome. The people of Rome were nervous, but didn't panic. They waited.

Hannibal decided against attack. Instead he continued south, looking for supplies and trying to persuade the people of other cities to join him against Rome.

Hannibal is defeated

Hannibal spent the next fifteen years in Italy. The Romans sent a number of armies to fight him, but he defeated them every time. Finally the Romans changed their tactics. Instead of fighting him, they decided to wear him down. They stopped any extra soldiers or supplies getting through to him and they refused to fight any more big battles.

Hannibal's army grew weaker with every year that passed. He had already decided that he was not strong enough to attack Rome, and few of the Italian tribes joined him. They all stayed loyal to Rome.

Meanwhile, the Roman army concentrated its efforts on attacking Carthage. After fifteen years in Italy, Hannibal was ordered home to help defend Carthage from the Romans.

Activity

You are one of Hannibal's soldiers. You have just heard that you are being called home from Italy. You are writing to your family at home in Carthage, to explain why the campaign has failed.
a) Do you think Hannibal is a good general? Tell them how he crossed the obstacles which were in the way of the army. Did he do well?
b) Should he have taken the elephants? Some people are grumbling that the elephants have held you up.
c) Some people are saying he should not have climbed the Alps during the winter. What do you think?
d) Others say he should have attacked Rome straight away. What do you think?

In 202BC, near Carthage, Hannibal was defeated by the Roman general Scipio. The Carthaginians were beaten. Their lands in southern Spain were taken by Rome. Fifty years later, the city of Carthage itself was totally destroyed, and its North African lands were also taken by Rome.

Rome was now the strongest power around the Mediterranean Sea, and her Empire grew rapidly. In the 70 years after the defeat of Hannibal, Macedonia (now south-east Europe), Greece and Asia Minor (part of modern Turkey) came under Roman rule. Egypt was under Rome's influence.

Some countries that the Romans conquered became PROVINCES. New Roman towns called COLONIES were established. Other neighbouring countries became allies. The defeat of Carthage meant that Rome was the master of the whole Mediterranean area. But as we shall see, the Romans still found it difficult to control all these lands.

1. Historians see Hannibal's defeat as a major turning point in Rome's history. How did the defeat of Hannibal change things for Rome?

9

How was Rome governed?

AFTER the Romans threw out the hated Etruscan King, Tarquin the Proud, they were determined not to allow one man to become so powerful again. Instead, they wanted to choose the people who would govern them. They developed a new kind of government which they called *res publica* which meant 'a matter for the people'. See if you think Roman government was really 'a matter for the people'.

▼ **SOURCE 1** The Republic

RES PUBLICA – THE REPUBLIC

THE CITIZENS OF ROME
Divided into two classes

The PATRICIANS (nobles who owned large estates and were descended from the founders of the city)

They all met in the ASSEMBLY Here they elected

elected

elected

ele

TWO CONSULS governed the city. They were elected for one year only and could not be elected again until 10 years had passed. They both had to agree before a decision could be made

THE MAGISTRATES
Officials who were appointed to be judges, to look after the city's finances and other jobs

advised

retired

THE SENATE. When magistrates retired they became members of the senate. They had a lot of experience and gave advice to the CONSULS. THE SENATE became very important and ended up controlling Rome.

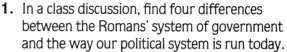

When the Romans spoke of 'the people' they meant Roman CITIZENS. This did not include the many slaves in Rome, most of whom were prisoners of war. Nor did it include women.
- Only Roman citizens were able to vote.
- Only Roman citizens could be elected into government jobs.
- All Roman citizens were expected to fight in the army when needed.

1. In a class discussion, find four differences between the Romans' system of government and the way our political system is run today.
2. How did the Romans make sure that no one man could become too powerful?
3. When Hannibal was invading Italy, the rulers of Rome had to make quick decisions.
a) Can you think of any features of the Roman system that would have made it difficult to reach quick decisions?
b) Can you think of changes that might make quick decisions easier in times of emergency?

The PLEBEIANS (ordinary peasant farmers and craftsmen)

In reality, Patricians and Plebeians were never equal, even though they had equal rights. Many Plebeians were poor and had to work, while many of the Patricians – who were very rich – had slaves and servants. This meant they could spend their time on politics. The result was that most of the magistrates and senators were Patricians.

All Roman citizens served in the army. As Rome conquered more territory, soldiers spent more time away from Italy. Many of the Patricians led Roman armies in the wars and returned home even richer, with many valuables from the conquered lands.

The Plebeians, however, were just ordinary soldiers. Some returned from the fighting to find their farms in ruins. They were forced to sell their land to the rich, and drifted into Rome to live in the crowded slums. The government tried to keep them happy with hand-outs of free bread, but there were sometimes very bad riots.

TRIBUNES were appointed to protect the ordinary people against unfair treatment

Activity

It is 133BC. A tribune called Tiberius Gracchus has suggested that the big estates of the Patricians should be divided up. The land should be shared out between the poor, who would then farm it.

Gracchus' idea is going to be debated in the Assembly.

Carry out this debate in your classroom. One person will be Gracchus. Other people will be Patricians and Plebeians. There might also be some women arguing that they should have a say.
a) What are the Patricians' arguments for keeping things as they are?
b) What are the Plebeians' arguments for sharing out the land?
c) What are the women's arguments for being involved in making decisions?

Did the Republic work?

The Republic under threat

IN THE first century BC, Rome was faced with many problems (see Source 1).

▼ **SOURCE 1** Map of the Roman Empire in 100BC

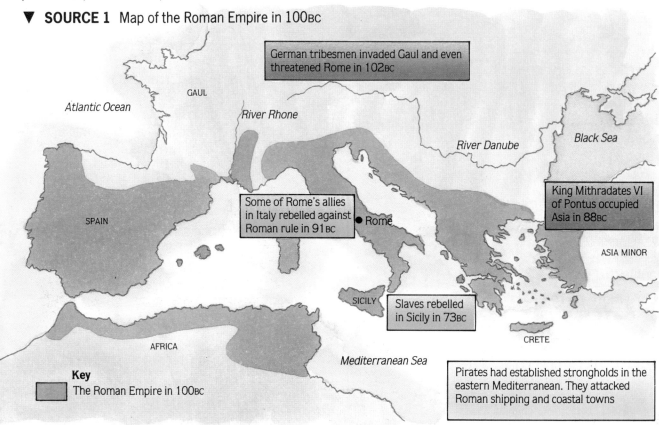

German tribesmen invaded Gaul and even threatened Rome in 102BC

GAUL

Atlantic Ocean

River Rhone

River Danube

Black Sea

King Mithradates VI of Pontus occupied Asia in 88BC

SPAIN

Some of Rome's allies in Italy rebelled against Roman rule in 91BC

● Rome

ASIA MINOR

SICILY

Slaves rebelled in Sicily in 73BC

CRETE

AFRICA

Mediterranean Sea

Pirates had established strongholds in the eastern Mediterranean. They attacked Roman shipping and coastal towns

Key
The Roman Empire in 100BC

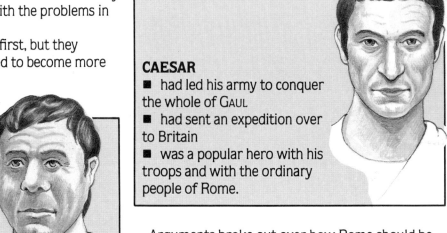

Rome depended on army generals like Pompey and Julius Caesar to deal with threats to Rome. They had been successful in dealing with the problems in Source 1.

The two men were friends at first, but they became deadly rivals as each tried to become more powerful than the other.

SOURCE 2

POMPEY
■ had cleared pirates out of the Mediterranean
■ had won back Asia Minor (modern Turkey)
■ had conquered Syria and Palestine
■ had the support of the Senate.

SOURCE 3

CAESAR
■ had led his army to conquer the whole of GAUL
■ had sent an expedition over to Britain
■ was a popular hero with his troops and with the ordinary people of Rome.

Arguments broke out over how Rome should be governed. Some Romans were beginning to think that Rome would be safer if one of these generals took over completely. They thought that the Republic wasn't very good at dealing with the problems Rome faced.

The SENATE disliked Caesar and supported Pompey (we'll see why very soon), and ordered Caesar to get rid of his army. Caesar ignored them, and in 48BC defeated Pompey in battle.

Most ordinary Romans were quite happy to let Caesar take over as 'DICTATOR for life', even though he had not been elected.

But this did not last very long. Sources 4 and 5 tell you what happened next.

▶ **SOURCE 5** Caesar's murder, painted in the nineteenth century

The murderers were all SENATORS. Most of them were Caesar's enemies but they also included Brutus, whom Caesar was very fond of.

SOURCE 4 Written by the Roman historian Suetonius, about 175 years after the events

"As Caesar took his seat in the Senate, the conspirators gathered about him as if to pay their respects. One of them, Casca, stabbed him just below the throat. As Caesar tried to leap to his feet, he was stopped by another wound. When he saw that he was beset on every side by daggers, he muffled his head in his robe. He was stabbed 23 times."

Why did they murder Caesar?

Many different explanations have been given for why the senators murdered Caesar:

- They thought he was becoming too powerful.
- Some thought he wanted to become King, and that would mean the end of the Republic.
- Some of the senators were jealous of him.
- The senators disliked Caesar because he was arrogant and acted as though he was superior.
- The Senate was worried that he was on the side of the Plebeians and wanted to make the Senate less powerful.

Now read Sources 6–12, which tell you more about Julius Caesar.

SOURCE 6 Some of Caesar's actions that had made him popular with the poor

- *Caesar helped the unemployed by selling them land cheaply.*
- *He provided building work in Rome.*
- *He made taxes fairer.*

SOURCE 7 From Cicero's letters. Cicero was an important Roman politician

a) Written after Julius Caesar had been to stay with him. Caesar brought with him many servants and friends who all needed entertaining

"Julius Caesar was not the sort of guest to whom you would say, 'Please come again on the way back'. Once is enough."

b) Written after Caesar ignored the rules for appointing consuls

"At one o'clock in the afternoon, Caesar announced the election of a consul to serve until 1 January, which was the very next morning. . . . You laugh. If you were here you'd weep. What if I told you everything? There were countless similar incidents."

DID THE REPUBLIC WORK?

SOURCE 8 The Roman writer Suetonius records the senators' criticism of Caesar

He accepted excessive honours. He became consul several times and dictator for life. He accepted honours that should only be given to a god: a gold throne, statues beside those of the gods, a special priest, and one of the months of the year was named after him.

At the Latin Festival someone placed on his statue a laurel wreath with a white ribbon tied to it [the white ribbon was the sign of a King]. The tribunes gave orders that the ribbon be removed, but Caesar told them off. From that time on he could not get rid of the rumours that he wanted to be King.

SOURCE 9 Written by the Greek historian Cassius Dio, about 270 years after the events

Caesar pardoned those who warred against him [in the war with Pompey] and gained a great reputation, both for bravery and for goodness.

SOURCE 10 Written by the Greek writer Plutarch, about 150 years after the events

It was unthinkable that Caesar would ever do so great a crime as destroy the Roman Republic.

SOURCE 11 Suetonius makes his own judgement

It was the following action that caused the deadly hatred of the Senate against him: when they approached him he refused to rise.

SOURCE 12 Some rumours about Caesar which were going around in Rome

■ He planned to move the capital of the Empire to Egypt.
■ He had ordered many opponents to be beheaded, or whipped to death, and he'd burned their homes.
■ He put his statue among the statues of kings.
■ He had love affairs with many men and women.

1. Read Sources 6–12. Decide whether any of the sources support or contradict the reasons for Caesar's murder given on page 13.
2. Do Sources 6–12 suggest any other reasons for Caesar's murder?
3. Working with a partner, decide which of the reasons is the most important. List them in order of importance. If two reasons seem equally important, put them side by side.
4. The picture in Source 5 is going to be used in a book about Caesar. You have been asked to write an explanation of Caesar's murder to go with the picture. In a headline and a single paragraph explain why you think the senators murdered Caesar.

The end of the Republic?

The people were outraged at Caesar's murder. The citizens of Rome took matters into their own hands. They gave Caesar's body a grand public cremation in the centre of the city, and then ran riot. They chased the murderers out of Rome, killed some of them and burned their houses.

Caesar left the vast majority of his wealth to his adopted son Octavian. But when Caesar's will was read out in public the citizens of Rome found they had each been left money.

If the murderers of Caesar had hoped for a return to the REPUBLIC, they were disappointed. Only months later, Octavian (who was only eighteen years old), helped by his supporters (including many soldiers loyal to Caesar), marched on Rome. They were determined to take revenge on Caesar's murderers. In the next five years 300 senators and 2000 other citizens were executed. In 42BC the last republican leaders, Brutus and Cassius, were defeated in battle.

Octavian was too clever to abolish the Republic and declare himself EMPEROR. But most historians agree that the Republic was ended, and that Octavian – who was given a new name, Augustus – was the first Emperor. The Roman Republic had become the Roman Empire.

See if you agree. Read the following sources and then answer the questions that follow.

SOURCE 13 Augustus ordered these things to be inscribed outside his grave for everybody to read

In my sixth and seventh consulships, after I had stamped out the civil wars, and at a time when I was in absolute control of everything, I transferred the Republic from my own control to the Senate and the people of Rome.

SOURCE 14 Some of the things that a biography by Suetonius says about Augustus

■ He first took the consulship by leading his armies against Rome and sending soldiers as messengers to demand the office for him. When the Senate hesitated, one of the soldiers threw back his cloak, and showing the hilt of his sword said, 'This will make him consul, if you do not'.
■ He thought of restoring the Republic but he decided it would be dangerous to share power between several people.

SOURCE 15 Written by a modern historian

The Plebeians continued to re-elect Augustus as consul every year. His popularity with them was overwhelming and gave him all the powers he needed.

SOURCE 16 In 27 BC, after Augustus handed back power to the Senate, the Senate passed a law giving the power back to him

. . . that he might have the right and power to do whatever he shall judge to be in the best interests of the state.

1. According to Source 14, how did Augustus become consul?
2. Did Augustus give back power to the Senate and people of Rome?
3. According to Source 13, why could Augustus not have done this earlier?
4. Why might the Plebeians keep on electing Augustus as consul?

AUGUSTUS

He sent soldiers to the senate to demand the office of consul for him.

The Plebeians re-elected Augustus as consul thirteen times.

A journey through Rome

UNDER Augustus the Roman Empire continued to grow. As it grew, Rome changed. The earliest Romans had been proud of their simple life. They worked hard. They were all willing to join the army when Rome was in danger. But the Empire quickly changed all that. Conquests brought great wealth to Rome. Many goods were imported, and large numbers of slaves were used to do all the hard work. All these things meant that life in Rome changed a great deal.

Augustus made many changes to Rome. He thought that the city was not as great as the capital of the Empire should be. He boasted that he found Rome built of sun-dried bricks and left it built of marble.

He built many public buildings. To guard against fires he employed night-watchmen, and to control floods he widened and cleared the River Tiber which had been full of rubbish.

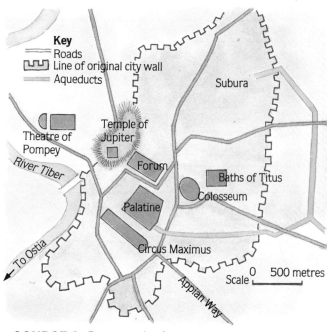

Key
- Roads
- Line of original city wall
- Aqueducts

Subura

Theatre of Pompey

Temple of Jupiter

River Tiber

Forum

Baths of Titus

Colosseum

Palatine

Circus Maximus

To Ostia

Appian Way

Scale 0 500 metres

SOURCE 1 Rome in the first century AD

Activity

What would Rome have looked like if you had visited it in the first century AD?

You are a merchant from the town of Wroxeter in far-away Britain. Sources 2–20 show you what you would have seen on your visit to Rome.

Read through pages 16–21, answering the questions as you go along. As you read about your visit to Rome, mark your route on your own copy of the map in Source 1.

You have arrived in Ostia, the port of Rome, on a cargo ship carrying wine and pottery from Gaul. The port is about 25 kilometres from Rome.

SOURCE 2 Written by the writer Aelius Aristides in the second century AD

So many merchant ships arrive in Rome with cargoes from everywhere, at all times of the year, that the city seems like the world's warehouse. The arrival and departure of ships never stops – it's amazing that the sea, not to mention the harbour, is big enough for all these merchant ships.

You could take a ferry boat to the centre of Rome, but you have had enough of boats. You decide to hire a carriage called a *raeda* (see Source 3).

SOURCE 3 A carving of a carriage

Your journey takes you along the Appian Way to the outskirts of the city. Rome has grown rapidly. It now has well over a million people, mostly living outside the lines of the original city wall. As your carriage drives along the Appian Way, you are surprised to see tombstones lining the road (see Source 4).

SOURCE 4 Tombstones on the Appian Way

SOURCE 5 Written by Paulus, a law writer, about AD200

It is not allowed to bring a corpse into a city, in case the sacred places of the city become polluted. A corpse cannot be buried or cremated within the city.

SOURCE 6 Inscription on a tombstone by the Appian Way

Stranger, my message is short. Stand here and read it. Here is the unlovely tomb of a lovely woman. Her parents gave her the name of Claudia. She loved her husband with all her heart. She had two sons, one of whom she buried. She was charming to talk to and gentle to be with. She looked after the house and spun wool. That's my last word. Go on your way.

1. Historians get much of their information about people in the Roman Empire from inscriptions on tombs. Write down three facts the tombstone tells us about Claudia.

Your carriage is now in a built-up area. Ahead, you can see the remains of the old city wall. Your carriage is not allowed into the city during daylight, so your driver stops at an inn by the Appian Gate. You pay your fare and have a drink at the tavern. Then, as the afternoon gets cooler, you set out for a walk through the centre of the city.

The streets are lined with houses, blocks of flats, shops and workshops. You stop to look at these as you pass by (see Sources 7 and 8).

SOURCE 7 A workshop: a cobbler and a rope-maker at work

SOURCE 8 A shop

Study Source 8 carefully.
2. What is being sold in the shop?
3. How are the goods displayed?
4. Which do you think are the customers and which is the shopkeeper? Explain your answer.

DRAWING BY ALAN SORRELL

SOURCE 9 Reconstruction of a street scene in Rome

SOURCE 10 Written by the humorous writer Juvenal in the second century AD

"*The fear of fires, the constant collapse of houses, the thousand dangers of a cruel city.*

However fast we hurry, there's a huge crowd ahead and a mob behind pushing and shoving. You get dug in the ribs by someone's elbow. Then someone hits you with a long pole, another with a beam from a building or a wine-barrel.

The streets are filthy — your legs are plastered with mud. A soldier's hob-nailed boot lands right on your toe. Togas which have just been patched are torn. A great trunk of a fir tree sways in its rumbling waggon and totters menacingly over the heads of the crowd."

1. Which things in Source 9 could have been reconstructed from ARCHAEOLOGICAL evidence?
2. Which things in the drawing could not have been reconstructed from archaeological evidence?
3. How could historians find out these things?
4. Which gives you the best impression of what it was like in the streets of Rome: Source 9 or Source 10? Explain your answer.

As you walk towards the centre of the city, you notice a huge arch crossing high above the streets (see Source 9). This is one of the AQUEDUCTS that bring water supplies into Rome. This one was repaired by Augustus. It takes water directly into the Palatine, which is where the Emperor lives.

At last you reach the centre of Rome. Here are all the important public buildings.

You arrive at a huge public bath-house. There are many of these in the city. These baths are used by everybody, rich and poor alike. They are cheap, and children are allowed in free. Romans spend hours there chatting with friends and conducting business, as well as bathing.

However they can be rather a nuisance if you live near one. Source 11 is what a Roman poet, Lucius Seneca, wrote about them in the first century AD.

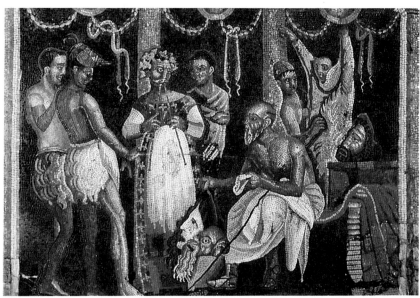

SOURCE 13 First-century mosaic showing actors at the theatre

SOURCE 11

"I live over the public baths. It's sickening. First, there are the 'strongmen' doing their exercises and swinging heavy lead weights about with grunts and groans. Next, the lazy ones, having a cheap massage. I can hear someone being slapped on the shoulders. Then there is the man who likes the sound of his own voice in the bath. And what about the ones who leap into the pool, making a huge splash?"

But the baths are not the only building for leisure and entertainment. Back in Britain some towns have a theatre, but here there are several to choose from. The Emperor Nero loved performances in a small theatre called an *odeon*. In fact, he used to perform himself (see Source 12).

SOURCE 12 Written by the Roman historian Suetonius

"It was forbidden to leave the theatre during a recital by Nero – however urgent the reason – and the gates were kept locked. Women in the audience gave birth, and some of the men were so bored that they pretended to be dead and were carried away to be buried."

You find somewhere to stay for the night in Subura, a busy area of Rome with many shops, taverns and flats. Late in the evening the streets are still teeming with people and very noisy. And when you go to bed for the night, the noise from the street outside seems to get worse, not better!

SOURCE 14 Written by Juvenal

"How can anyone sleep in lodgings here? It's only the rich who get any sleep. The noise of the carts thundering along the narrow streets, and the language of the drivers when they get stuck in a traffic jam, would wake even the heaviest sleeper."

SOURCE 15 A recent account of life in Augustus' Rome

"No traffic was allowed in the centre of Rome during the day, so . . . as night fell, the darkened streets became crowded with cattle going to market, people moving house, people emptying out the cess pits, farmers with their carts carrying oil and wine to deliver to the shops, animal cages on the way to the circus, soldiers moving military supplies."

5. Why do you think no heavy traffic was allowed in central Rome during the day?

A JOURNEY THROUGH ROME

In the morning you step out of your lodgings to find the streets deserted! This can only mean one thing. The chariot races are taking place at the Circus Maximus (see Source 16). As you get closer you can hear the roar of the crowd.

▼ **SOURCE 16** A drawing of the Circus Maximus. The stadium held 250,000 spectators, but not always safely. In the time of the Emperor Nero 13,000 people were killed in a single accident, when banks of seating collapsed

SOURCE 17 Pliny, a Roman writer, describes the chariot races. Four chariots raced each other seven times around the track (five miles). Each team wore different colours: the Reds, the Blues, the Greens and the Whites

“If you've seen one race you've seen them all. I cannot understand why so many thousands want to see chariots racing. Why don't they grow up? I wouldn't mind, if they went to see the skill of the charioteers. But all they support is the colour of the driver's tunic. If they swapped colours in mid-race, I swear they'd follow the colours and change their support too.”

On the next day, you see the Colosseum, a vast AMPITHEATRE, where GLADIATORS and wild animals from all around the Empire fight to the death. You have seen gladiators in Britain, but nothing on this scale. The Colosseum holds 50,000 spectators and the shows go on for weeks! (See page 50.)

1. Before you leave Rome you are going to visit one of the entertainments – the baths, the chariot racing, the theatre or the gladiator fights. Look back at all the information on pages 16–21. Which do you choose, and why? Mark the route to the entertainment you choose on your map.

Now it is time for you to complete the business you came to Rome to discuss. The Romans might discuss business matters at the baths, or even at the public toilets (see Source 18), but you go to the heart of Rome – the Forum (see Source 19). This is an enormous area full of magnificent buildings which are all used for government or religion.

At the centre of the Forum is the Temple of Julius Caesar. It is built over the spot where his body was cremated.

SOURCE 18 A public toilet. There were a large number of public toilets, like this one, in Rome. The toilet became a meeting place for Romans, where business or politics could be discussed, or gossip exchanged

SOURCE 19 An artist's reconstruction of the Forum. The huge building on the left is the Basilica, Rome's business centre

SOURCE 20 Written by the architect Vitruvius in 27 BC

"In the Forum both public and private business is controlled by the town's officials. The site of the Basilica should be fixed next to the Forum in as warm an area as possible so that in winter businessmen may meet there without being troubled by the weather."

It is time for you to leave Rome. You take a Tiber ferry back to Ostia. On the way, you think back over your time in Rome.

Like most people in the Roman Empire, you believe that your life is controlled by gods and goddesses. You make regular offerings (gifts) to the gods at home to earn their approval so that your business will do well. Today, your last day in Rome, you decide to make an offering in the Temple of Jupiter (the King of the gods). You walk up a hill to reach it. From the top you can see many other temples. All the main gods have at least one temple in Rome.

1. When you get back home to Wroxeter, you are asked to produce a two-page leaflet advertising Rome as a good place to visit. Choose features of Rome that would most appeal to Roman citizens living in the rest of the Empire. You can use words and pictures from this book.
2. Do you think that the attractions you have included in your leaflet would appeal to people today?

Life in Rome

SO FAR, you have been looking at Rome from the point of view of a visitor. But what was it like to live in Rome? That would depend a great deal on whether you were rich or poor.

Rome's success in conquering other countries made it a very wealthy city. But this just meant that the gap between the rich and the poor widened. Up on the hills around Rome were elegant mansions owned by the rich. In the city itself were street after street of ramshackle blocks of flats. Almost all of Rome's one million people lived cramped into these poorly-built blocks.

1. Source 3 shows two blocks of flats. Can you see the following:
   - the rich family
   - their slave cooking dinner
   - the poor families
   - the tavern?
2. Write two or more sentences summing up the contrasting living conditions of rich and poor Roman families living in blocks of flats.

SOURCE 1 Written by the Roman writer Juvenal in the first century AD

❝We live in a city shored up with slender props — for that's how the landlords stop the houses from falling down. I would like to live in a place that's free from fires and alarms.❞

SOURCE 2 Written by the politician and historian Tacitus in the first century AD

❝Rome has narrow winding alleyways, irregular streets with tall buildings where the sun never reaches.❞

▼ **SOURCE 3** An artist's reconstruction of flats in Rome

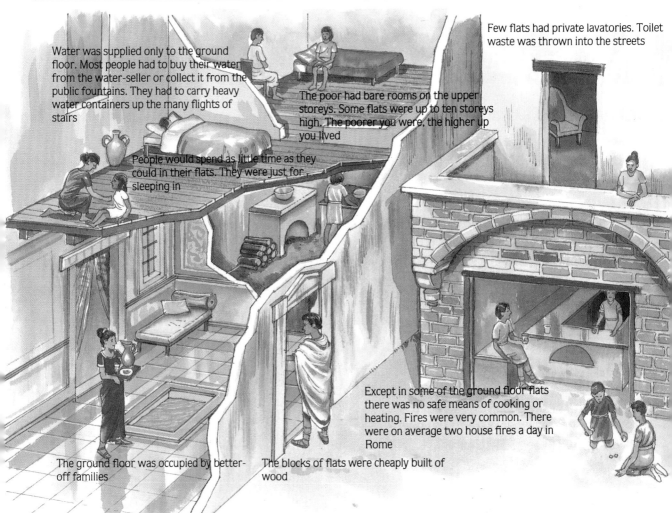

Water was supplied only to the ground floor. Most people had to buy their water from the water-seller or collect it from the public fountains. They had to carry heavy water containers up the many flights of stairs

The poor had bare rooms on the upper storeys. Some flats were up to ten storeys high. The poorer you were, the higher up you lived

People would spend as little time as they could in their flats. They were just for sleeping in

Few flats had private lavatories. Toilet waste was thrown into the streets

Except in some of the ground floor flats there was no safe means of cooking or heating. Fires were very common. There were on average two house fires a day in Rome

The ground floor was occupied by better-off families

The blocks of flats were cheaply built of wood

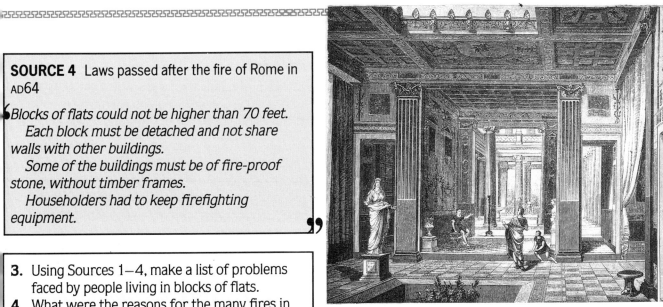

SOURCE 4 Laws passed after the fire of Rome in AD64

Blocks of flats could not be higher than 70 feet.
Each block must be detached and not share walls with other buildings.
Some of the buildings must be of fire-proof stone, without timber frames.
Householders had to keep firefighting equipment.

3. Using Sources 1–4, make a list of problems faced by people living in blocks of flats.
4. What were the reasons for the many fires in Rome? Why did the fires spread so easily?
5. Do you think the measures described in Source 4 would be helpful? What other actions could the authorities take to solve the problem?

SOURCE 6 An artist's reconstruction of the inside

6. Pick three features of Sources 5 and 6 that you would not expect to find in an English house today, and explain why they were popular in first-century Italy.
7. Describe any similarities between the houses and living conditions in Sources 1–6 and houses or flats that you know today.

Outside the city centre, on the hills overlooking Rome, stood the grand mansions of the richest Romans. Sources 5 and 6 show what ARCHAEOLOGISTS believe these looked like.

▼ **SOURCE 5** Floor plan and external view of a Roman mansion

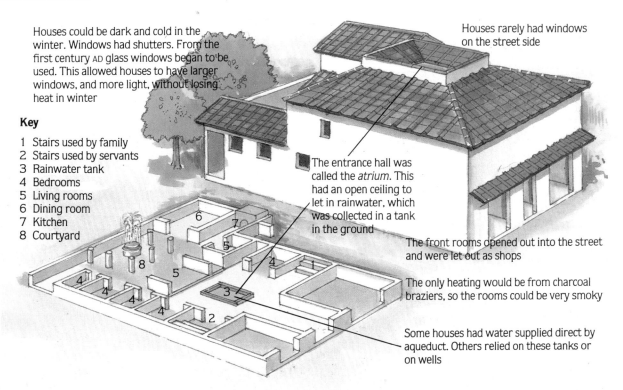

Houses could be dark and cold in the winter. Windows had shutters. From the first century AD glass windows began to be used. This allowed houses to have larger windows, and more light, without losing heat in winter

Houses rarely had windows on the street side

Key

1 Stairs used by family
2 Stairs used by servants
3 Rainwater tank
4 Bedrooms
5 Living rooms
6 Dining room
7 Kitchen
8 Courtyard

The entrance hall was called the *atrium*. This had an open ceiling to let in rainwater, which was collected in a tank in the ground

The front rooms opened out into the street and were let out as shops

The only heating would be from charcoal braziers, so the rooms could be very smoky

Some houses had water supplied direct by aqueduct. Others relied on these tanks or on wells

Family life

The Roman family was often bigger than most modern British families. For rich families, it included not only the mother, father and children, but also other relatives living in the house and all the household slaves. The father was head of the family. He had power over everybody in his house, from his wife to his slaves.

The life women led depended a lot on their social status. Wealthy women often had a lot of independence, especially if they were widows. Women could own and inherit property, and a few wealthy women managed their own businesses. Many middle-class women shared the work in crafts and trades with their husbands, especially in silver-working and perfumery. Women could become priestesses, hairdressers or midwives, and there were some female doctors, but men kept most jobs to themselves.

At the other end of the scale, many women were slaves, doing jobs ranging from lady's maid to farmworker. Some were even GLADIATORS.

> **SOURCE 7** Inscription on a tombstone praising a 'perfect' wife
>
> *Here lies Amyone, wife of Marcus. She was most good and beautiful, a spinner of wool, obedient, chaste and stay-at-home.*

> **SOURCE 8** A Roman writer describes the kind of wife he wouldn't like to have
>
> *. . . a flatchested, straightfaced woman who dashes about all over town, turning up at all-male gatherings, telling the army generals in uniform just what to do — and all this while her husband is there as well.*

> **SOURCE 9** An account by a Roman writer of how women protested about a law which banned them from wearing colourful clothes and riding in carriages during wartime. The woman won and the law was abolished
>
> *The women could not be kept indoors, either by the magistrates or their husbands. They blocked all the streets to the city and besieged the doors of the magistrates who were preventing the law being abolished.*

SOURCE 10 Painting of a Roman woman, from a coffin lid found in Egypt. The painting shows the woman as her relatives would like to remember her, but probably not as she was just before she died!

SOURCE 11 A woman innkeeper

▲ **SOURCE 12** A carving showing the stages in a boy's life:
1. His mother feeds him
2. His father carries him
3. He rides on a miniature goat chariot
4. He tells his father what he has learned at school

Women played the main role in bringing up the children. Roman parents were encouraged by the government to have large families, but most Romans hoped to have sons rather than daughters. In the fourth century, the SENATE had to pass a law forbidding people to leave newborn baby girls out in the open to die.

Boys in rich families were taught by tutors or went to school, but most children could not read or write. They were sent out to work at an early age.

SOURCE 13 Women slaves fighting as gladiators. Their stage names were Achillia and Amazon

SOURCE 14 A child's toy made of toxic lead

Study Sources 7–13 carefully.
1. What can they tell us about:
a) what some men thought the perfect Roman wife should be like
b) how women really behaved
c) what parts of Roman life women were able to join in
d) how important women were in family life?

2. What impression does Source 12 give you of the life of a child in Rome?
3. Divide into groups – if possible, some boys, some girls and some mixed.
a) Use the evidence on these two pages to make statements on the status of women in first-century Rome. How different or similar is it to the situation in Britain nowadays?
b) Compare your statements with other groups.

Food and diet

The poor did not have kitchens and could not do any cooking. If they could afford it, they bought hot food from one of the many bars in the streets.

Their diet was one of bread, wheatmeal porridge, beans, lentils and a little meat. Many poor Romans depended on free hand-outs to survive.

> **SOURCE 15** Extracts from Augustus' record of his own achievements
>
> *In my eleventh year of power I gave free grain to at least 250,000 people.*
>
> *In my thirteenth year of power I gave free grain to 200,000 people.*
>
> *Whenever the government did not have enough money, I gave free grain from my own granary to over 100,000 people.*

> **SOURCE 17** The recipe for the writer Cicero's favourite meal
>
> *Take the flesh of a large salt water fish, filleted. Mix it with brains, chicken's liver, hard-boiled eggs and cheese. Sprinkle it with a sauce of pepper, honey and oil and then cook it in oil over a slow fire. Finally bind it together with raw eggs.*

1. Look at Source 16. Make a list of similarities and differences to a modern kitchen. Mention:
   - how the food is cooked or heated
   - how food is stored
   - what the utensils are made of.

For wealthy Romans, on the other hand, eating was a major part of a day's activity. The main meal started at about three o'clock in the afternoon and went on for several hours, with many courses. The meal was a social occasion and there would be entertainment between courses, such as dancers or gladiatorial fights.

The food was cooked and served by slaves.

People ate with their fingers. They drank wine, which was usually mixed with water.

Olives were often eaten as a first course.

Fish was very popular, and stuffed dormice were regarded as a delicacy. There was not much meat on them, but that did not matter to the Romans, as they had lots of courses. A very strong-tasting sauce called *garum* was used to help cover up the taste of the fish and meat, which were often not very fresh. How the food looked was as important as how it tasted.

Fruits like figs and grapes were served for the dessert courses.

▶ **SOURCE 16** A modern reconstruction of the kitchen in a Roman house

Shopping

At first, the main market in Rome was in the FORUM. When this became too crowded, new markets were built near to the River Tiber. There was a cattle market, a vegetable and fruit market and a fish market. As well as this, certain streets specialised in one kind of shop. But the great shopping street of Rome – the Street of the Etruscans – had shops and workshops of all sorts.

North of the Forum was the working-class district of Subura. It was full of small shops where the poor shopped.

Activity

Work in groups. Each group has to run the household of a rich Roman family and draw up a shopping list. There is going to be an important dinner party, and you have to stock up with the clothes and goods that the household needs.

First, identify the shops and workshops shown in Sources 18–22. Your teacher will give you clues if you need help. Then draw up a shopping list. Include at least five items that a rich household would need for a special meal like the ones described above, and five other general items you would need for the household. Alongside each item, show which shop you would buy this from (look back at Sources 7 and 8 on page 17 as well).

▲ SOURCE 18

▲ SOURCE 19

▲ SOURCE 20

▲ SOURCE 21

▲ SOURCE 22

27

How was Rome fed and supplied?

IN 50BC most of what Rome needed still came from Italy itself. But the city was growing rapidly, and 100 years later the situation had changed.

> **SOURCE 1** Written by Aelius Aristoides about Rome in the first century AD
>
> 66 *Egypt, Sicily and the civilised parts of Africa are your farms.* 99

1. Look at Source 1. What do you think the writer means?

2. Look at Source 2. Where did the following goods come from?
   - timber
   - wine
   - fishpaste
   - papyrus.
3. Did most goods come by water or by road?
4. Where is the nearest supplier of corn?
5. Which of the imports shown would be used for:
   - eating and cooking
   - building
   - clothing?

By the middle of the first century, most of what Rome needed was imported from various parts of its enormous EMPIRE. Italy did not produce goods of its own. Instead, the PROVINCES of the Empire either paid for Rome's supplies by taxes or supplied it with goods. Source 2 shows you how Rome was supplied in the first century AD.

▼ **SOURCE 2** Map showing the main goods and products supplied to Rome by the provinces in the first century AD

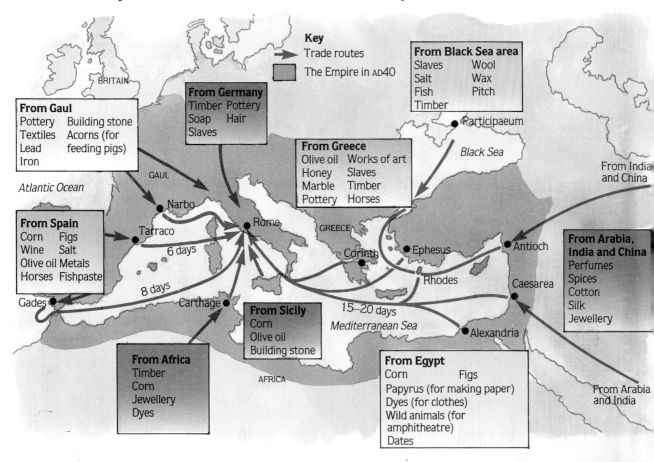

Key
→ Trade routes
▢ The Empire in AD40

From Black Sea area
Slaves   Wool
Salt   Wax
Fish   Pitch
Timber

From Germany
Timber Pottery
Soap   Hair
Slaves

From Gaul
Pottery   Building stone
Textiles   Acorns (for
Lead   feeding pigs)
Iron

From Greece
Olive oil Works of art
Honey   Slaves
Marble   Timber
Pottery   Horses

From India and China

From Spain
Corn   Figs
Wine   Salt
Olive oil Metals
Horses Fishpaste

From Arabia, India and China
Perfumes
Spices
Cotton
Silk
Jewellery

From Sicily
Corn
Olive oil
Building stone

From Africa
Timber
Corn
Jewellery
Dyes

From Egypt
Corn   Figs
Papyrus (for making paper)
Dyes (for clothes)
Wild animals (for amphitheatre)
Dates

From Arabia and India

Britain
Atlantic Ocean
Gaul
Narbo
Tarraco
6 days
8 days
Gades
Carthage
Rome
Greece
Corinth
Ephesus
Rhodes
Panticipaeum
Black Sea
Antioch
Caesarea
Alexandria
15–20 days
Mediterranean Sea
Africa

Corn was the most important import. Most emperors tried to keep the poor people of Rome on their side by supplying cheap (or often free) corn. When they didn't do this they faced riots, and their position as Emperor might even be threatened. So vast amounts of corn were imported (see Source 3).

Most of this trade came through Ostia, which grew into a massive port with warehouses, customs offices, and ship-building yards.

Goods were then transported along the river or canal to Rome (see Source 5).

After the fire of AD94 there were so many ships carrying building materials that this route was almost completely blocked.

SOURCE 3 A corn ship, from a first-century wall painting

6. Look at this list of jobs done by Romans in the first century AD
   - barge workers
   - cobblers
   - rope-makers
   - lawyers
   - dock labourers
   - doctors
   - warehousemen
   - brick-makers
   - corn-measurers

a) Which of these jobs are being done in Sources 3–5?

b) Which of these jobs might need to be done at Ostia? Explain your answer.

SOURCE 4 An antelope being loaded on board a ship bound for Rome. It is being taken to be killed in the amphitheatre

SOURCE 5 Barges, towed by slaves, carrying a cargo of wine

Does Rome need another province?

IT IS AD43. You are the Emperor Claudius. Your position as Emperor is not secure. There has already been one attempted rebellion against you, and there is a shortage of grain in Rome.

As you can see from Source 2 on the previous page, GAUL has been conquered. It has been a Roman PROVINCE for 90 years. If the Empire is going to keep expanding, Britain is the obvious next step. Previous emperors thought the same. Augustus even raised an invasion army – but he had to put down a rebellion in Gaul and never got to Britain.

Now it's your turn. What should you do about Britain? Should you invade it?

There are a number of things you need to take into account to decide whether to invade:

■ Can you keep up a profitable trade with Britain if you don't invade?

■ Will an invasion be successful? Can you beat the Britons? A victory would do your reputation good. Every Emperor needs a military victory to help win support back in Rome.

■ Will it be worth it financially? Are you likely to get more money in taxes from the Britons than it would cost you to keep Britain under control?

■ Will it help security on your borders?

■ Does Britain have resources that you want to exploit?

Sources 1–8 show some of the information you know about Britain. Read through them all and answer the questions before deciding whether to invade Britain.

---

1. Read Sources 1–4. What kind of place do the writers think Britain was?
2. Are some of the descriptions more reliable than others? Explain why.
3. What do the sources disagree about? Why do you think they disagree?
4. Write down three facts that Claudius would have known about Britain from Sources 1–4, and three opinions.

SOURCE 1 A description written in the first century BC by a Roman poet, Horace. He never visited Britain

Britain is at the very end of the earth. The Britons are savage towards foreigners. The seas around Britain are full of sea-monsters.

SOURCE 2 From Julius Caesar's accounts of his invasions of Britain in 55BC and in 54BC. He invaded because British tribes were helping the Gauls in their fight against Roman rule

All Britons dye themselves with woad, which produces a blue dye and makes them look wild in battle.

The population of Britain is very large, and there are many farmhouses. There is a large number of cattle. Most of the tribes living inland do not grow grain. They live on milk and meat and wear skins.

For coins they use bronze, gold or iron. Tin is found inland and small quantities of iron near the coast. The bronze they use is imported. There is timber of every kind.

The Britons' method of fighting is from chariots, dashing about all over the battle field hurling their spears. Our men were unnerved by these tactics, which were strange to them.

SOURCE 3 Written by the Roman politician Cicero at the time of Caesar's invasion. He had not been to Britain

We know there is not a trace of silver in the island, and that the only hope of plunder is slaves.

SOURCE 4 A description written 60 years after Caesar's invasion by the Greek writer Strabo. He did not visit Britain

Their way of life is a bit like that of the Gauls but much cruder and more barbaric. For example, although they have plenty of milk, some of them do not know how to make cheese. Nor do they know anything about farming.

They have more rain than snow, and on days when there is no rain the fog hangs about for so long that the sun shines for about three or four hours a day.

Grain, cattle, gold, silver and iron are found in Britain. They are exported with hides, slaves and excellent hunting dogs.

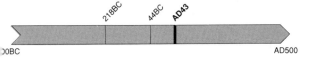

SOURCE 5 Two events in Britain in AD41

a) *Cunobelinus, chief of the Catuvellauni tribe, died. His sons were anti-Roman.*

b) *A Briton called Berikos was driven out of the island as a result of the civil war, and came to Rome to try to persuade Claudius to send a force to invade.*

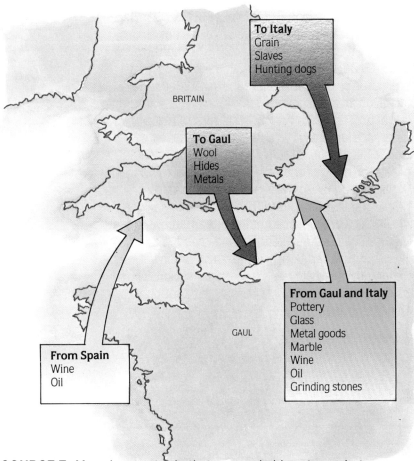

To Italy
Grain
Slaves
Hunting dogs

BRITAIN

To Gaul
Wool
Hides
Metals

From Gaul and Italy
Pottery
Glass
Metal goods
Marble
Wine
Oil
Grinding stones

GAUL

From Spain
Wine
Oil

SOURCE 6 A Roman coin showing a picture of a Celtic chieftain that the Romans had defeated. The Celts were the people who lived in Britain and Gaul

SOURCE 7 Map showing trade that was probably going on between Britain and the Roman Empire in AD40

SOURCE 8 Written by the historian Strabo just after Augustus had called off his planned invasion of Britain in 26BC

Although the Romans could have possessed Britain, they scorned to do so. They saw there was nothing at all to fear from the Britons, since they are not strong enough to cross over the ocean and attack us.

Some of the British chieftains have become friends to Augustus. They have made the island virtually a Roman possession.

The Britons are likely to put up with heavy duties on their imports and exports. There is no need to keep troops there.

It would require at least one legion [5000 soldiers] to collect taxes from them. The cost of the troops would be as much as the Britons would pay in taxes. Besides, there would be some danger in using force.

5. Add to your list any new facts that Sources 5–8 tell you about Britain.

Activity

Now decide whether it is a good idea to invade Britain. Get into pairs.

1. On a scale of one to five indicate whether a successful invasion might be good or bad for:

	Bad			Good	
■ trade	1	2	3	4	5
■ security of the border	1	2	3	4	5
■ making you more popular	1	2	3	4	5

2. How likely are you to win? Very likely? Don't know? Very unlikely?

3. What's your decision? Will you invade?

4. Now, on your own, write a speech explaining your decision. Say which of the reasons was most important in influencing you for or against an invasion.

Life in the provinces

CLAUDIUS did invade Britain. In AD43 he organised a successful campaign. There was hardly any resistance from the British, who were caught off guard. Claudius arrived for the last sixteen days, to receive the surrender of eleven English kings. He was given an immediate 'triumph' in Rome — a special procession to honour a successful military leader. A triumphal arch was built in Rome to honour him. A special coin was made, which would spread the news of the new province all around the Empire. Claudius' son was renamed Brittanicus.

So Britain became just another Roman PROVINCE. In this section we will be finding out about life in the Roman provinces, including Britain.

Look at Sources 1—4. They all show life in various Roman provinces at roughly the same period. Try to match up each picture with the correct caption from the box opposite.

▲ **SOURCE 1**

◀ **SOURCE 2**

▲ **SOURCE 3**

▲ **SOURCE 4**

Captions
Artist's reconstruction of a village in the province of Gaul
Labourers at work on a farm in Germany. From a wall painting made in the third century
A reconstructed farmhouse in southern Britain
Scenes on a farm in North Africa, from a third-century mosaic

In northern parts of the Empire, such as Britain, most farms were smallholdings, farmed by individual families. The families sometimes lived by themselves and sometimes in villages.

In other parts of the Empire, such as North Africa or Spain, there were large estates producing grapes, wine and olive oil, a lot of which was exported to Rome.

Some of these estates were divided into two parts. One part was farmed by the owner, using slaves or paid labourers. The rest was divided into small plots which were rented to tenants. They had to pay one third of their produce as rent and work on the owner's land for six days a year.

Look again at Sources 1–4.

1. What is each farmhouse made of?
2. Which ones do you think are owned by estate owners and which by peasant farmers?
3. What jobs can you see being done in Source 2?
4. Are any of these jobs mentioned in the calendar in Source 5?
5. For which part of the Roman Empire do you think this calendar was made: Britain, Spain or Germany? Explain your answer. You might find it helpful to refer to Source 2 on page 28.
6. Do you agree or disagree with this statement?
   - 'Farming was much the same all over the Empire.'

   Explain why.

SOURCE 5 An agricultural calendar

December *Tend vines. Sow beans. Cut wood. Gather and sell olives*

January *Sharpen stakes. Cut willows and reeds*

February *Weed fields. Tend vines. Burn reeds*

March *Prop up and prune vines. Sow three-month wheat*

April *Count sheep*

May *Clear weeds from grain fields. Shear sheep. Wash wool. Teach oxen to pull carts. C[...] animal fodder*

June *Mow hay. Tend vines*

July *Harvest barley and beans*

August *Prepare stakes. Harvest wheat. Burn stubble*

September *Smear wine casks with pitch. Gather fruit*

October *Harvest grapes*

November *Sow wheat and barley. Dig trenches to plant trees*

Lullingstone villa – a study in change

At Lullingstone, on the banks of the River Darent in Kent, ARCHAEOLOGISTS have found the remains of a Roman VILLA. The buildings have been completely excavated and the evidence tells us a lot about how the building and the people living there changed over 350 years.

Stage 1: Up to AD80

Archaeologists have found the remains of a CELTIC farm. There was not enough evidence to reconstruct what it looked like, but it was probably similar to the one shown in Source 4 on the previous page.

Stage 2: AD80–280

In about AD80 a new square house called a villa was built, made of flint and mortar. It was carefully constructed and was much larger than a Celtic farmhouse. This was a new style of building in Britain, but was popular all over the Roman Empire.

■ There was a large storeroom under the ground.
■ The house measured twenty by fifteen metres.
■ It had five rooms, with a corridor running the length of the house and a small entrance porch to one side.

---

1. Look at Source 4 on page 32. What are the main differences between the Celtic farmhouse and the villa described in Stage 2?
2. Why have archaeologists found many more remains of the villa than of the Celtic farmhouse?

Stage 3: AD280–300

In AD280 the farmhouse was extended and improved at great expense (see Source 6). Yet it was lived in for only twenty years.

Various objects dating from this period have been found on the site, including an expensive gold ring and a statue (probably of one of the owner's ancestors) carved from Greek marble by Roman artists.

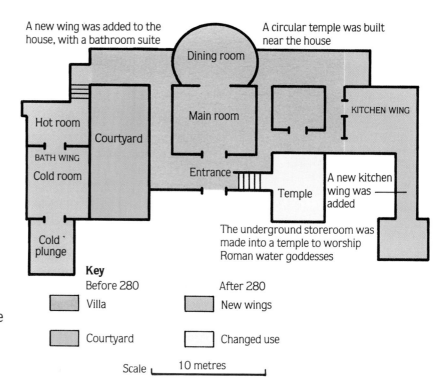

A new wing was added to the house, with a bathroom suite

A circular temple was built near the house

The underground storeroom was made into a temple to worship Roman water goddesses

A new kitchen wing was added

Key

Before 280
- Villa
- Courtyard

After 280
- New wings
- Changed use

Scale | 10 metres

SOURCE 6 Plan of the ground floor of the villa in AD280 (Stage 3)

---

3. What evidence is there that the owner of the villa during Stage 3 was rich?
4. What evidence is there about the religious beliefs of the owner?
5. Does the villa seem to be being used in a different way than it was in Stage 2?

Stage 4: AD300–360

From AD300 the villa fell into disrepair for several years. For part of this time it was used as a small factory for TANNING leather. Then in AD330 a new series of repairs and extensions began.

The improvements included:

■ a new dining room
■ expensive new MOSAIC floors laid in the dining room and the living room showing the Romans' favourite gods
■ a large granary built near to the house.

Source 7 shows the villa during this period.

---

6. What sort of person do you think the new owner is?

▲ SOURCE 7 A reconstruction of the house in about AD360

SOURCE 9 From a modern book about life in Roman Britain

❝Large parts of the Empire were in decline in the fourth century. However, this was Britain's most prosperous period. For the first time wealthy villas became common everywhere, except in the north and west.❞

SOURCE 8 One of the mosaic floors

> **7.** Look at Source 8. Can you think of any reasons why mosaics would be an expensive way to cover the floor?

Stage 5: AD360–430

In AD370, just ten years after the Stage 4 improvements were made, one room in the house was changed into a Christian chapel. No other changes were made. Even after the house fell into disrepair again, the chapel remained in use until the fifth century, when the villa burnt down.

> **8.** What evidence is there of changes in religious beliefs by the owners during the five stages?
> **9.** At which stage would you rather have lived in the villa?
> **10.** Read Source 9. Does the evidence from Lullingstone:
> - support the view in Source 9 *or*
> - disagree with this view *or*
> - not help in deciding if this view is accurate?

Activity

You have just got a job helping the information officer at Lullingstone. You have been asked to produce a short information sheet for school parties visiting the villa. It should include:
- a title for each stage
- a three-line description of the main changes that took place at each stage (use drawings to help you if you wish).

To make the information sheet more interesting, add your ideas about why the changes happened, and who lived there at each stage. Use the evidence to explain and support your ideas.

Use the completed information sheets to make a wall display.

How did the Romans control the Empire?

BY AD100 the Roman Empire stretched almost 3000 miles, from Scotland to the Middle East. It had a population of about 50 million people from many different races, who spoke many different languages and all worshipped their own gods.

In this section we explore how the Romans controlled this massive Empire. Did they do it by force and repression, or by treating the people well?

Organising the Empire

As we saw on page 32, the Romans divided their Empire into PROVINCES. Most provinces were controlled by a GOVERNOR, who made regular inspections of his province and held courts of law. He had a staff of 30–40 officials to help him. They included lawyers, clerks and tax collectors.

Each province paid taxes to Rome. These had to pay for the running of the province and leave Rome with a profit. Taxes were often paid in goods such as grain.

Good communications between Rome and the provinces were essential. They were provided by sea routes and the roads the Romans built. In Britain alone, 6500 miles of road were built in 100 years.

Such an efficient road system meant that the Roman army could travel very quickly to a trouble spot, or to put down a rebellion. When Julius Caesar was leading his Roman army to conquer Gaul, he travelled 800 miles in just eight days.

The army

Let's look at how the army helped Rome to keep control of its Empire.

---

1. Look at Source 1 carefully. Can you see the following features?
   - German prisoners of war
   - soldiers mounted on horses
   - prisoners being forced to behead their own countrymen.
   Draw the scene and label all of these things.

▼ **SOURCE 1** A scene from Marcus Aurelius' column. The column was built to honour Marcus Aurelius' successful campaign against tribes in Germany

The legions

The army was organised into legions. There were about 30 in the whole Empire. Each legion was made up of 60 centuries, each with 80 men called legionaries. Centurions were in charge of the centuries. Each legion also had 120 cavalry. There were 150,000 legionaries in total.

The soldiers in the legions served for sixteen years. They had to be Roman citizens, and most of them were volunteers. More and more, recruits came from the provinces where the legions were serving. Many were the sons of ex-soldiers who had settled there. For all these reasons, men became very proud of their legion.

The *auxilia*

These army units were made up of conquered armies and friendly tribes. The soldiers served for 25 years. They were not Roman citizens, but received citizenship at the end of their service. Many were volunteers, recruited in the province where the unit was stationed. Their armour and weapons were similar to the legionaries', but of inferior quality. Altogether, there were about 227,000 *auxilia* in the Empire, including some cavalry.

Tactics

The Romans' tactics were not very complicated. The Romans depended on their better training and discipline to win battles.

The foot-soldiers, with their shields, formed a solid barrier in the centre. Archers standing behind them fired a hail of arrows over their heads at the enemy. The cavalry fought on the flanks and were especially used for cutting down the enemy once they were retreating.

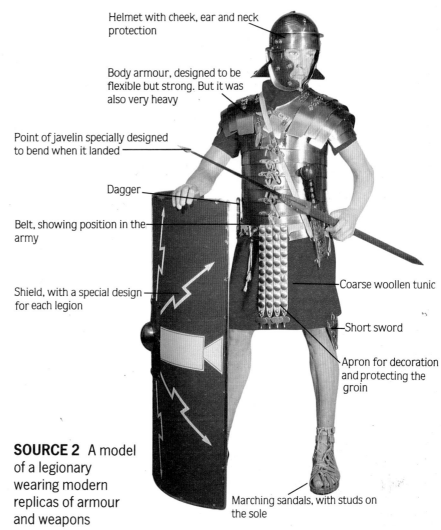

Helmet with cheek, ear and neck protection

Body armour, designed to be flexible but strong. But it was also very heavy

Point of javelin specially designed to bend when it landed

Dagger

Belt, showing position in the army

Shield, with a special design for each legion

Coarse woollen tunic

Short sword

Apron for decoration and protecting the groin

Marching sandals, with studs on the sole

SOURCE 2 A model of a legionary wearing modern replicas of armour and weapons

---

2. Choose three items of the legionary's equipment from Source 2 and explain how they would be useful in a battle.

3. The beginnings and endings of the following sentences have been mixed up. Using the information on these two pages, match the correct heads and tails. There are two tails for each head. Write the complete sentences in your book.

Heads	Tails
Legionaries	ran a province
	became Roman citizens when they finished their army service
Auxiliaries	collected taxes and held law courts
	served for 16 years
	had to be Roman citizens
The governor	served for 25 years

HOW DID THE ROMANS CONTROL THE EMPIRE?

Rebellion!

As you can see from Source 1 on the previous page, the Roman army could be very cruel in dealing with enemies. For example, in the province of Dacia (modern Romania), the Romans forced 100,000 local people to move right out of the province into another country. They replaced them with a completely new population from the province of Dalmatia, 400 miles away, who were more friendly to the Romans. Even so, the Romans were not always successful in keeping the peace, as the following case study from Britain shows.

In AD61 Britain had been a Roman province for less than twenty years. The Romans had not yet conquered even half of Britain (see Source 5). What's more, the estimate that Britain could be controlled by just one LEGION of the Roman army was proving to be a bad miscalculation. Four legions had been stationed in Britain since the invasion and had been kept fairly busy.

In AD61, Suetonius, the GOVERNOR of Britain, decided to conquer the Isle of Anglesey, just off Wales. Many rebellious Britons, led by the DRUID priests, were hiding there. Suetonius took two legions with him. This left the south of England almost bare of Roman troops.

While he was away, the Britons' anger against the Romans bubbled up into a full-scale rebellion.

SOURCE 3 The Roman historian Tacitus describes why the Iceni tribe rebelled

The King of the Iceni tribe had left his huge treasure in equal shares to his two daughters and the Emperor. But Roman tax collectors looted his lands, whipped his wife Boudicca and assaulted her two daughters. Leading members of the Iceni tribe lost their homes and lands. The relatives of the King were made slaves.

1. According to Sources 3 and 4 what caused the rebellion?
2. Are there some causes which had been building up for longer than others? Explain your answer.

▶ **SOURCE 5** The tribal areas of Britain

SOURCE 4 Tacitus describes why the Iceni's neighbours, the Trinovantes, joined the rebellion

What chiefly made the Trinovantes angry was how the Roman veterans had behaved when they founded the colony at Colchester. They treated the Britons cruelly. They drove them from their homes and called them slaves.

Another cause of anger was the temple built in honour of Emperor Claudius. To the British it was a symbol of everlasting slavery. The Roman priests made the Britons pay heavy taxes to use the temple.

The Britons defeated the Romans' Ninth Legion. Then they attacked Colchester and completely destroyed it. Archaeologists have found a layer of black soot, blackened pottery and melted glass across the whole area, dating from AD61. Every man, woman and child was massacred. The rebels went on and did the same in London and St Albans.

When Suetonius got word of this, he sent orders for the Second Legion to come from Gloucester to support him. He quickly set off back from Wales.

But the Second Legion failed to respond and suddenly Suetonius found himself face to face with a much larger force of Britons. Who would win?

Boudicca, the Queen of the Iceni, thought she would win.

Key
- - - Approximate tribal boundaries
Roman province in AD61
Roads

SOURCE 6 In his account of the rebellion, the Roman historian Tacitus wrote down the sort of things that he thought Boudicca would have said

❝*The Romans will never face the din and roar of all our thousands. There are more of us and we are braver.*

If we ever choose to retreat, we hide in the swamps and mountains. They cannot chase anybody or run away, because of their heavy armour.

They need bread and wine and oil, if they cannot get these, they cannot survive.' ❞

SOURCE 8 A statue of Boudicca on her chariot, made in 1902

3. Look at Source 6. Why did Boudicca think she would win? Do you agree with her?
4. Look at Source 8. What impression does this give you of Boudicca?
5. This statue stands outside the Houses of Parliament in London. Does this mean that people in Britain are ashamed or proud of Boudicca?

SOURCE 9 From Tacitus' account of the rebellion

❝*Suetonius' army was about 10,000 men strong. He chose a spot circled by woods. It had a narrow entrance and dense trees behind it. So he had no fear of an ambush. The enemy had to come at him from the front, across an open plain. He drew up his soldiers in order. The legions were in the centre. The auxiliaries were kept at the back for when they were needed. The cavalry were at the sides.*

A huge number of Britons came to the battle field. They did not draw up in organised lines. Separate bands rushed up and down shouting. So sure were they of winning that they put their wives in carts on the edge of the plain.

The battle began. The narrow passage into the clearing slowed down the enemy attack. Then the Romans rushed forward in a wedge. The auxiliaries followed. The cavalry charged the enemy. The Britons fled, but got tangled up in their wagons at the rear. A dreadful slaughter followed. Neither men nor women were spared. Some writers say about 80,000 Britons were killed. The Romans lost about 4000 men. Boudicca took poison before she could be captured. ❞

Key
✕ Possible site of battle

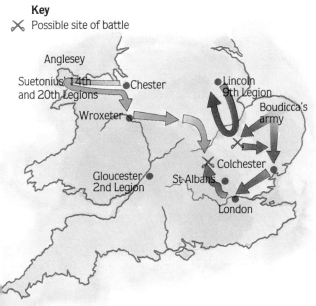

SOURCE 7 Movements of the rebels and the Roman army

6. Draw a plan of the battle site, showing the woods and the armies drawn up for battle.
7. Draw a plan of the battle scene, showing the movements of the armies.
8. Why did the Romans win?

HOW DID THE ROMANS CONTROL THE EMPIRE?

There is evidence of a change of policy in Britain after Boudicca's rebellion was put down. A new governor, called Agricola, was sent to Britain. Source 10 tells you how he governed Britain.

SOURCE 10 A description of Agricola, governor of Britain after Boudicca's rebellion, by Tacitus

❝He had learned from what had happened to others that an army can do little if the government is unfair. For government jobs he chose men he knew would not be greedy. He made the corn tax less heavy.

He tried to get them to live in peace. He gave them help to build temples, public squares and good houses. He gave the sons of chiefs a Roman education. As a result the Britons were eager to speak Latin and everywhere you could see the toga [the Roman national dress] being worn. Gradually, the natives were tempted by shops, baths and rich banquets.❞

Sources 3, 4, 6, 9 and 10 were all written by Tacitus, a Roman historian. He was the son-in-law of Agricola, and was writing at a time when Agricola's reputation was suffering in Rome. He had not seen the events he described, nor visited Britain.

However, Agricola had been a young soldier in Suetonius' army at the time of Boudicca's rebellion. There are no other accounts of the rebellion.

---

1. From what you now know about Tacitus say:
a) where you think he may have got his information about the rebellion from
b) whether you think his evidence will be reliable?
2. Can you think of any events in Sources 7–10 that Agricola could have seen for himself?
3. Do you think Source 10 is a reliable account of what Agricola actually did?
4. You are Agricola. Pick three of your actions from Source 10 and explain why you think they will help control the province and prevent any more rebellions.

Why did the Romans build towns?

In the eastern parts of the Empire great towns existed before the Romans came. Many of these towns were left to govern themselves and the local way of life was left untouched. But in the Western Empire towns were almost unknown before the Romans arrived.

When they conquered a new province, such as Gaul or Britain, the Romans set up three kinds of towns:

■ The most important were called colonies. Ex-soldiers were given free land in the colonies when they retired from the army.

---

1. Why do you think the Romans wanted their ex-soldiers to settle down in the new colonies?
2. Look back at Source 4 on page 38. What did the British most hate about the colony of Colchester?

■ Slightly less important than the colonies were the towns called *municipia*. Only Roman citizens could live in these towns, and they governed themselves. Their buildings and government were supposed to be like Rome's and were meant to show the local TRIBES the great advantages that came with Roman rule.

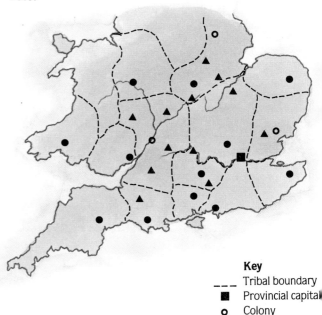

Key
- - - Tribal boundary
■ Provincial capital
○ Colony
● Civitas
▲ Municipium

SOURCE 11 Towns built by the Romans in Britain

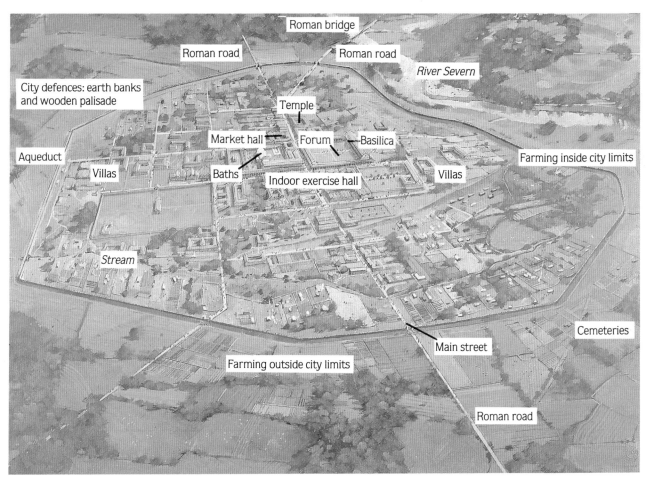

Roman bridge

Roman road

Roman road

River Severn

City defences: earth banks and wooden palisade

Temple

Market hall

Forum

Basilica

Aqueduct

Farming inside city limits

Villas

Baths

Indoor exercise hall

Villas

Stream

Cemeteries

Main street

Farming outside city limits

Roman road

SOURCE 12 Reconstruction drawing of Wroxeter, a Roman *civitas* in Britain as it was in AD150

■ In each tribal area the Romans set up a town called a *civitas*. This was controlled directly by the GOVERNOR of the province, but he allowed friendly tribes to play a part in governing themselves. The towns were named after the local tribe.

Wroxeter was originally the site of an important Roman fort, from AD48–90. The Romans used it as a base for their conquest of North Wales. Once Wales had been conquered, they literally packed up the fort and moved to Chester. The Wroxeter site was then used as the base for a brand new *civitas* for the Cornovii tribe. Its Roman name was Viroconium Cornoviorum. Source 12 shows the town as it was after the main public buildings were completed around AD150.

3. Look back at pages 16–21, which describe a merchant's visit to Rome. Wroxeter was the merchant's home town. Use Source 12 to draw up lists of the differences and the similarities he would have noticed between Rome and Wroxeter.

Activity

Work in pairs. One of you is a British chieftain who supports the Romans. You are trying to persuade another chief to do the same. How can you convince the other chief of the advantages of Roman rule and the dangers in opposing it?

The other chief is determined not to accept the Romans. How are you going to convince your partner that he/she is wrong to support the Romans?

Before you start, make a list of three arguments in your favour. Support them with evidence from pages 36–41.

41

The frontier

BRITAIN was one of the last provinces the Romans conquered. In the early days of the Empire, they did not pay much attention to defending their new provinces from attack. Rome must have seemed so strong that defence was not needed.

In the second century, however, the Emperor Hadrian was having second thoughts about the Roman frontiers. Hadrian believed the Empire should not keep trying to expand. Instead, he wanted to establish fixed frontiers that could be defended.

Activity

You are an adviser to Hadrian. Source 1 shows you the extent of the Empire in AD120. Prepare a short report to Hadrian on where new defences may be needed, and where he should consider changing the boundaries of the Empire. In particular, what should he do about the areas of the frontier where there are problems (marked A, B, C and D on Source 1)?

Mention the following in your report:

- which parts of the Empire have strong natural boundaries such as mountains, deserts, seas or wide rivers, which make them easy to defend
- which parts of the Empire are threatened by strong or warlike neighbours, and how you would strengthen the frontier against them
- where you would withdraw from some occupied land to make the frontier easier to defend, or where you would expand by conquering troublesome tribes
- how this helps with the problem of the frontiers at A, B, C and D.

Your teacher will tell you whether you reached the same conclusions as Hadrian.

SOURCE 1 The Empire in AD120

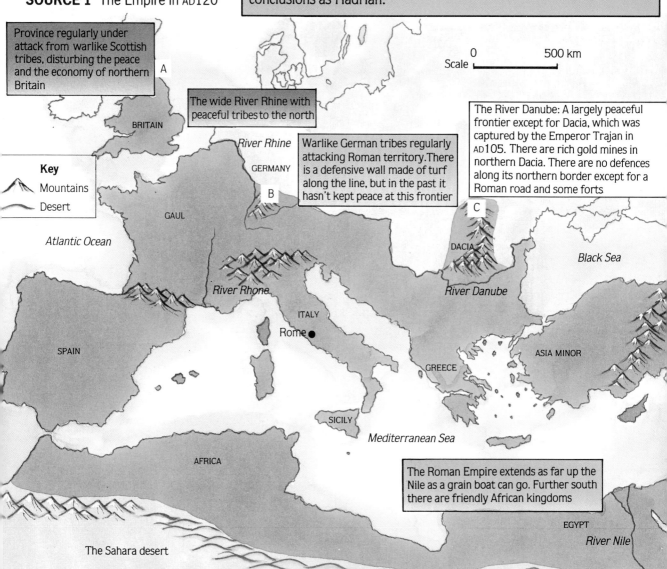

Province regularly under attack from warlike Scottish tribes, disturbing the peace and the economy of northern Britain

The wide River Rhine with peaceful tribes to the north

Warlike German tribes regularly attacking Roman territory. There is a defensive wall made of turf along the line, but in the past it hasn't kept peace at this frontier

The River Danube: A largely peaceful frontier except for Dacia, which was captured by the Emperor Trajan in AD105. There are rich gold mines in northern Dacia. There are no defences along its northern border except for a Roman road and some forts

The Roman Empire extends as far up the Nile as a grain boat can go. Further south there are friendly African kingdoms

Key

- Mountains
- Desert

Atlantic Ocean

BRITAIN

River Rhine

GERMANY

GAUL

River Rhone

ITALY

Rome

SPAIN

DACIA

River Danube

Black Sea

GREECE

ASIA MINOR

SICILY

Mediterranean Sea

AFRICA

EGYPT

River Nile

The Sahara desert

Scale 0 — 500 km

The Wall

One of the most famous frontiers is Hadrian's Wall, built in the north of Britain in AD120. Like all the Romans' frontier defences, it served various purposes:

■ to show the people of the Empire that the frontier was now fixed, and fixed at a sensible point that the Romans would be able to defend

■ to keep out hostile tribes and to separate the friendly tribes on the Roman side of the frontier from the hostile ones on the other side

■ to help a Roman way of life to settle in: the Wall would allow people to set up towns and build villas without the constant danger of attack

■ to keep the soldiers busy and disciplined, building and maintaining the Wall.

Votadini – friendly to the Romans. Had been allowed to keep their hill fort at Traprain Hill

Selgovae – enemies of the Romans, who had destroyed their hill fort base at Eildon

Brigantes – defeated by Rome in AD71. Kept largely under control since then

▲ **SOURCE 2** Northern England

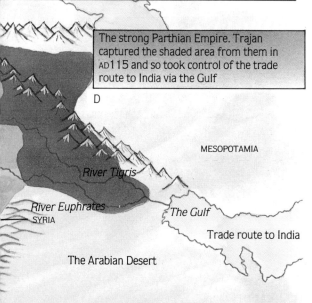

The strong Parthian Empire. Trajan captured the shaded area from them in AD115 and so took control of the trade route to India via the Gulf

1. Look at Source 2. You have been given the job of deciding where the wall should be. Two possible lines are shown.

   You must take into account the four points on the left. Which line will you take?

SOURCE 3 Hadrian's Wall

How successful was the Wall?

SOURCE 4 Findings from aerial surveys of archaeological sites on both sides of the Wall

❝■ There are three times as many settlements south of the Wall as north of the Wall.
■ There are many more rectangular sites (a typical Roman way of building) south of the Wall.
■ More sites south of the Wall are surrounded by cultivated fields.
■ Many more of the settlements north of the Wall are surrounded by defensive ditches.
■ There were no villas, and only a few small towns, north of the Wall. ❞

1. What does Source 4 tell us about the differences between life north and south of the Wall?
2. Does Source 4 prove that the Wall was successful in
a) separating hostile tribes from friendly tribes
b) helping a Roman way of life to settle in on the Roman side of the Wall?

Life as a soldier

What was life really like for soldiers in the Roman army? Sources 5–15 give you a range of viewpoints and different pieces of evidence. From the evidence given try to find out:

■ what kind of work a soldier did when he wasn't fighting

■ what kind of family life a soldier could have

■ what discipline was like in the army

■ what complaints soldiers had about life in the army

■ what rewards soldiers got for being in the army.

> **SOURCE 5** From army records found at Hadrian's Wall
>
> **April 25** In the workshops 343 men. Of these 12 making shoes, 18 building a bath-house. Other jobs: plasterers and working in the hospital.

> **SOURCE 6** From army records found in Egypt
>
> Titus Flavius Valens:
> January 15 – making papyrus
> January 17 – working in the coin mint
> January 18 – working in the granary.

> **SOURCE 7** The wage records of one soldier for four months
>
> Pay received: 75 denarii
> Deductions:
>   bedding   3
>   rations   20
>   boots and straps   3
>   Saturnalia [winter feast]   5
>   tent   15
>   uniform   –
>   arms and armour   –
>   Total deductions: 46
> Into savings bank: 29

> **SOURCE 8** Advice to the emperor Valens in AD369
>
> The strength of the army is sometimes reduced by military disasters and by desertions arising from boredom with camp duties.

> **SOURCE 9** Recent excavations in Roman forts have identified the soldier's diet
>
> ■ The bones of the ox are most frequently found. Sheep, pork and ham were also popular. Poultry and fish also formed part of the diet.
> ■ Grain was the basic foodstuff. It was made into bread and used as the basis of soups, porridge and pasta.
> ■ Each soldier got through a third of a ton of grain each year. Every Roman fort in Britain had sufficient supplies to last a year.
> ■ Rations while on campaign took the form of hard biscuits.
> ■ Blackberries, strawberries and cherries and beans and lentils were also eaten.
> ■ Both beer and wine were drunk. There were no dining halls. The troops either ate in the open or in their barrack rooms.
> ■ While on the march, soldiers carried rations for three days, a bronze food-box, a kettle and a portable hand-mill. Each soldier baked his own bread.

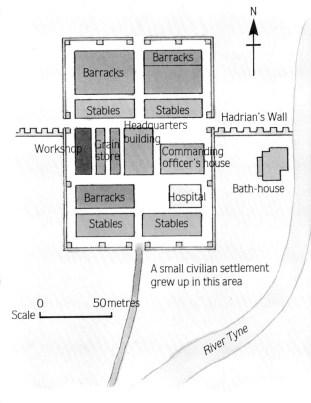

SOURCE 10 Chesters fort on Hadrian's Wall

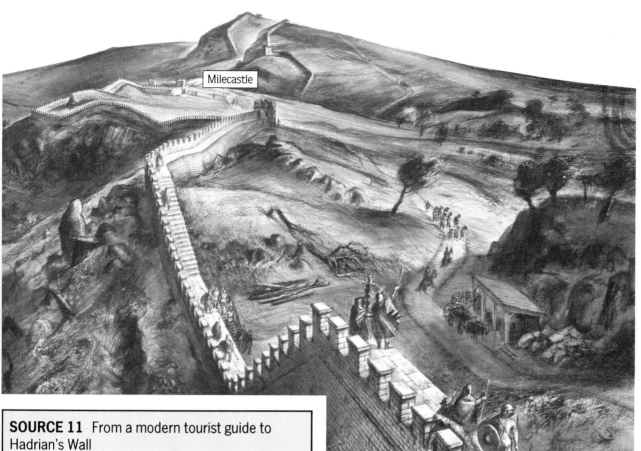

Milecastle

SOURCE 11 From a modern tourist guide to Hadrian's Wall

Every army has its camp followers. Civilian settlements grew up outside forts. As the army moved on, some of these people would move on with it. One important group in the civilian settlement would be the soldiers' wives and families. A Roman soldier was not allowed to marry, but there was nothing to stop him from having a relationship, and children, with a local woman. These 'marriages' were recognised in Roman law when the soldier retired.

SOURCE 12 Augustus decrees special privileges to military veterans in 31 BC

I have decided that all veterans shall be exempt from taxation, exempt from (further) military service and exempt from compulsory public services.

SOURCE 13 Suetonius describes Augustus' treatment of soldiers

If a company broke in battle, Augustus ordered the survivors to draw lots, then executed every tenth man and fed the remainder on barley bread instead of the usual wheat ration.

SOURCE 14 An artist's reconstruction of Roman soldiers on duty on Hadrian's Wall. The soldiers' barracks were in the milecastle

SOURCE 15 Speech by a leader of an army mutiny in the first century AD

Most of us grow old with bodies maimed with wounds. We are sent to soaking swamps and mountainous wastes. We get paid 1½ denarii a day, and out of this clothing, arms and tents have to be bought. Of floggings, and hard winters, of boring month after month, there is no end.

1. The speaker in Source 15 is trying to persuade men to join a mutiny. Do you think his account of army life can be trusted? Use the other sources to explain your answer.

Activity

Work in groups. Make a wall display about life in the Roman army. Include extracts from the evidence on this page, and add drawings or diagrams.

How civilised were the Romans?

WHAT does it mean to be civilised? It might mean any of the following to us today:

- to be clean
- to be tolerant of people who have different views
- to be advanced in science
- to like good art and literature
- to treat people well
- to value all life.

You might want to add to this list.

The Romans regarded themselves as civilised, but do you think that they really were? And did being civilised mean something different to them than it does to us today?

Let's look at some of the achievements that the Romans were most proud of.

- Their system of law. Throughout the Empire they organised courts to try to give people a fair trial.
- Their literature. In the first century BC and first century AD there was an explosion of literary activity in Italy. Poets, historians and philosophers became celebrities.
- The Romans made many new discoveries in medicine and surgery. One of the most famous doctors in the history of medicine was Galen. He was born a Greek, learned his surgery skills in a gladiator school in Roman Egypt, and then came to work in Rome itself.

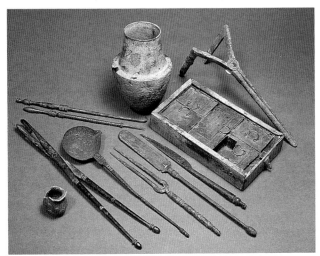

SOURCE 1 Roman surgical and midwifery instruments

---

1. What do you think each of the instruments in Source 1 is used for?
2. Why might a gladiator school be a good place to learn surgery?

- The Romans were also very proud of their achievements in technology. They were very clever at making things. They applied all branches of maths and science to solving difficult practical problems: supplying water to cities, grinding corn more efficiently, or putting up buildings that were bigger and grander than anyone had built before.

SOURCE 2 An aqueduct in Segovia, Spain, built in the second century AD. The water is carried along the top level

Keeping clean

Now let's look at one particular area of Roman achievement – water supply and hygiene. We have already seen (on page 18) how Augustus repaired the Roman water supply. All around the Mediterranean, Roman engineers built impressive waterworks to deliver fresh water to the cities and towns of the Empire.

SOURCE 3 Written by Frontinus, Water Commissioner for Rome in AD97. His aqueducts brought in about 1000 million litres of water a day

❝My job concerns the health of the city, and so this task has always been handled by the most important men in the state. Now nine aqueducts bring water into the city.

The new Anio aqueduct is taken from a river which is muddy. A special filter tank was placed at the beginning of the aqueduct, where the soil could settle and the water clarify before going along the channel.❞

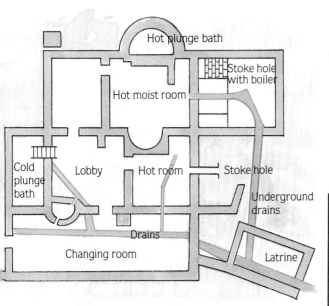

▲ **SOURCE 4** A plan of the bath-house at the Roman fort of Vindolanda

▶ **SOURCE 5**
How the baths were heated

SOURCE 6 Written by Strabo, a Greek who visited Rome in the first century

Water is brought into the city through aqueducts in such quantities that it is like a river flowing through the city. Almost every house has cisterns and water pipes and fountains

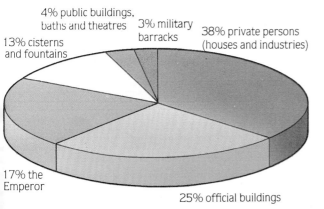

4% public buildings, baths and theatres

3% military barracks

38% private persons (houses and industries)

13% cisterns and fountains

17% the Emperor

25% official buildings

SOURCE 7 Figures for the distribution of the water supply in Rome in the first century AD

1. What evidence is there of the importance the Romans placed on clean water?
2. Do you think the water was shared out fairly?
3. Refer back to the information on page 22. Does this agree with Source 6? Explain your answer.

Activity

One other feature of Roman life that is important in deciding how civilised the Romans were is their art and architecture. You have seen examples of both in this unit. Now we'll look at some in more detail.

Choose one of the following two tasks. Work in groups.

1. Art

You have been asked to select pieces of art for an exhibition of the best of Roman art.

With your group, look through the whole of this unit and pick out at least three items that you would like to display in your Roman art exhibition.

You could choose from:
- the sculptures on pages 6, 25 and 36
- the MOSAICS on pages 19, 35 and 56
- the paintings on pages 2, 24 and 29
- the metalwork on the cover or on page 4.

Once you have chosen your three items, make a catalogue for your exhibition. Write a short paragraph for each item, describing what it's made of, when it was made (if you can find that out), and any special features, and explaining why you have chosen it.

Compare your choice with the choices other groups have made.

2. Architecture

Choose one of the following buildings: The Colosseum (page 50), the Roman Forum (page 21), the Circus Maximus (page 20), or Lullingstone Roman Villa (page 35).

Make a big outline drawing of the building, and stick labels to it to show its features. For example, say what materials it is made of, how big it is, what it was used for, how it is decorated, and the problems the Romans had to overcome to build it.

Slaves

The Romans took slavery for granted. For them a country without slaves was uncivilised.

From the third century BC, slaves flooded into Rome. Most were prisoners of war. Julius Caesar's conquest of GAUL alone brought in half a million slaves in five years. They were sold in the great slave markets in Rome and in other cities.

Some slaves worked and lived in rich people's houses. Others worked in mines or on large farming estates. But they all had one thing in common. They were the property of their master. They had no rights at all.

Were all slaves treated badly? The evidence in Sources 8–17 should help you to answer this question.

> **SOURCE 8** Written by a modern historian
>
> 66 *The worst ill-treatment of slaves was in the great barracks and concentration camps of the large ranches and plantations, and the squalor of the mines. The average age of death of these men was about 21.* 99

> **SOURCE 9** Columella, a Spanish landowner, gives advice to owners of slaves working on farms
>
> 66 *In the care and clothing of the slave household you should have an eye to usefulness rather than appearance, taking care to keep the slaves protected against the wind and the rain with long-sleeved leather tunics, patchwork garments or hooded cloaks. If you do this, no weather is so unbearable that some work may not be done in the open.* 99

SOURCE 10 An iron collar for a slave. The writing says: 'I have run away. Catch me. If you take me back to my master Zoninus you'll be rewarded.' The collar was riveted on

SOURCE 11 A tombstone for a slave erected by his master. Part of the inscription reads, 'the most faithful slave'

> **SOURCE 12**
> a) Written by the Roman writer Pliny to the Emperor Trajan
>
> 66 *I find in several cities certain persons who work and are paid as public slaves or as clerks in the civil service, despite being condemned to the mines and the public games. How should I deal with them?*
>
> b) Trajan's reply
>
> 66 *Those whose sentences have not been reversed should be sent back to their punishments, but let those who have grown old work at the public baths, cleanse the sewers or repair the streets.*

SOURCE 13 The writer Seneca writing to a friend about how slaves should be treated

I am glad to learn from those who bring news from you that you live on friendly terms with your slaves. This is right for a sensible and well educated man like yourself.

'They are slaves,' people say. No. They are men.

SOURCE 16 From a modern history of the Roman Empire

When wars became less frequent, the supply of slaves began to dry up and they became more expensive. The Emperor Claudius stopped masters killing their slaves without good reason, and Domitian stopped the castration of slaves for commercial reasons.

SOURCE 14 A carving from a Roman tomb from AD100. A stone carving is being lifted by a crane powered by slaves walking around inside a treadmill wheel

SOURCE 17 Reconstruction of mills built in France in AD310. Together, the eight mills could grind as much corn in one hour as 800 slaves could have done previously

SOURCE 15 A Roman historian explains the causes of a slave revolt in Sicily in the first century

The Sicilians brought the slaves down in droves from the markets and immediately branded them with marks on their bodies. Oppressed by hard work and beatings, the slaves could endure it no longer.

After one revolt 6000 slaves were crucified along the Appian Way (a road leading into Rome).

1. List all the different jobs slaves did according to Sources 8–17.
2. What evidence is there that slaves were treated badly?
3. What evidence is there that slaves were treated well?
4. What evidence is there in Sources 16 and 17 that the situation of slaves changed as time went by? How did it change?
5. From the evidence, how do you think a Roman would justify owning slaves?
6. Do you think the Romans were wrong to keep slaves? Give your reasons, and refer to the evidence in Sources 8–17.

The murderous games

Source 18 shows one of the grandest buildings in Rome. Most of it is still standing today. The Romans reserved their best architecture for their most important buildings. And yet this magnificent building was created to allow people to watch gladiators fighting to the death, criminals being executed publicly and prisoners of war being mauled by wild animals.

SOURCE 19 A nineteenth-century view of Roman gladiators fighting in the Colosseum

Source 19 shows the professional fighters – the gladiators – fighting in the arena. The gladiators were mostly slaves and criminals, and had been highly trained in special gladiator schools. There were some women gladiators (see page 25). If gladiators were lucky and survived their many fights they could win their freedom.

The gladiator fights started around 260BC. The Romans believed that the souls of the dead needed human blood, and so at funerals they killed prisoners or slaves. Over the next 200 years the gladiator shows developed out of this. In 65BC, Julius Caesar held funeral games for his father where 640 gladiators fought, and criminals were forced to fight with wild beasts.

Soon the gladiator fights were held purely for enjoyment. Members of rich families paid for the games to be held and tried to make theirs the biggest and bloodiest games.

But the most spectacular shows were organised by the Emperors. Along with hand-outs of free grain, the spectacular and bloody shows were the best way of keeping the ordinary Romans on the Emperor's side. The Emperor Trajan held games in

▼ **SOURCE 18** The Colosseum in Rome – the most magnificent amphitheatre in the Roman Empire

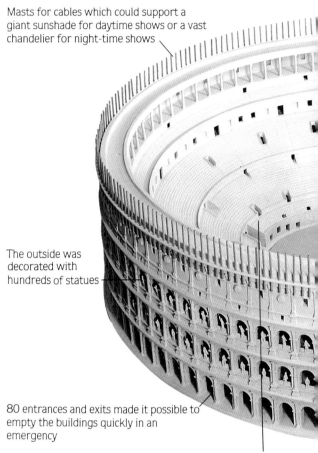

Masts for cables which could support a giant sunshade for daytime shows or a vast chandelier for night-time shows

The outside was decorated with hundreds of statues

80 entrances and exits made it possible to empty the buildings quickly in an emergency

Shows were free, but seats nearest the arena were reserved for rich people

AD108 lasting 123 days, where 9138 gladiators fought and 11,000 animals were killed. On a single day 3000 men were killed.

Going to watch the fights could be dangerous. One day, when they ran out of criminals, the Emperor Caligula ordered that a whole section of the crowd should be thrown to the wild beasts.

However, not all Romans liked the games.

SOURCE 20 From a letter written by Cicero to a friend in the first century BC

❝ *What pleasure can it possibly be to a man of culture when either a puny human being is mangled by a powerful beast, or a splendid animal is transfixed with a hunting spear?*

Seating for 50,000 people to watch men and animals fighting each other to the death

The arena floor could be made watertight and flooded for mock naval battles

The arena floor was made of sand to absorb the blood of the victims

Underneath the arena was a maze of corridors and rooms to keep the gladiators, wild animals and prisoners before they were taken up to the arena for their fight to the death. Hidden trap-doors and ingenious machines allowed fighters and animals to appear from beneath the earth

For many Romans, however, the gladiators were glamorous figures, like modern film stars. MOSAICS, statues and drawings were made showing top gladiators. At Pompeii, you can still see messages that girls scratched into the wall about their heart-throbs. Some gladiators even volunteered for the job. In Source 22 the writer Juvenal writes about a senator's wife who eloped to Egypt with her favourite fighter.

SOURCE 22

66 What did she see in him to make her put up with being called 'The Gladiator's Moll'? He wasn't exactly young, and he had a dud arm. Besides, his face looked a proper mess, helmet-scarred, a great wart on his nose, an unpleasant discharge always trickling from one eye. But he was a gladiator. This made her prefer him to her children, her country, her sister and her husband. 99

1. Use the information on this page to write two paragraphs about why you think the games were so popular with the ordinary Romans.
2. Is there any evidence that not all Romans liked the games?
3. Work in pairs. You have been given the opportunity to interview a) a gladiator, and b) an Emperor, about the games. What questions do you want to ask each of them? Draw up a list of questions. What answers would you expect them to give?

SOURCE 21 Written by the Roman philosopher Seneca

6 I arrived at the Colosseum in the middle of the day. A mass execution of criminals was taking place. This was meant to be entertainment for the crowd while they waited for the gladiators.

No sooner has a man killed his rival than the crowd shout for him to kill another, or be killed. In the end every fighter dies. And all this with half the seats still empty.

You may object that the victims are murderers and thieves, but even if they deserve to suffer, why watch their sufferings? 99

1. Use Sources 1, 3, 13 and 20 to describe how civilised the Romans were.
2. If you use Sources 8, 9, 18 and 21 to describe how civilised the Romans were, how does your view change?

How tolerant were the Romans?

YOU may think that one important part of being civilised is to be tolerant of other people's beliefs. We are now going to investigate whether the Romans were tolerant or not.

The Romans governed many different races, who worshipped many different gods. How tolerant were the Romans of the different religious beliefs of the people they conquered?

> **SOURCE 1** Written by Polybius, a Greek visitor to Rome in the second century AD
>
> 66 What keeps the Empire united is religion. It is cloaked in so much pomp, and plays such a large part in private and public affairs, that nothing can fight its influence. The government encourages it for the sake of the common people, whose lawless desires and violent anger are kept under control by invisible terrors and great ceremonies. 99

1. What does Polybius tell us about the general attitude of the Roman government towards religion?
2. Is he stating facts or opinions? Explain your answer.

Roman religion would not be regarded as a religion by many people today. It did not involve any emotional or spiritual commitment. The Romans' approach was a practical one. They carried out the right actions, and in return the gods gave them a more comfortable and successful life.

People prayed and made offerings at temples to ask for help or to thank the gods for a favour.

There were few full-time PRIESTS. Most priests were important officials in the government, for whom being a priest was just one of several jobs. The Emperor was the chief priest. From the first century AD on, emperors were worshipped as gods after they died.

People also worshipped at home. They had household gods, who were seen as the guardians of the house. Houses had a SHRINE called the *lararium* where family ceremonies took place (see Source 2).

As the Romans conquered new territories, they came across new gods and goddesses. Let's look at three examples and see how the Romans dealt with them.

SOURCE 2 A *lararium*

Britain: Sulis

The Britons worshipped many of their own gods. At the hot springs at Bath they worshipped a goddess called Sulis. When the Romans built a town there and developed the baths they called the town Aquae Sulis (Waters of Sulis) and built a temple to the goddess. They combined the worship of Sulis with worship of their own goddess Minerva.

Persia: Mithras

Mithras was a Persian god concerned with the struggle between good and evil. The religion had many secret rituals and practices. It was a favourite religion of many Roman soldiers. The religion was for men only.

Greece: Asclepios

Asclepios was a Greek god who was adopted by the Romans. They built temples to him in Rome. They believed that if you were ill and slept at Asclepios' temple the god would cure you during the night.

1. According to these examples, how did the Romans deal with the gods and goddesses of people they conquered?
2. Why do you think they had this policy?

One important thing about all of these foreign gods, as far as the Romans were concerned, was that they could be worshipped alongside Roman gods. In fact, Roman gods had a lot in common with them. As long as their priests did not tell people to reject Roman rule, and as long as the people in the provinces continued to worship the Emperor and did not cause trouble, the Romans did not mind which gods they followed.

However, we are now going to look at three other case studies, which show that the Romans had a different attitude to religions which brought their followers into conflict with the rules or the needs of the Empire.

Case study 1: the Druids

The DRUIDS were priests in GAUL and Britain. They claimed they were the only people who knew the secrets of the gods. They were respected by the leaders of the TRIBES. They were often asked for advice. They understood the cycles of the seasons and had made calendars, showing which months were good for certain activities.

The Romans were determined to wipe out the Druids. They chased them all the way to their stronghold on the island of Anglesey, off the Welsh coast, and killed all of them. Why did the Romans treat the Druids this way? Sources 3 and 4 suggest one reason.

SOURCE 4 A picture of a Druid human sacrifice, drawn in 1676. It was based on a description written by Julius Caesar after his invasion of Britain in 54BC (although he almost certainly didn't see a sacrifice)

SOURCE 3 Written by the Roman historian Tacitus

The Druids covered their altars with the blood of their prisoners and the ripped-out guts of men sacrificed to their gods.

After conquering Anglesey [in AD61], Suetonius' men hacked down the religious woods, dedicated to devil worship and foul ceremonies.

Tacitus also offers us some other information (see Source 5):

SOURCE 5

■ *Anglesey was a popular hiding place for rebellious Britons.*
■ *When the Britons fought, the Druids stood in ranks, their hands uplifted, calling to the gods for help.*

1. When Suetonius attacked Anglesey it was only about 200 years since the Romans had stopped human sacrifices in their own religion. What do you think Romans would feel about a religion that still included human sacrifice? Do you think this would explain their dislike of the Druids?

2. Do the two statements in Source 5 suggest reasons why the Romans finished off the Druids? Explain your answer.

HOW TOLERANT WERE THE ROMANS?

At the other end of the Empire the Romans found themselves facing problems with two other religious groups, the Jews and the Christians.

Case study 2: the Jews

The home of the Jewish religion was the tiny kingdom of Judaea. Source 6 shows that this area was vital to Rome for many reasons.

Unlike Britain, Judaea was not a Roman province. But it was dominated by Rome. From time to time parts of Judaea were absorbed into the Roman province of Syria. At other times Rome appointed a governor to run Judaea. But as long as it was peaceful the Romans saw no need officially to make it a province.

Until 4BC Judaea was ruled by a strong King, Herod the Great. He was a keen supporter of the Romans and a friend of the Roman Emperor Augustus. At this time the Romans treated the Jews well. For example:

■ The Jews were excused service in the Roman army because it would involve them breaking some of their religious rules.

■ The Romans turned a blind eye to features of the Jewish religion that they disagreed with — for example the idea that there was only one God.

■ The Roman Emperor Augustus — who was not a Jew — paid for daily sacrifices in the Jews' Temple in Jerusalem.

Early in the first century AD most Jewish leaders were pro-Roman. When one of the kings of Judaea started breaking Jewish religious laws the Jews' leaders appealed directly to Rome for help and the King was removed.

Not all Jews lived in Judaea. There were Jewish communities in other cities in the Empire. Source 7, for example, concerns the Jews living in Rome.

SOURCE 7 A decree of Augustus in AD2 or 3

66 *Since the Jewish nation has been found well disposed to the Roman people, it has been decided that the Jews may follow their own customs . . . And if anyone is caught stealing their sacred items, his property shall be confiscated.*

---

1. From the evidence so far choose two words from the following list which best describe the attitude of the Romans to the Jewish religion, Then write four sentences explaining why you have chosen these two words.
   - critical
   - friendly
   - supporting
   - angry
   - tolerant
   - intolerant

Over the next 60 years the situation began to change. Herod had been a strong King. But his successors were the opposite. Judaea had one political crisis after another. Some Roman officials who were sent to help sort out these problems made them worse. For example, Pontius Pilate upset the Jews by breaking their religious rules and helped to stir up disagreements between opposing groups of Jews.

By AD60 there were some Jewish groups, including many chief priests, who supported Rome. Other groups, such as the poorer priests and a group called the Zealots, were opposed to the Romans and to any Jews who supported Rome.

Things came to a head in AD66. The Zealots revolted. They drove the Roman soldiers out of Jerusalem and took control of the Temple.

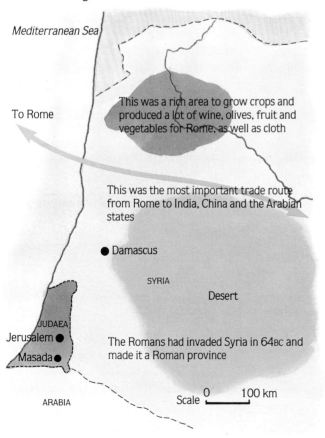

Mediterranean Sea

To Rome

This was a rich area to grow crops and produced a lot of wine, olives, fruit and vegetables for Rome, as well as cloth

This was the most important trade route from Rome to India, China and the Arabian states

● Damascus

SYRIA

Desert

JUDAEA
Jerusalem ●
Masada ●

The Romans had invaded Syria in 64BC and made it a Roman province

ARABIA

Scale 0 ___ 100 km

SOURCE 6 Syria and Judaea in the first century AD

The Roman Emperor sent an army of 50,000 soldiers to Judaea. They dealt harshly with the rebels. Up to one million Jews were killed. Thousands of others were transported to their deaths in AMPHITHEATRES. Jerusalem was captured. The Zealots were burned alive in the Temple. And Titus, one of the Roman generals, sacrificed a pig in the Temple, which was a terrible insult to the Jews.

The revolt was crushed, but that was not the end of the Zealots' resistance. In AD73 one group took over the mountain fortress of Masada.

SOURCE 8 The Jewish historian Josephus tells the story

The new governor in Judaea was Flavius Silva. He saw that only one fortress held out against the Romans. The fortress was Masada. He built a siege wall right round the fortress, with camps so that no one could escape.

The Romans occupied a spur of rock and built a solid earth platform on top. On this they built a base of stones, and on this a tower 27 m high, protected all over with iron plates. This tower was for catapults and stone throwers. A great battering ram was brought up to the platform and swung continuously against the fortress wall until it was smashed.

Josephus records the end of the battle. First, he makes up words which the Jewish leader might have said (see Source 10).

SOURCE 10

❝'It is clear that at daybreak our resistance will come to an end. But we are free to choose an honourable way to die with those we love. Let us die without becoming slaves to our enemies.'

Ten were chosen by lot to be the executioners of the rest, and everyone – men with their wives and children – lay down and offered their throats to those who had to perform the painful duty. So finally the nine presented their throats, and the one man left set fire to the palace and drove his sword through his own body and fell down beside his family. **❞**

2. Make a tracing of the outline of the fortress of Masada in Source 9. Mark on it where you think the Romans built the siege wall, the earth platform and the tower.
3. Are there any parts of Josephus' account that you think cannot be trusted?
4. Why do you think the Romans treated the Jewish rebels so harshly?
5. Why do you think the Jews at Masada killed themselves?

SOURCE 9 Photograph of Masada

Spur of rock occupied by Romans

Pathway to the fortress

Herod's palace

Case study 3: the Christians

The Christians were followers of Jesus Christ. Christianity began life as an offshoot from the Jewish religion. In around AD30 Jewish leaders in Judaea were worried about a new PROPHET, Jesus.

> **SOURCE 11** From an account of the events written some years later
>
> *Jesus was called by his followers Christ (the chosen one of God). His own people, the Jews, did not like this. They brought him to trial and handed him over to the Roman governor, Pontius Pilate, to be executed.*

Pilate saw no reason to crucify Jesus. But he bowed to Jewish pressure, and, because he feared a riot, he agreed to crucify Jesus. However, Jesus' followers did not give up. Not many years later the new religion of Christianity (named after Christ) was spreading around the Roman Empire, and even to Rome itself.

> **SOURCE 12** Written by the historian Tacitus about events in AD64. The city of Rome had been badly damaged by a massive fire
>
> *Nero [the Roman Emperor] put the blame for the fire on the Christians. Accordingly, they were all arrested. An enormous number were convicted. Mockery of every sort was added to their deaths. They were covered with the skins of beasts, and torn apart by dogs; or were nailed to crosses; or were condemned to the flames and burnt to serve as lighting when the sun had gone down.*

> **1.** Look at Source 12. How has the attitude of the Romans towards the Christians changed since AD30?

Sources 13–17 will help you decide for yourself why the Romans changed their minds about the Christians.

Some of the Christian leaders began to spread Christianity well beyond Syria. They included Paul, who was a Roman citizen. He made three journeys to cities in Asia, Macedonia and Achaea to teach people about Christianity. Eventually he was arrested and taken to Rome and was probably executed in AD66.

Christians like Paul taught that there was only one God. They wouldn't make offerings to any of the Romans' gods.

> **SOURCE 13** An extract from the *Acts of the Apostles*. In Ephesus (in the Roman province of Asia Minor) a silversmith complained that Paul was ruining his business of making silver models of Roman gods
>
> *Paul is telling them that gods made by human hands are not gods at all. There is danger for us here. Not only that our line of business will get a bad name, but also that the temple of Diana – the goddess who is worshipped by everyone in Asia and in all the world – will come to mean nothing.*

> **SOURCE 14** In the third century, Christians had to take a loyalty test. This is the sort of certificate they were given if they passed
>
> *We, Aurelia Bellias, daughter of Peteres, and her daughter Capinis, have always sacrificed to the gods, and now in your presence have sacrificed and eaten the sacred offerings.*

SOURCE 15 Written by the Emperor Trajan to one of his officials

Christians should be punished unless they prove they are not Christian by worshipping our gods. 99

---

2. According to Sources 14 and 15, how did Christians prove they were loyal to the Emperor?

3. Not all Christians were prepared to do this. Can you think of reasons why they might not want to?

SOURCE 16 Written by a modern religious writer

The real strength of Christianity, which made it outstrip all other religions, was its message of love and hope for everybody. This love and hope was extended to women, and even the poor and those that society had rejected. 99

▼ **SOURCE 17** A mosaic showing Christians being killed by wild animals in an amphitheatre

The persecution of Christians continued for many years. They suffered many extreme punishments.

For safety, Christians in Rome started to meet in secret in underground caves. This made the government even more suspicious, because they thought the Christians were plotting against the government.

Despite this persecution, Christianity continued to spread and grow, and 250 years after St Paul's journeys to the Mediterranean, Christianity was the most popular religion in the Empire.

Now look back at Sources 13–17 and use evidence from them to answer these questions.

4. How did the Romans treat Christians?

5. Why were the Romans worried about the Christians?

6. Can you find any evidence to explain why Christianity was so popular?

Different outcomes

The Druids were wiped out. The Jews survived as a persecuted minority in the Empire. But Christianity grew, until in 337 the Emperor Constantine became a Christian and Christianity became the official religion of the Empire. By 400 the Romans were spreading Christianity into the provinces, and the traditional religions of the Empire were themselves being put down.

---

1. On pages 52–57 we have studied the Roman treatment of three different religious groups. Do you think the Romans were right to be worried about:
- the Druids
- the Jews
- the Christians?

2. How could they have dealt with each group other than the way they did?

Activity

You have been asked to write a list of guidelines for government officials in first-century Rome, to help them decide whether a new religion is to be tolerated or not. Work in groups, and using any of the evidence on pages 52–57 write at least three guidelines.

Problems in the Empire

IN AD369 an anonymous writer sent a document to the Emperor Valens. Like many other people in the Empire, he was very worried about the problems facing it. In his 'treatise' he describes the problems and suggests some solutions, which are occasionally rather far-fetched.

> **SOURCE 1** From the introduction to the treatise
>
> *I shall describe:*
> - *how taxes can be reduced by half*
> - *how settlers can be persuaded to develop frontier lands without anxiety*
> - *how the gold and silver you [the Emperor] own can be doubled*
> - *how you can please the soldiers by giving them more rewards than usual.*
>
> *I shall also show:*
> - *how a particularly fast warship is able, through a brilliant invention, to defeat ten other ships and sink them, without need for a large crew*
> - *how a new invention can allow a horse to charge the enemy lines without needing a rider on his back*
> - *how a new type of military bridge has been invented which can be carried around by a small number of men and 50 packhorses.*

---

1. What evidence is there in Source 1 that:
- the government was running out of money
- people felt they were paying too much tax
- the army could not afford to pay as many soldiers as it needed?

The writer then goes on to explain his ideas about why things have gone wrong and various things he believes the Emperor should do:

> **SOURCE 2** Extracts from the treatise
>
> - *Public grants have made the rich even more extravagant, while the poor are driven by their problems into crime.*
> - *Now, in addition, comes the appalling greed of the provincial governors, which ruins the taxpayers.*
> - *The vast spending on the army must be stopped.*
> - *Above all, it must be recognised that wild nations are pressing upon the Roman Empire and howling round about it everywhere. Treacherous barbarians, protected by natural defences, are attacking every frontier. The state must take care of the frontier.*
> - *When you've dealt with all these, one thing remains to you, Emperor – to get rid of dishonest laws.*

The problems of the Roman Empire have been a favourite subject for historians to write about. Sources 4–6 come from three different histories of the Empire. They give us some extra information about some of the problems already mentioned, and add some new problems as well.

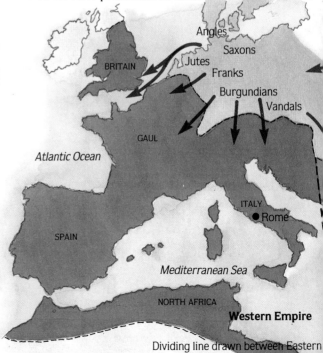

▶ **SOURCE 3** The Roman Empire and the barbarian tribes which threatened it. Since AD330 the Empire had been ruled from the Eastern capital, Constantinople

600BC | 218BC | 44BC | AD43 | AD120 | AD369 | AD500

SOURCE 4

The Empire's biggest single expenditure was the army. To pay for the army taxes had risen so much that an ordinary Roman was paying up to one third of his income in taxes and another one third in rent.

SOURCE 5

With no fixed method of choosing the next Emperor, there was nothing to stop cruel and selfish men from fighting for power. Time after time, successful generals marched their legions into Rome and killed the reigning Emperor, only to suffer the same fate themselves. In the space of 73 years there were 23 emperors, 20 of whom were murdered.

SOURCE 6

By the fourth century it was becoming very clear that the defensive system set up during the second century had a major flaw. It was too much like a lobster. Once attackers got through the armoured outer shell, there was nothing inside but undefended fleshy parts.

The Roman road system, which had served the Roman army so well when they were always on the attack, had allowed invaders to push deep into the Empire as soon as they got through the walls.

SOURCE 7 Border security was increased all over the Empire. Even in far-away Britain in the fourth century, the Romans built a series of coastal defences called the forts of the Saxon shore. This one is Pevensey Castle in Sussex

Huns

Eastern Goths

Western Goths

Black Sea

Constantinople

ASIA MINOR

Eastern Empire

Activity

Work in pairs or groups.
1. Using all the sources on this page, make a list of problems facing the Empire.
2. Write each problem on a separate piece of paper.
3. Arrange the problems in order of importance. Put the biggest problem first. If you think two problems are equally important place them alongside each other.
4. Take the problems in order, starting from the top. In your group, try to think of solutions to that problem.
5. Sometimes your solutions to one problem might make another problem worse. Check each of your solutions against the other problems.
6. Now, on your own, write a 'Discussion paper' to be presented to the Emperor's advisers.
   a) Set out the problems facing the Empire.
   b) Suggest solutions that can be adopted.

59

PROBLEMS IN THE EMPIRE

The decline of the West

The BARBARIAN tribes first crossed the Rhine in AD406. There had been regular raids for as long as the Empire had existed, but now the worn out Roman army and its inefficient leaders couldn't resist any longer. German tribesmen poured into the Empire looking for land to settle in. In 410 they reached Rome itself, and stripped it of many of its treasures.

The government in Rome sent a famous message to the British leaders. The British had appealed for help to fight off barbarian tribes who were making regular raids on the English coast. The British got the message back, 'You must look to your own defences.' In other words, the Romans meant 'We've got enough problems of our own in Rome. Please look after your own problems yourselves.'

In 476 the last western Emperor, Romulus Augustulus, lost his power. A barbarian King, Ordovocar, took over Italy and ruled his kingdom from Rome. Throughout Western Europe the Roman influence gradually, rather than suddenly, gave way to the new influence of the barbarian tribes.

---

1. Compare Source 8 with Source 3 on the previous page. Describe the changes that have happened in 100 years.

▼ **SOURCE 8** What had happened to the Roman Empire by AD476

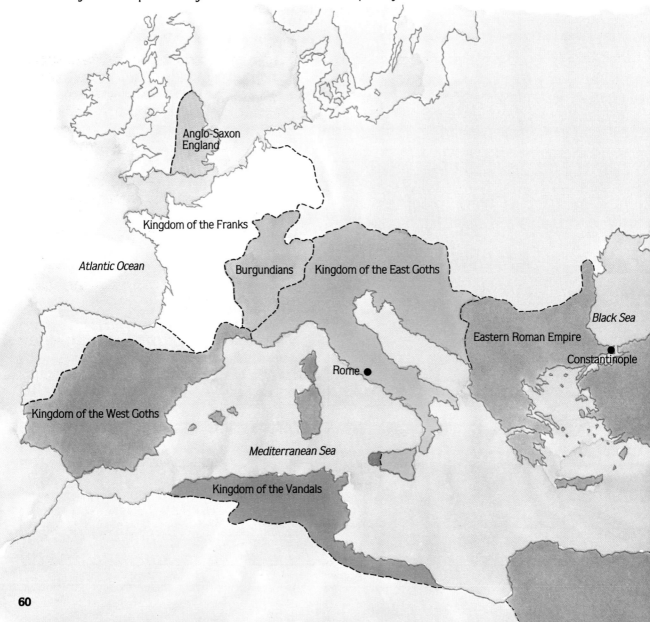

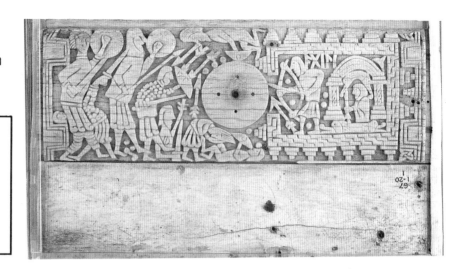

► **SOURCE 9** This ivory box, showing an attack on a Roman-held town, was made by Frankish craftsmen in the fifth century

2. Look at Source 9. Can you find:
- the Frankish attackers
- archers falling from the walls of the town
- townspeople sheltering in a church.

The survival of the East

After the Emperor Constantine moved the capital of the Empire to Constantinople in AD330, the Eastern Empire was wealthier and more populated than the West. The Pope, head of the Christian Church (now the official religion of the Empire), was in Rome, but the important affairs of the Empire were dealt with from Constantinople. And although the Eastern Empire suffered economic problems and barbarian attacks as well, it survived for a further 1000 years. It remained a powerful force around the Mediterranean until it was overrun by invaders in 1453.

The story of the Eastern Empire, under its new name, the Byzantine Empire, will be picked up again in the third unit in this book.

1. What date would you choose as the date of the end of the Roman Empire? Here are some possibilities. You might want to add a different date altogether.
395: when the Empire officially split in two
410: when Rome was sacked by barbarian invaders
476: when the last western Emperor was removed
1453: when the Eastern Empire was destroyed.

Take a vote in the class to see which is the favourite date.

What have the Romans given us?

Is THERE any evidence that even though the Roman Empire declined its influence continued?

Roads
■ In Britain, several of our main roads – e.g. the A1 (London to Scotland) or the A5 (London to North Wales) – follow the old lines of Roman roads.

Places and place names
■ Some of our most important cities were founded by the Romans, e.g. London.
■ Some places take their names from their Roman name, e.g. London from *Londinium*.

Calendar
■ The calendar we use today, with 365 days in a year, is based on the one developed by Julius Caesar.
■ All the months of the year take their names from the Roman months.
■ Some days of the week are named after Roman gods.

1. Which month is named after Julius Caesar, and which one after Mars, the god of war?
2. Which day of the week is named after Saturn, the Roman god of farmers?

Literature
■ Many stories, plays, poems and histories have survived from the Roman period. Probably the most famous is the *Aeneid*, written by Virgil.

Language
■ Latin is still spoken in some sections of the Roman Catholic Church. Until ten years ago all services in Roman Catholic churches were said in Latin.
■ Latin has influenced the way European languages such as French, Spanish, Italian and English have developed.
■ All British coins have a Latin inscription.
■ We've borrowed many words from Latin to use in English, e.g. *versus, et cetera, exit*.

3. Look at a pound coin. See if you can work out where the Latin is.

Religion
■ Christianity was adopted as the official religion of the Roman Empire in AD337 and remains the dominant religion in most countries which once formed a part of the Empire.

Buildings
■ Some Roman buildings – e.g. the Roman baths in Bath – are still standing today, which shows how well built they were.
■ Roman styles have been copied in many places at different times, e.g. public buildings such as museums, town halls and even schools built in Britain in the nineteenth century.

Health and medicine
■ Roman ideas about public health, surgery and patient care were picked up by ISLAMIC doctors and later by European doctors.

Science
■ In science, plants, animals, insects and even mushrooms are known officially by Latin names.

Law
■ Aspects of British law – the way the courts are run, names of officials and the way cases are recorded – have all developed from Roman law.

Activity
Historians call the influence a society has on societies that come after it a legacy. What is the Roman legacy?

Work in small groups.
1. Write out each of the pieces of information on this page on a separate piece of card.
2. Sort the cards into three piles:
a) things that still play a part in your life today
b) things that don't play a part in your life today
c) things you cannot decide about.
   You may need to refer to earlier pages in the unit for more information about a subject.
3. You are going to have a class debate. Prepare a case for or against this statement: 'The Romans have no relevance for us today.' You should consider:
■ whether the Roman legacy plays a part in *your* life today.
■ whether the Roman legacy plays a part in *other people's* lives today.

MEDIEVAL REALMS

super omnem terram:
tis es super omnes de

500BC

0

AD500

AD1000

AD1500

What were the Middle Ages like?

"*The medieval period began in 1066 when William of Normandy invaded England and defeated the English army at the Battle of Hastings. It continued full of battles and corpses until another battle in 1485 brought this violent period to a close.*"

LOOK at these two collections of sources. All the paintings come from the Middle Ages, and the photograph is of a church which was built during the Middle Ages. However, the two collections give very different impressions of what the Middle Ages were like.

After you have finished this unit on Medieval Realms, you will be able to make up your own mind about what the Middle Ages were like.

COLLECTION A

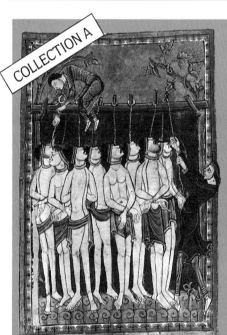

SOURCE 1

SOURCE 2

SOURCE 3

SOURCE 4

SOURCE 5

SOURCE 6

SOURCE 7

SOURCE 8

SOURCE 9

SOURCE 10

1. Explain what is happening in each of the sources in Collection A.
2. Use the sources in Collection A to write a description of what the Middle Ages were like.
   You could use some of these words in your description:

   peaceful   clever   dangerous
   cruel   violent   hardworking.

3. Explain what is happening in each of the sources in Collection B.

4. Use the sources in Collection B to write a description of what the Middle Ages were like. You could use some of the words in the list on the left in your description.
5. Historians disagree about what the Middle Ages were like. How do the two collections of sources help to explain why historians have different views of the Middle Ages?

England in the 1060s

ENGLAND in the 1060s was a very different place from the Roman province in AD400. There were probably about 1½ million people living in England, compared with 47 million today. Much of the southern half of the country was still covered by forest. Here and there were small villages where the forest had been cleared and the land was farmed. The northern and western parts of the country were even more thinly populated (see Source 1).

Nearly everyone worked on the land. There were few towns – probably only about twenty with a population of more than 1000. The largest of these towns are marked on Source 1.

England was governed by King Edward the Confessor, but he had trouble in keeping the country under control. Source 2 shows that England was divided into a number of earldoms, each ruled over by a powerful leader called an earl. These earls were meant to be loyal to the King, but sometimes they rebelled against him.

England was not a well defended country. There were hardly any castles, and most towns or villages were simply protected by earth embankments, like the ones shown in Source 3.

SOURCE 3 The remains of the earth embankments surrounding Wareham in Dorset

On the edge of Europe

England's connections with Scandinavia were much closer than with the rest of Europe. Earlier in the century, England had been part of the great VIKING EMPIRE of King Cnut of Denmark and Norway (see Source 4).

SOURCE 1 England's population in the 1060s. The largest towns are also shown

Key
Population per km²
- 6 and over
- 4 to 6
- 2 to 4
- Under 2
- No data
- Towns with more than 3000 inhabitants

SCOTLAND
WALES
York
Lincoln
Norwich
Stamford
Thetford
Wallingford
London
Winchester

Key
1 Morcar
2 Edwin
3 Gyrth
4 Harold
5 Waltheof
6 Leofwine

WALES

SOURCE 2
English earldoms

However, two developments were going to bring about much more contact between England and mainland Europe.

Across the English Channel, Normandy was a growing power. William, Duke of Normandy, had recently defeated some of the neighbouring countries. The Normans were even trying to conquer the island of Sicily. William also had ambitions to become King of England: if this happened England's connections with the rest of Europe would become much stronger.

England had one important thing in common with the rest of Europe. It was a Christian country and belonged to the Roman Catholic Church. The head of the Church was the Pope in Rome. He was in charge of all the BISHOPS and PRIESTS in England and the rest of the Christian countries of Europe – together known as Christendom.

SOURCE 4 King Cnut's Scandinavian Empire, 1016–1034

NORWAY

DENMARK

ENGLAND

English Channel

ENGLAND

NORMANDY

BYZANTINE EMPIRE

Rome

Constantinople

Sicily

ISLAMIC EMPIRE

Jerusalem

SOURCE 5 Europe and the Middle East in the 1060s

The other great religion at this time was ISLAM (see Unit C, pages 154–215). You can see the Islamic Empire in Source 5. The Islamic people, or MUSLIMS, had control of the HOLY LAND and the city of Jerusalem. The Pope was determined to conquer the Holy Land. In 1095 he announced a CRUSADE against the Muslims. If England took part it would mean co-operating closely with the rest of Europe.

SOURCE 6 Descriptions of the English and the Normans in the 1060s written by William of Malmesbury, a monk, about 70 years later. He was half English and half Norman by birth

a) *The English, at that time, wore short garments reaching to the midknee; they had their hair cropped; their beards shaven; their arms covered with golden bracelets; their skins covered with punctured designs. Drinking parties were very common and they drank until they were sick. Drunkenness weakens the human mind and they often fought with rashness and fury rather than with military skill.*

b) *The Normans were very particular in their dress and ate and drank with care and not to excess. They were used to war, and could hardly live without it. They were fierce in rushing against the enemy, and where strength failed they tricked and deceived the enemy.*

---

1. The beginnings and endings of the following sentences have been mixed up. Using the information on these two pages, match the correct heads and tails.

Heads	Tails
King Cnut	were the two great religions of the time.
Edward the Confessor	wanted the European rulers to go on a Crusade to conquer the Holy Land.
Christianity and Islam	ruled over a great Scandinavian Empire.
The Normans	ruled over England in the 1060s.
The Pope	hoped to conquer England and Sicily.

2. Read Source 6 carefully. What were the differences between the Normans and the English?

3. Do you think William of Malmesbury's descriptions can be trusted?

4. Give at least three reasons why, if William of Normandy wanted to invade England, the Normans might find it easy to defeat the English.

5. Say whether you agree or disagree with each of these statements, and explain why:
   ■ 'In the 1060s England had little contact with the rest of Europe.'
   ■ 'England was likely to become more involved in Europe in the future.'

6. How was England in the 1060s different from England under Roman rule? The following headings will help you: towns, defence, trade, contact with Europe.

From across the water

THE month is September, the year 1066. It is early in the morning, about six o'clock. A boy and a girl sit near the ruins of the old Roman fort at Pevensey on the south coast of England. For a few moments they have escaped their daily chores.

After milking the family cow and eating a breakfast of warm milk and hard black bread, they have crept away to their favourite place on the cliffs to watch the dawn over the sea. It is getting lighter now and from their position on the cliffs they have a good view of the beach and the sea. The strong wind coming off the sea makes them shiver.

They are just about to leave when the girl notices some unfamiliar smudges on the horizon. What can they be? As the light grows stronger the smudges become clearer. They are ships, hundreds of them, and the wind is speeding them towards the beach.

Without knowing it, the boy and girl are seeing the beginning of one of the most important events in English history – the Norman Invasion.

SOURCE 1 This picture comes from the Bayeux Tapestry. The Normans had it embroidered in Kent in the 1070s to tell the story of their invasion of England

SOURCE 3 From the Bayeux Tapestry

SOURCE 4 From the Bayeux Tapestry

Captions

The Norman fleet approaches the coast of England

The Norman army lands

The Normans round up sheep and cows

The Normans prepare a feast

SOURCE 2 From the Bayeux Tapestry

1. Match the captions to the pictures in Sources 1–4.
2. List the pictures in the correct order.
3. Look carefully at Source 1.
   a) Describe how the two cooks (A) are cooking the meat.
   b) Why do you think the baker (B) is using a large pair of tongs?
   c) Can you see where the food is being taken indoors?
   d) Why is the table (C) made of shields?
   e) Why do you think this man (D) is blowing a horn?
4. Imagine you are the girl or boy watching the invasion from the old Roman fort. Describe the landing of the Norman army and what happens after they have landed. Try to include as much detail as you can find in Sources 1–4 about their ships, their clothing, their weapons and tools, and what they are doing.

Why was 1066 a year of crisis?

IN 1066 England was invaded twice, there were two bloody battles for the English throne, and England had three different kings! Why was 1066 such a year of crisis in England?

One reason was that on 5 January 1066 the King of England, Edward the Confessor, died without any children. There were three people claiming to be the next King of England.

Edward's death certainly sparked off the crisis of 1066, but in fact trouble had been brewing for a long time. Edward had done well to stay in control of England until 1066. To understand why 1066 turned into such a year of violence, we must look at what had been happening during the years before.

SOURCE 1   England (including Wessex), Norway, Denmark and Normandy

The Earls of Wessex

Harold Godwineson belonged to the most powerful family in England. They already controlled Wessex, but had ambitions to rule England. In 1051, Harold and his father rebelled against Edward, but were defeated and driven from the country. Harold returned the next year and soon became the most powerful nobleman in England. He thought he had the best claim to the throne because he was Edward's brother-in-law. Harold was also the only Englishman claiming the throne.

SOURCE 2   Written in about 1120 by a monk who was trained in Normandy

66While the crowds watched King Edward's funeral, Harold had himself crowned King alone by Archbishop Stigund, without the common consent of the other bishops and nobles. When the English learned that Harold had taken the throne they were moved to anger; some of the most powerful were ready to resist him by force.99

SOURCE 3   From a book in praise of the Godwine family, written in 1066 by a foreign monk

66Archbishop Stigund whispered in Harold's ear that the King was broken with age and knew not what he said.
Stretching forth his hand to Harold, Edward said, 'I commend all the kingdom to your protection.'99

England and Normandy

When King Cnut invaded England in 1016, Edward the Confessor, who was then a young boy, fled to Normandy for protection. He stayed there until 1042, when he became King of England. As King, he had to protect his throne from Viking attacks and from the powerful Earls of Wessex.

In 1051 Harold Godwineson of Wessex rebelled against Edward. Edward asked his cousin **William, Duke of Normandy**, for help. William

1. Why did Harold Godwineson think he should be King of England?
2. Do you think his claim was a good one?

England and Norway

In the 860s VIKINGS from Norway had invaded England and had settled in the north. In 1016 the Viking King Cnut had become King of England, Denmark and Norway. England was ruled by Norwegian kings until 1042, when the English Edward the Confessor seized the throne. The Norwegians planned two invasions in the 1040s, but they never happened.

The King of Norway in 1066 was **Harald Hardraada**. Harald wanted to rebuild the great Viking Empire of King Cnut. He also felt that he had a right to be King of England (see Source 4). He made raids on the English coast, and he planned a full-scale invasion of England. There were many people from Viking families in the north of England who might help him.

1. Why did Harald Hardraada think he should be King of England?
2. Do you think his claim was a good one?

KING CNUT
King of England 1016-1035
(also King of Denmark and Norway)

his son

KING HARTHACNUT
King of England 1040-1042
(also King of Denmark)

promises English throne to

KING MAGNUS OF NORWAY

Claim passed on to next King of Norway

HARALD HARDRAADA

SOURCE 4 Harald Hardraada's claim to the English throne

---

sent soldiers to live in England. Also, in 1051, according to Norman sources, Edward made William his heir.

1. Sources 5, 6 and 7 are all about the same event. What details does Source 6 give which are not in Sources 5 and 7?
2. Why do you think Source 6 includes these details when the other two sources do not?

◄ **SOURCE 5** An extract from the Bayeux Tapestry showing Harold swearing his loyalty to William as the next King of England

SOURCE 6 Written in about 1120 by Eadmer, an Englishman who hated the Norman kings

66 In 1064 Harold asked King Edward for permission to go to Normandy to set free his nephew who was being held there as a hostage.

William told Harold that King Edward had promised him that he would succeed him on the throne. William went on to say this: 'If you agree to support me in this project I will let you have your nephew.'

Harold saw there was danger whatever way he turned. He could not see any way to escape without agreeing to all that William wished. So he agreed. 99

SOURCE 7 Written around 1071 by William of Poitiers, who had served as a Norman soldier

66 King Edward, who loved William as a brother, felt the hour of his death approaching. He sent Harold to William to confirm his promise of the throne by an oath. When they came together, Harold swore loyalty to William. 99

3. Why did William think he should be King of England?
4. Do you think William's claim was a good one?

Activity

Divide into groups. Each group must decide who has the best claim to the English throne. Prepare a wall display or poster to convince people that your candidate's claims are good ones.

WHY WAS 1066 A YEAR OF CRISIS?

Harold defends England

King Edward died on 5 January 1066. The next day, Harold Godwineson was crowned as king. But he must have known that he would have to fight both Harald Hardraada and William to stay king.

Throughout the summer of 1066 both William of Normandy and Harald Hardraada prepared their invasion fleets. Harold Godwineson prepared his defences and waited. William threatened the south coast, while Harald Hardraada threatened the north (see Source 8). Harold had to decide which coast to defend first.

The threat to the south coast

In January 1066 William started to build a fleet and gather his army together. By 12 August he was ready. He had 5000 foot-soldiers, and 2000 KNIGHTS on horseback. The most difficult part of the operation would be transporting these soldiers across the English Channel.

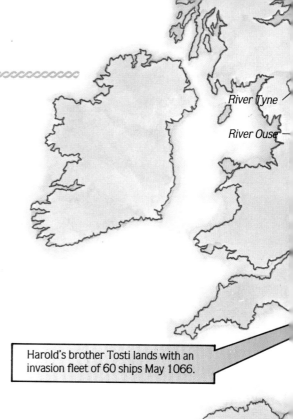

River Tyne

River Ouse

Harold's brother Tosti lands with an invasion fleet of 60 ships May 1066.

SOURCE 8 Threats to Harold in 1066

SOURCE 9 Extracts from the Bayeux Tapestry showing William's preparations for the invasion

The wind was blowing in the wrong direction and so William waited. Harold Godwineson knew that William might invade at any moment.

William was not the only threat to the south coast. Tosti (Harold Godwineson's exiled brother) wanted revenge on Harold and had gathered together a fleet of 60 ships (see Source 10).

SOURCE 10 Written by Simeon of Durham a few years after the events it describes

66 *Tosti landed at the Isle of Wight in May. After forcing the islanders to pay him money, he departed, and went along the south coast to the port of Sandwich, committing ravages. King Harold, who was then in London, ordered a large fleet and an army to be assembled. Tosti, being informed of this, withdrew.*

King Harold went to Sandwich and there waited for his fleet. When it had assembled, he went to the Isle of Wight, and as William was preparing to come with an army he kept watch the whole summer. But by 8 September provisions were growing scarce and Harold sent his navy and army home. 99

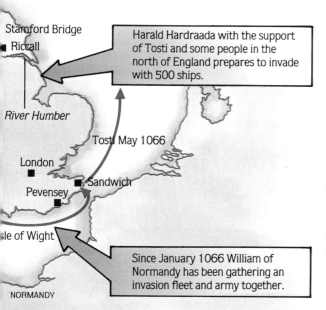

Stamford Bridge
Riccall

Harald Hardraada with the support of Tosti and some people in the north of England prepares to invade with 500 ships.

River Humber

Tosti May 1066

London

Sandwich

Pevensey

Isle of Wight

Since January 1066 William of Normandy has been gathering an invasion fleet and army together.

NORMANDY

The threat to the north coast

Harald Hardraada had also been making preparations to invade. He had support from the people of the Orkneys, which belonged to him, and from Tosti and his fleet of ships, which had gone north. He also hoped for help from Malcolm, King of Scotland, and even from people in the north of England who were from VIKING families.

> **SOURCE 11** From an account by William of Malmesbury, written about 70 years after the events it describes
>
> *In late May Tosti arrived on the Humber with a fleet of 60 ships, but was quickly driven away by Earl Edwin and Earl Morcar. He set sail for Scotland with only twelve ships. When he heard that Harald Hardraada was planning an attack on England with over 500 ships and 10,000 men, Tosti put himself under his command.*

1. Put yourself in Harold Godwineson's position in the summer of 1066. You have news of William's invasion preparations, but you also know about Tosti and Harald Hardraada.
   - Do you guard the south coast?
   - Do you guard the north?
   - Do you split your forces and guard both?
   Explain carefully which course of action you would have taken. You must take into account who was the stronger, and who was likely to attack first.

On 20 September Harald Hardraada arrived at the mouth of the River Tyne with a powerful fleet of more than 500 ships. Earl Tosti joined him with his fleet. They sailed up the Ouse and landed at Riccall. The two brothers Earls Edwin and Morcar fought a battle with the Norwegians, but after a long fight the English fled. Many of them were killed.

Harold was now in a desperate position. After the long wait on the south coast he had just sent his soldiers and sailors home. He now had to gather his army together again, march hundreds of miles north, defeat the Norwegians and return south before the wind changed and allowed William to invade!

Source 12 tells us what then happened on 25 September.

> **SOURCE 12** From the Anglo-Saxon Chronicle, which was written by the English a long time after the events it describes. The writer was very much on Harold's side
>
> *Then came our King Harold on the Norwegians unawares, and met them beyond York at Stamford with a great host of English folk; there was that day a very fierce battle fought on both sides. Harald Hardraada was killed, and Earl Tosti; the Norwegians that were left were put to flight, and the English fiercely struck them from behind, until some of them came to the ships. Some drowned, some were burnt, some died in various ways, so that there were few left. Only 24 ships returned to Norway.*

This was a great victory for Harold against one of the greatest warriors of the time. But on the night of 27 September (two days later), the direction of the wind along the south coast changed and William's invasion fleet set sail. It landed at Pevensey, on the Sussex coast, early next morning.

Just think how Harold must have felt when he heard this news!

2. Harold had won a great victory in the north. Was his position now stronger or weaker than it was before Harald Hardraada's invasion?

Harold v. William: who will win?

LOOK at the timeline. It shows the events in the months and days leading up to the Battle of Hastings, and the different ways the two sides got ready for it.

As you study the timeline and all the sources on these two pages, remember that:

■ William waited until the weather was suitable to cross the English Channel. He did not lose his patience and try to go too early.

■ Harold had chosen to take the English throne and so was a target for both Harald Hardraada and William.

■ Harold chose to guard the south coast and so had to dash up north quickly.

■ Harold had to dash back from the north and attack William before he was really ready.

SOURCE 1 Written in about 1115 by Florence of Worcester, a monk

❝Harold marched his army towards London by forced marches; and, although he knew that he had lost some of his best men in the recent battle, and that half of his troops were not yet assembled, he did not hesitate to meet the enemy.

William, Count of the Normans, had arrived with a countless host of horsemen, slingers, archers and foot-soldiers, and had brought with him also powerful help from all parts of France.❞

1. Looking at the timeline and all the sources on this page, which army do you think would be best prepared for the battle? Give reasons.

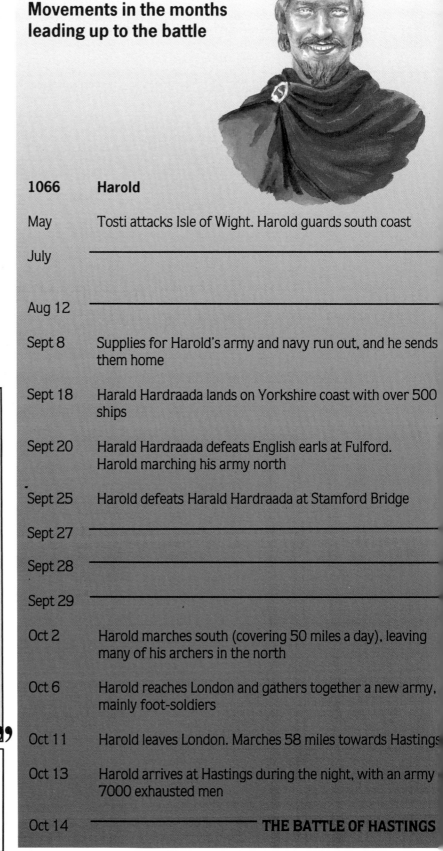

Movements in the months leading up to the battle

1066	Harold
May	Tosti attacks Isle of Wight. Harold guards south coast
July	
Aug 12	
Sept 8	Supplies for Harold's army and navy run out, and he sends them home
Sept 18	Harald Hardraada lands on Yorkshire coast with over 500 ships
Sept 20	Harald Hardraada defeats English earls at Fulford. Harold marching his army north
Sept 25	Harold defeats Harald Hardraada at Stamford Bridge
Sept 27	
Sept 28	
Sept 29	
Oct 2	Harold marches south (covering 50 miles a day), leaving many of his archers in the north
Oct 6	Harold reaches London and gathers together a new army, mainly foot-soldiers
Oct 11	Harold leaves London. Marches 58 miles towards Hastings
Oct 13	Harold arrives at Hastings during the night, with an army 7000 exhausted men
Oct 14	**THE BATTLE OF HASTINGS**

William

William continues to prepare his fleet: arms and people are gathered together

Fleet assembles ready to invade

William waiting in France for the wind to change

The wind changes direction and William's fleet leaves France

William's fleet lands early in the morning

Occupies Hastings, prepares for battle

SOURCE 2 The Normans having time to relax

SOURCE 3 The Norman cavalry ready for battle

SOURCE 4 Written by William of Malmesbury, 70 years later

66*Harold, elated by his success at Stamford Bridge, decided to give no part of the spoils to his soldiers. Many left his army as he was proceeding to the Battle of Hastings, so he had very few soldiers with him.*99

SOURCE 5 Harold's and William's movements

You may already have made up your mind about which side was likely to win the battle, but we need to see what actually happened. Was there any chance that Harold could win?

HAROLD V. WILLIAM: WHO WILL WIN?

SOURCE 6 A scene from the Bayeux Tapestry

What happened in the battle?

SOURCE 7 A Norman account by William of Poitiers. He was not at the battle

66 *William's army advanced steadily in good order. The crossbowmen were at the front. Next came the infantry, and the knights were at the back.*

Harold's army was a vast host, gathered from all the provinces of England and reinforced by their allies the Danes. They did not care to fight on equal terms, so they took up their position on a hill with a forest behind them. They dismounted and drew themselves up in close order on foot.

The Norman foot-soldiers then attacked, but it seemed they would be overwhelmed by the English missiles. Then our knights crashed into the enemy with their shields. The English remained on high ground and kept close order. They were superior in numbers and in the way their spears broke our shields. Thus they pushed our knights down the hill.

William stood out boldly in front of those in flight, and restored their courage. Our men marched up the hill a second time. They realised that they would suffer heavy losses, but then remembered the trick of retreating. They turned round and pretended to flee. Several thousand English quickly gave pursuit. The Normans suddenly turned their horses, surrounded the enemy and cut them down. Twice this trick was used with great success. 99

1. Look at Source 6. Explain which soldiers are the Normans and which are the English. Read Source 7 – this will help you to decide.
2. Describe in as much detail as you can what is happening. Include:
   - the number of soldiers on each side
   - the number dead
   - how the Normans are armed
   - whether the English are armed in the same way
   - how the English have organised their defence.

SOURCE 8 An English account from the Anglo-Saxon Chronicle

66 *William took Harold by surprise before his men were ready for battle. The English army had a very small space; and many soldiers, seeing the difficult position, deserted King Harold. Even so, he fought bravely from dawn to dusk, and the enemy's army made little impression on him until, after a great slaughter on both sides, the King fell.* 9

3. In what ways do Sources 7 and 8 differ?
4. Why do you think they give such different accounts?
5. Were there any moments in the battle when Harold could have won?

76

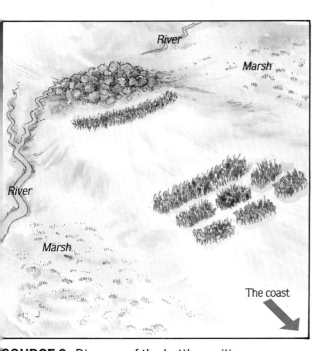

SOURCE 9 Diagram of the battle positions

6. Using Source 9 as a start, draw a detailed map of the beginning of the battle. Put in the hill, the forest, and the different lines of Norman soldiers. Then draw another plan with arrows and labels explaining what you think happened in the battle. Make sure you understand the events before the battle as well as those during the battle.

Activity

Work in groups. Using all the evidence on the last four pages, make up your mind why William won. Was it:
■ because of his own skill *or*
■ because Harold made mistakes *or*
■ because Harold was unlucky *or*
■ by a combination of all three?

How did Harold die?

SOURCE 10 From the Bayeux Tapestry. The words mean 'King Harold is killed'

1. What does Source 10 tell you about how Harold died?

Question 1 is not easy, because the Tapestry shows two soldiers dying. The one on the left is pulling an arrow from his eye. The one on the right is being chopped down with a sword. Which one is meant to be Harold? Look at Sources 11 and 12. Do they solve the problem?

SOURCE 11 An account of Harold's death written by a French bishop just two years after the battle – well before the Bayeux Tapestry was embroidered

❝With the point of his lance the first knight pierced Harold's shield and chest, drenching the ground with blood. With his sword the second knight cut off his head. The third disembowelled him with his javelin. The fourth hacked off his leg.❞

SOURCE 12 An account written about 150 years after the battle

❝Harold fell, his brain pierced by an arrow.❞

2. Why do you think the accounts differ?
3. Could both the men in the Tapestry be Harold?
4. What problems would historians face if they tried to use this evidence to find out how Harold died?

How did William gain control?

PUT yourself in William's place just after the Battle of Hastings. You have defeated Harold. But there is a long way to go before you can say that you have conquered England. So far all you have conquered is a small corner of England. How you deal with the remaining problems will also have an important effect on the English. Will they be worse off or better off?

Some of the problems (shown in Source 1) are short-term. They pose an immediate threat to you and need to be dealt with straight away. But they can be solved by swift and decisive action.

The other problems do not pose an immediate threat. They need thinking about carefully and may take years to deal with.

---

1. Which of the problems in Source 1 are short-term ones and need to be dealt with immediately?

2. In what order would you deal with them?

Sources 2–6 show how William dealt with the short-term problems.

SOURCE 2 Written by William of Poitiers in around 1071. He fought for William of Normandy

66 *Then William marched to Dover, which was held by a large force. The English were stricken with fear and prepared to surrender unconditionally, but our men, greedy for booty, set fire to the castle and the greater part of it was destroyed. The Duke, unwilling that those who had offered to surrender should suffer loss, gave them money for the damage. Having taken possession of the castle, the Duke spent eight days adding new fortifications to it.* 99

SOURCE 3 Florence of Worcester describing William's movements before he went to London

66 *Earl William was laying waste Sussex, Kent, Hampshire, Surrey, Middlesex and Hertfordshire and ceased not from burning villages and slaughtering the inhabitants. He was then met by the Earls Edwin and Morcar and Londoners of the better sort, who submitted to him.* 99

SOURCE 1 Map of England showing some of the problems William faced in 1066

SCOTLAND

1. Many of the English lords do not want to accept you as King. You cannot trust them to keep their parts of the country under control. You need to find a way of keeping the whole country under control.

2. You need to collect taxes, but you do not know how much wealth there is in the country and who owns what.

▶ **SOURCE 4** Norman soldiers attacking Englishmen. A picture from a medieval manuscript

5. There is still a threat of invasions from Scandinavia, supported by an English rebellion in the north of England.

ork

4. London is England's capital city. You must take control of it quickly. Some of Harold's troops did not come with him to Hastings. Many of them are still in London.

London

Dover

3. There is a very strong castle full of English soldiers at Dover. If things go wrong for you they could cut off your route back to Normandy.

Hastings

SOURCE 5 Written about 60 years after the events described, by a monk trained in Normandy

66 *The royal forces approached York, only to learn that the Danes had fled. The King ordered his men to repair the castles in the city. He himself continued to comb forests and remote mountainous places, stopping at nothing to hunt out the enemy hidden there. He cut down many in his vengeance; destroyed the lairs of others; harried the land, and burned homes to ashes. Nowhere else had William shown such cruelty. He made no effort to control his fury and punished the innocent with the guilty. In his anger he ordered that all crops, herds and food of every kind should be brought together and burned to ashes, so that the whole region north of the Humber might be stripped of all means of sustenance. As a result of this such a terrible famine fell upon the humble and defenceless people that more than 100,000 Christian folk of both sexes, young and old alike, perished of hunger.* 99

SOURCE 6 Florence of Worcester describing conditions about twenty years after the Conquest

66 *So severe was the famine in most parts of the kingdom, that men were driven to feed on the flesh of horses, dogs, cats and even of human beings.* 99

3. Which of William's problems are Sources 2, 3 and 5 about?
4. Describe in your own words how William dealt with each of these problems.
5. Which problems has William not dealt with?

Activity

a) You are an English earl. Prepare a speech to give to William, complaining about the brutal way he is treating the English.
b) Now write a reply from William to the English earl, explaining why you have to use such methods.

HOW DID WILLIAM GAIN CONTROL?

By the early 1070s William had put down all the rebellions against his rule. He could now think about the long-term problems. How could he make sure that the whole country was under control, and how could he find out what everybody owned so that he could tax them?

The Feudal System

The ownership of land was dramatically changed by William. Many of the English earls died in the great battles of 1066. Others were killed in the later rebellions, or fled abroad. William took land from many of the surviving English landowners. He needed landowners he could depend on:

- to protect the country from invasion
- to keep the English under control
- to collect taxes.

Source 7 shows who held land in England by the end of William's reign.

In theory, all the land in England belonged to the King, but he could not look after it all himself so he granted some of the land to the men who had helped him conquer England. One of these men was his brother, Odo of Bayeux, who was given over 400 estates all round the country.

In return for this land, tenants-in-chief (BARONS) like Odo had to send William KNIGHTS for his army for 40 days a year. This gave William an army of about 4000 men. The diagram in Source 8 shows how this system worked.

Odo had 184 estates in Kent but kept only seven of them. The rest he granted to men who had fought with him at Hastings. These men did not do any of the farming of their lands themselves. They used the PEASANTS who lived on these estates.

---

1. William needed to do the following:
  - reward his followers
  - keep law and order all over the country
  - raise money
  - raise an army.

  Which two of these needs are dealt with by the Feudal System?
- a) Divide your page into four boxes. In two of the four boxes use a drawing with some writing to show how the Feudal System helped solve these two needs.
- b) Which of the four needs did the Feudal System not help solve?

SOURCE 7

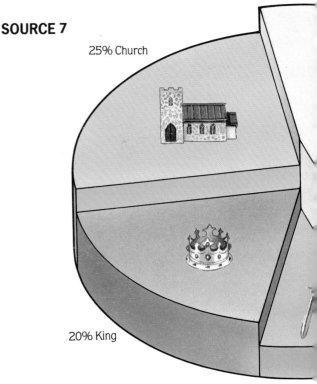

25% Church

20% King

8% English earls

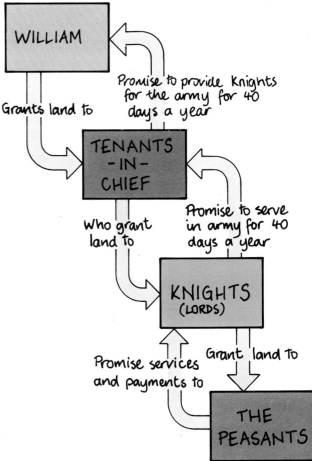

SOURCE 8 How the Feudal System worked

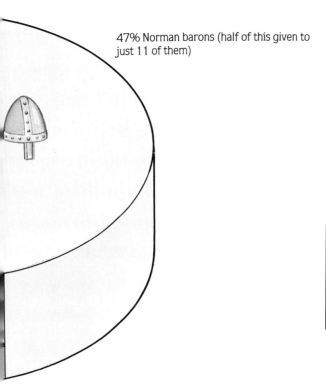

47% Norman barons (half of this given to just 11 of them)

The Domesday Book

In 1085 William had to bring a large army over from Normandy because of a threatened invasion. The invasion never came, but the army had to be paid for. William was already taxing people according to the value of their land. But no one had ever bothered to find out exactly how much everyone owned. There might be some people who were not paying as much tax as they should.

Read Source 9, which explains William's solution.

SOURCE 9 From the Ely Inquiry

The King's officials met the priest, the reeve and six men from each village. They inquired what the manor was called, and who held it in the time of King Edward; who holds it now; how many hides there are, how many ploughs, how many villeins, how many cottars; how many slaves, how many freemen; how much woodland, how much meadow; how many mills, what the estate is worth now. And it was also to be noted whether more could be taken from the estate than is now being taken.

Remember that this happened only twenty years after the Conquest. Although the survey caused some riots, the officials managed to travel about and get this information from 13,000 villages. A second group followed them, checking everything. It was all finished within a year. Only the far north, Wales, Scotland and some large towns like London were not covered. The results of the survey were written down in the Domesday Book.

You can see the kind of information they recorded in Source 5 on page 86.

1. William used his own officials and not the BARONS to carry out this inquiry. Why was this?
2. Does the success of this inquiry show that William was completely in control of the country?

The sheriffs

Before the time of William, law and order were kept and taxes collected by the SHERIFFS and the shire courts. The sheriffs were appointed by the King. William made the job more important by making the BARONS into sheriffs. The sheriffs paid the King a lump sum, and then kept all the fines they collected. They often taxed the poor too heavily, and even evicted peasants from their homes. The system of law and order became more efficient but it is doubtful whether it was very fair.

1. Look back at the four boxes you made for question 1 on the opposite page. Fill in the two empty boxes to show how William solved his other problems.
2. Which of the following statements does everyone in the class agree are right?
   ■ 'William invaded England in September 1066.'
   ■ 'William had the best claim to the English throne.'
   ■ 'William was a cruel king.'
   ■ 'William gave land to many of his followers.'
3. Which of the statements is there disagreement about?
4. Are the statements everyone agreed about stating facts or opinions?
5. How about the statements people disagreed about? Are they facts or opinions?

Castle building

William was convinced that one of the reasons why he had been able to conquer England was because it had hardly any castles. He had used castles very successfully to control Normandy.

Some English villages or small towns, called *burhs*, were surrounded by large earth ramparts (see Source 10). The local people were expected to defend them in times of danger. But they were nothing like the castles the Normans built (see Sources 11–13).

Source 11 shows a castle that the Normans built at Dinan in Normandy.

SOURCE 10 Wallingford, showing the line of the ramparts

SOURCE 11 Castle of Dinan, from the Bayeux Tapestry

---

1. Draw an outline picture of Source 11 and label:
   - the different methods being used to attack the castle
   - how the soldiers are defending the castle
   - the drawbridge and the moat
   - the soldier who is surrendering the castle.

SOURCE 13 The 'White Tower' at the Tower of London, the first stone keep built by William

SOURCE 12 Modern drawing of the motte and bailey castle at Pickering

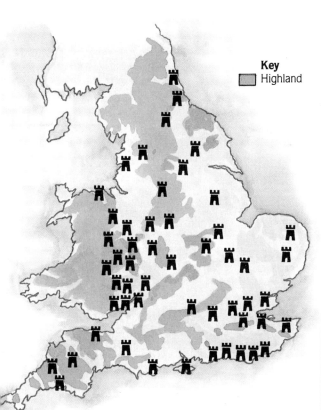

Key
Highland

SOURCE 14 Map showing the castles built in England and Wales by the end of William's reign. In Gloucester 16 houses were destroyed to make way for the new castle, in Cambridge 27, in Lincoln 166

William had castles built all over England. Like the ones in Normandy, they consisted of a motte and a bailey. The motte was a large mound, usually about 50 feet high, and was built at one side of a circular bailey. The whole construction was built from earth and wood and could be finished in a couple of weeks.

A castle provided safety for a baron and his family. At first, barons lived in the bailey and retreated to the motte to escape from danger, but later they lived in stone keeps like the one in Source 13. The castle was also a base for the baron's soldiers to control the surrounding countryside. Anybody wanting to conquer this part of the country would have to capture the castle before they could move on. Law courts were held at the castle, and people paid their taxes there.

2. Look at Source 12. Describe the features which would make it easy to defend.
3. Why do you think the Normans built the first castles of wood?
4. Later in William's reign castles like the one in Source 13 began to be built. What are the advantages of this kind of castle?
5. Using Sources 10–14, describe the stages of the development of castles from the English burh to the Norman stone keep.

How do we reconstruct medieval villages?

NEARLY everybody in the Middle Ages lived in the country. Here and there in the countryside were small clusters of houses with sometimes a hundred, sometimes several hundred people. These villages, with the land around them, were called manors and were held and controlled by a lord or lady of the manor.

What did these villages look like? We are going to look at the evidence left behind, to see if this question can be answered.

The village of Wharram Percy in Yorkshire

The first village we are going to look at, Wharram Percy, no longer exists. Apart from the church, there are no buildings left standing, just fields. But because the land has not been built on by later generations there are many remains for the ARCHAEOLOGISTS to excavate.

Wharram Percy, like some other MEDIEVAL villages, was deserted about 500 years ago. Until the 1940s, almost everyone had forgotten that there was ever a village called Wharram Percy. After the villagers left, the houses fell down and grass grew over the foundations and streets. But over the last 50 years, using evidence such as Sources 1 and 2, archaeologists have not only rediscovered the village but have been able to reconstruct what it was like.

> **SOURCE 1** Evidence noticed by archaeologists
> - A parish church stands isolated in the middle of fields.
> - Three fields close to the church are called 'Water Lane', 'Towngate' and 'Town Street'.

◄ **SOURCE 2** A photograph of Wharram Percy from the air. Photographs like this were taken for the first time in the 1940s. They can show details of what is just below the surface of the ground

> 1. Look at Sources 1 and 2. What evidence can you find that there was once a village at Wharram Percy?

When archaeologists visited the area they had to struggle through overgrown footpaths, rotting footbridges and broken stiles. They found grass fields which had not been ploughed for hundreds of years. In these fields they found the stone foundations of rows of rectangular houses. Can you see these in the photograph?

> 2. Why do you think it took so long for Wharram Percy to be discovered?

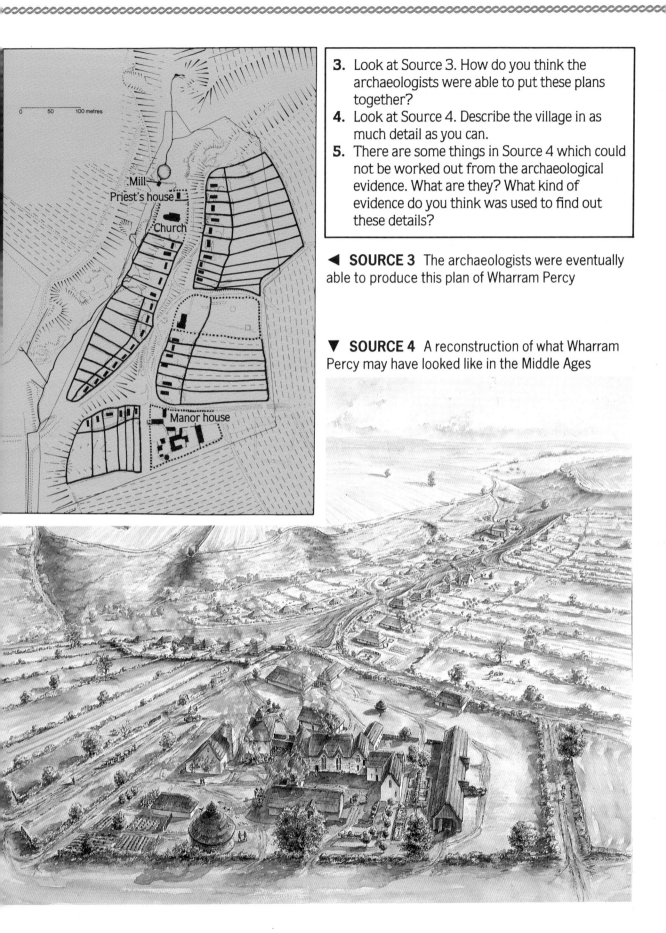

3. Look at Source 3. How do you think the archaeologists were able to put these plans together?
4. Look at Source 4. Describe the village in as much detail as you can.
5. There are some things in Source 4 which could not be worked out from the archaeological evidence. What are they? What kind of evidence do you think was used to find out these details?

◄ **SOURCE 3** The archaeologists were eventually able to produce this plan of Wharram Percy

▼ **SOURCE 4** A reconstruction of what Wharram Percy may have looked like in the Middle Ages

Mill

Priest's house

Church

Manor house

0   50   100 metres

The village of Elton in Cambridgeshire

We are now going to see how written and pictorial evidence can help us find out about medieval villages. Much of the evidence we will use in this section is about the village of Elton. Unlike Wharram Percy, Elton is still a thriving village today. All the medieval buildings were destroyed long ago. Archaeologists have not been able to excavate the ruins. Yet we can still work out what life in Elton was like, even if we can't find out everything we would like to know.

The MANOR of Elton belonged to the Abbot of Abbey Ramsey, who also held 23 other manors. He did not live in Elton and rarely visited it. His officials ran the manor for him. They had to keep law and order in the manor. They also had to keep records of all the money spent or received. As far as the Abbot was concerned, Elton existed just to provide the Abbey with food, materials and money.

The first evidence we have is from the Domesday Book. In the 1080s William I sent his officials to every part of England to find out what everybody owned so that he could tax them properly. This is what the officials wrote about Elton:

> **SOURCE 5** From the Domesday Book
>
> In Elton the Abbot of Ramsey had 10 hides of land. There are now 4 ploughs on the demesne. There are 28 villeins having 20 ploughs. There is a church and a priest, and 2 mills with an income of 40s a year. There are 170 acres of meadow.

> **SOURCE 6** From another royal survey 100 years later
>
> 2 water mills and a fulling mill also belonged to the Abbot, also fishing rights on the river.

SOURCE 8 A peasant's house in a medieval village

> **SOURCE 7** From the thirteenth-century records of money spent by the lord
>
> **1286** 6d paid for branches for the barn and the sheepfold.
>
> **1297** 12d paid for the hiring of one ship for carrying 1200 bundles of rushes from Wytlesmare to Elton.
>
> 12d paid to a carpenter for work on the chapel 12 working days.
>
> 2s paid to a man thatching the barn during 32 days with board.
>
> 1d for a bolt for the door of the little barn.
>
> 6d to a carpenter for making gates before the hall and barn during 6 days.
>
> 2d to a mason for repairing the walls before the great barn.
>
> 5s 2d for 4 men slating the chapel for 3 weeks.
>
> 7d paid to 2 carpenters for $3\frac{1}{2}$ days for repairing the building between the two mills.
>
> 7d paid to a man for thatching the mills.

Most of the evidence is about the buildings around the manor house, which belonged to the lord. Pictures from other villages can help us discover what these buildings in Elton might have looked like.

1. Which of the buildings shown in Sources 8–11 are mentioned in Sources 5–7?

SOURCE 9

SOURCE 10

nostras

Quomodo miseretur pater filiorú misertus est dominus timentibus se: quoniam ipse cognouit figmen

SOURCE 11

SOURCE 12 From the fourteenth-century records of money spent by the lord of Elton

1307 15d for a thatcher hired for 20 days to thatch the stable, the dovecote and the sheepfold.

4d for a mason to mend the wall between the manor house and the granary.

1311 4d paid for stone bought to mend the foundations of the mills.

3s 8d for 38 wooden boards for the wheels of the mills.

9d paid to a mason for mending the dairy.

8d paid to a mason for making one piece of the wall of the pound.

6d paid to a carpenter for making new beams for the kiln.

1313 2d paid to a carpenter for mending the common privy.

20d paid to 2 carpenters for erecting and mending the dovecote next to the chapel.

6d for a thatcher to thatch the ox-shed.

1324 16d paid to one slater for mending the roof of the manor house, kitchen and bakehouse during 16 days with food.

1345 3s 11d for stones and slates for making a new oven and furnace in the manor.

1350 12d for a mason for repairing the walls of the manor house after the flood.

SOURCE 15 A barn

SOURCE 13 From the records of money paid to the lord of Elton

1296 22d for letting the boat from time to time.

3s 4d rent from Adam Bird for an oven, and 8s 4d from Henry the smith for another oven.

13s 9d profit from the pound.

1307 6d from Robert the smith for one smithy.

1350 40s rent for the 3 mills, 2 grist and 1 fulling.

SOURCE 16 A manor house

SOURCE 14 From cases in the manorial court of Elton

1308 Thomas de Chauseye carried away the door posts of the house of Richard son of Ellis, and broke the thatch of his wall. Fine of 6d.

SOURCE 17 Baking bread or firing pots in an oven

SOURCE 18 A blacksmith's smithy

---

1. Use Sources 5–18 to complete this table about the buildings in Elton:

Type of building	What was it made of?	What was it used for?	Where was it?
sheepfold	branches and thatch	keeping the sheep in	near the manor house

2. On your outline map of Elton (which you can get from your teacher), draw in the buildings where you think they would have been. Explain why you have put them in those particular places.
3. You have now used archaeological evidence to find out about Wharram Percy, and documentary evidence to find out about Elton. Which type of evidence was more useful? Give three reasons for your answer.

Living in a medieval village

THE lord of the manor did not farm all the land in Elton. The part which he did farm himself was called the demesne. The rest was farmed by the villagers.

Most of the villagers in Elton in the twelfth century can be divided into two groups – 48 VILLEINS and 22 FREEMEN. The villeins worked on the lord's land. In return they each had land to farm for themselves. The freemen paid rent to the lord to have their own land.

1. Look at the information on this page. What are the main differences between the villein and the freeman?
2. Are there any ways in which they are similar?
3. Would you rather have been a villein or a freeman?

The villeins
They were under the lord's control in many ways.

Services
The villeins had to do services for the lord. They had to do WEEK-WORK every week of the year:
■ ploughing the lord's land – one day a week all year
■ other jobs such as weeding, hay-making, ditching, repairing the mills, making and mending fences and carting – two days a week for most of the year, but five days a week during the harvest.

Payments
The villeins also had to make payments to the lord in the place of doing certain services for him. Here are some examples.
■ wardpenny – 20d a year, paid instead of guard duty
■ maltsilver – 10d a year, paid instead of making malt for the lord.

Control
The villeins had to attend the manorial court. If they did not they were fined. They also had to serve on the JURY if chosen.

Villeins needed the lord's permission to live outside the manor. Villeins also needed the lord's permission for their daughters to get married.

When the son or daughter of a villein took over their parents' land they had to pay the lord money.

The villeins and the freemen
There were also a number of services and payments which were made by all the villagers, whether they were freemen or villeins.

Services
BOON-WORK varied according to how much work the lord needed done. Most of it was done by the villeins, but the freemen could be made to do it as well. It usually consisted of:
■ ploughing in early winter, spring and summer
■ collecting the harvest during August and September
■ hay-making. The peasants often worked the whole week until all the hay was in.

Payments
■ All the villagers had to use the lord's mills for grinding their corn into flour. They paid for this either with money or by giving the lord some of their corn. If they were caught using a hand-mill of their own they were punished in the manorial court.
■ It was a fire risk to bake bread in the villagers' own houses, so the lord built two ovens. These were rented by bakers, who charged the villagers for their services. The smithy was run in the same way.
■ Many of the women brewed their own ale (beer), but they could only sell it once it had been tested by the ale tasters and at a price set by the lord.

As we have already seen, the lord of the manor rarely visited Elton. His officials ran the manor for him.

Source 1 shows how the lord's officials were expected to make sure that the villagers carried out all these services.

SOURCE 1 From a thirteenth-century guide for manor officials

The steward
He should instruct the bailiffs who are beneath him. He should visit each of the manors two or three times a year and inquire about rents and services.

The bailiff
Every morning he should examine the corn, meadows and woods. He should see that the ploughs are yoked in the morning so that they may do their proper ploughing every day.

The reeve
The reeve should be chosen by the whole village. He must see that everyone rise in the morning to do their work and that the lands are well ploughed and sown with good clean seed. He should each year with the bailiff work out the services owed in the manor.

SOURCE 2

SOURCE 3 Peasants being supervised by the bailiff

4. Describe what is happening in each of Sources 2–4. For each picture, say whether it is week-work or boon-work and whether it is villeins or freemen or either doing the work.

Activity
You are the Abbot of Ramsey's STEWARD visiting Elton. Draw up a medieval CHARTER for either a villein or a freeman, listing the services and payments which are due to the lord. Design it in the style of a medieval document (see Source 24 on page 107).

SOURCE 4

LIVING IN A MEDIEVAL VILLAGE

The peasants' year

Both the men and the women of the medieval village worked hard and carried out very important jobs. Much of the time they worked side by side, but they also had their own separate jobs to do.

Many of the jobs in Source 5 were done by both men and women.

SOURCE 5

All year round
Firewood had to be collected, drainage ditches had to be dug, the animals had to be looked after and the peasant's house had to be repaired.

November
Some of the animals were butchered and the meat was salted and smoked so that it would keep through the winter.

October
The field was sown with winter corn.

August and September
This was harvest time. All the family helped. The men would scythe the crop until they had enough for a sheaf. The women tied up the sheaf. The sheaves could not be left in the field overnight because they would rot. They all had to be carted from the field. Both the scything and the carting were dangerous jobs. The carts were loaded high and a fall meant a broken neck. The carts also had to be driven carefully or they would overturn.

The grain then had to be separated from its stalk and from the husks. This was called winnowing. The grain was stored in the lord's barn or, if it was the peasants' own grain, in the lofts of their houses. The lord provided food and drink and gave all the workers a feast when the harvest had been completed.

January
Much time was spent on work around the house — getting firewood and turfs, planting vegetables in the garden.

February
Ploughing began. Women or children helped to drive the oxen. The soil was sometimes prepared with manure.

March
The seed for the oats and barley had to be sown. A harrow was then used to cover the seeds over with soil. Other jobs included weeding, chasing away birds and ploughing the fallow (empty) field to stop weeds growing.

June
The sheep were sheared and the hay harvest in the meadow began. The hay was cut and then stacked in the barn. The cattle were allowed into the field to eat the stubble.

July
The fallow field was ploughed again. Hemp and flax were gathered in by the women, and laid out to dry ready for spinning.

Remember that as well as all this work on their own land, the VILLEINS had to do their services for the lord. In Elton that meant three days a week of ploughing and other jobs, but five days a week during the harvest. What's more, in extra busy times, such as during winter ploughing, hay-making and harvesting, the lord could make the peasants work for him for even longer.

1. Now study Sources 6–10 and match each one with a month of the year.
2. Which was the busiest time of the year for the medieval peasant: spring, summer, autumn or winter?

◀ SOURCE 6

SOURCE 7

SOURCE 7

◀ SOURCE 8

▲ SOURCE 9

▲ SOURCE 10

> **3.** Some villeins paid the lord a fine (money) instead of labour services. Why do you think they did this?

Women in the village

Women were allowed to hold land in the village. When a man died, the lord of the manor would normally expect the land to stay with the same family. The man's widow would have the land for as long as she lived and it would then go to the eldest son. But if the widow had no grown-up sons the land could be a problem, as she would not be able to do all the work herself. Source 11 shows one woman's solution.

> **SOURCE 11**   From Elton manorial court records
>
> 66 *Agnes, widow of Thomas Bird, surrendered to Thomas all the land she holds on condition that he will provide for her:*
> - *a quarter of wheat six times a year*
> - *five cart-loads of sea coal on 1 November*
> - *a suitable house, 30 feet long and 14 feet wide*
> - *and Thomas will carry out all services owed to the lord.* 99

As we have seen, the women did help with the farming. But they also had many other jobs to do.

Look at Source 12. The figures come from the records of the Coroner's Courts in the fourteenth century. These courts investigated people's deaths. The first graph shows where in the village men and women died. The second shows what the men and women were doing when they died.

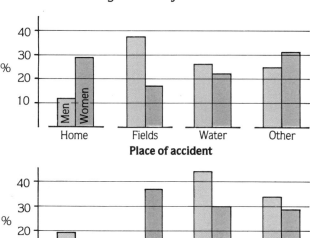

Place of accident

Activity at death

SOURCE 12

1. Which of the statements below do the figures in Source 12 support the most?
   - 'Women only worked at home. They never helped in the fields.'
   - 'Women did not work as hard as men.'
   - 'Women worked at home more than the men did, but they also worked at other kinds of jobs around the village and in the fields.'
2. Which of these statements do the figures show to be untrue?
3. Which of these statements do the figures tell us nothing about?
4. Using the figures in Source 12 and what you already know about the work women did, say whether you agree with this statement or not:
   - 'Women worked in the fields as much as the men, but they did the less dangerous jobs.'
5. Using the sources on pages 92–95 decide what might be particularly dangerous jobs in the fields, at home or in transport.

The women at work

Before dawn the fire had to be lit. This often meant going out and collecting straw to light the embers. The morning porridge was heated over the fire.

Cleaning the house took little time. The houses were small and the floor was covered in straw. Even though chickens, pigs and other animals wandered in and out of the house, the women still tried to keep their houses clean. Archaeologists have found that many floors were swept so often that the brooms left U-shaped depressions.

Water for cooking, washing and drinking had to be carried from the well to the house. Washing clothes, which was done by hand, was a hard job. Other jobs included cutting wood, baking bread in the lord's ovens and taking grain to the mill.

It was also normal for women to do some farm work every day. The cows had to be milked, the chickens, and usually a pig, had to be looked after. The garden was important as it produced the family's vegetables. When their help was needed in the fields, women hoed, weeded, tied the sheaves and helped with the ploughing. They had to collect firewood, carrying bundles of sticks on their backs.

On top of all this, there were the children to look after. Babies were often wrapped in swaddling clothes. This meant that they could not crawl about.

Older babies were often tied into their cradles. During the busy times, the women had to go and work in the fields or the family would starve. They left their babies at home, or sometimes took them with them. The swaddled babies could be put in trees. Once a child was about five years old it would look after younger children.

Women earned extra money by brewing beer – a very dangerous job, as it involved carrying twelve-gallon vats of hot liquid. Many women spun thread and always took their spindle with them to do some spinning in spare moments. The thread was sometimes made into rough cloth for the family, but more often it was sold to a weaver. Women also earned wages as thatchers and labourers.

1. Now look at Sources 13–15. Which parts of the above description can be supported by this evidence? Does any of this evidence contradict the description?
2. Was the work women did in the village just as important as the work done by the men? Give your reasons.
3. History books written earlier in the twentieth century largely ignored the contribution women made to the medieval village. Books written today have a lot more about women. In the class, discuss why you think this is.

SOURCE 14 Women fetching water

SOURCE 15 Woman taking grain to the mill

SOURCE 13 Woman spinning

Activity

You are either a woman or a man. Write and illustrate a diary for two days in either January or September. Work in pairs. Compare your diary with your partner's.

Field systems

The open field system

THE best land in England for growing crops was in the Midlands. The land was divided into two, three or sometimes four enormous fields. These fields were completely open – they had no fences, walls, ditches or hedges around them (see Source 1).

Each field was divided into furlongs, which were sub-divided into strips. The villagers had strips scattered across all the fields. One villager's strips are shown in red on Source 1.

Between the strips was raised unploughed land.

The peasants had to agree which crop was going to be grown in each of the fields. This was usually fixed by tradition, or in the manorial court.

One of the fields would be left fallow, or empty, to allow the soil to recover. This would be a different field each year (see Source 2).

The village also had meadows, which were fenced. These grew grass for hay. Once the hay had been harvested animals were allowed to graze there.

There was also waste or common land which was used for grazing cattle.

	Year 1	Year 2	Year 3
Field 1	Wheat	Oats	
Field 2	Oats	Fallow	
Field 3	Fallow	Wheat	

SOURCE 2 Diagram to show crop rotation

---

1. Copy Source 2. Fill in the column for Year 3.

SOURCE 3 From *Piers Plowman*, a poem written in the fourteenth century

"If I went to plough I pinched so narrowly that I would steal a foot of land from my neighbour; and if I reaped I would reach into my neighbour's land."

SOURCE 4 From manorial court records of the fourteenth century

"To stop people stealing other people's land the Lord of the Manor insists that boundary stones shall be put in to separate people's strips.

Seven tenants are fined 6d each because they have ploughed the pathways between the strips."

---

2. The open field system is often described as very wasteful. Can you think of ways in which it did waste time and land?

3. Look at Sources 3 and 4. What other problems did the open field system cause?

4. If the open field system was so wasteful, why was it used?

SOURCE 1 The open field system

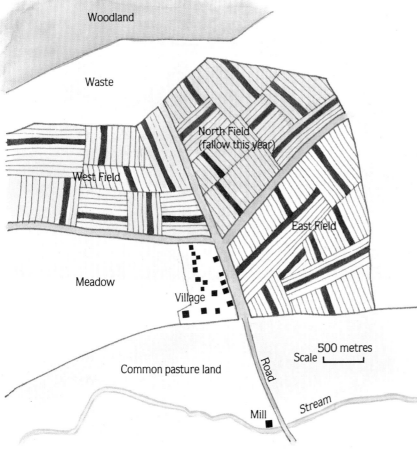

Woodland

Waste

North Field (fallow this year)

West Field

East Field

Meadow

Village

Common pasture land

Road

Scale 500 metres

Mill

Stream

The infield–outfield system

This system was found in highland areas like Scotland, parts of northern England and Devon and Cornwall. The land was more suitable for keeping animals than for growing crops, and most of the farmer's time was spent looking after the animals.

The infield was the best land, nearest the village (see Source 5). Each villager's strips would be scattered throughout the field. They grew just enough cereal crops to feed their families. The main crop was oats, but different crops were grown in different parts of the field every year.

The infield was used every year and was heavily manured.

Further from the village was the outfield. This was poor quality land and was not manured. It was used to grow crops for a few years but was soon exhausted. It was then used for grazing cattle or for growing grass, while another outfield was created for crops.

Key
- Infield–outfield
- Open field system

▲ **SOURCE 6** Map showing field systems in most common use in various areas of Britain

▼ **SOURCE 5** The infield–outfield system

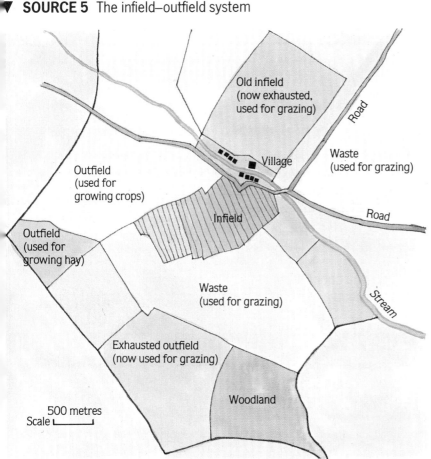

1. What were the main differences between the infield–outfield system and the open field system?
2. Look at Source 6. Why did different parts of the country have different field systems?

The poor and the rich at home

The poor

A GREAT deal of evidence survives about the lives of the wealthy in medieval times. Written sources, pictures, and the homes and belongings of the rich have survived.

With poorer people, however, we need to bear in mind the following:
- Most could not read or write, and the rich did not usually bother to write about them.
- Their houses were made of wood, branches, clay and straw.
- They had few belongings. These were often of poor quality.

---

1. Do you think we have much evidence about the lives of the poor?

Sources 1 and 2 show some of the things historians have worked out about the lives of poor people.

SOURCE 1 An account from a recent history book

Life for the peasants was miserable. They lived in single room hovels with no light. The floors were covered with rushes where the rubbish collected and rotted. In the middle of the hovel was a fire. It must have been very smoky in there, and to make it worse the animals were brought in at night. There was never any time for sport or entertainment and they never ate anything but bread and cheese.

SOURCE 2 A modern drawing of a medieval peasant's house

2. List the main things that Sources 1 and 2 agree about.

3. What impression do they give you about the lives of poor people?

4. Compare Sources 1 and 2. Does the written evidence tell you more about the peasants' living conditions than the picture does? Explain your answer.

Sources 3–8 show some of the evidence that has survived about the lives of the poor.

SOURCE 3 From the account book of a fifteenth-century manor, showing food provided by the lord to celebrate their Saint's Day

Beef, four calves, two half sheep, a breast of mutton, a breast of veal, five lambs, six pigs, seven rabbits; eggs, butter, milk and cream; pepper, vinegar, cloves, sugar, dates and honey.

SOURCE 4 Extracts from manorial court records

66 John Raynald broke into and entered at night the Lord's park where he took 17 oak trees which he used to repair his house.

John Shephard is fined because the clay he took to place on the outside of his walls of his house was taken from the common roadway.

John Yude wants to lease one of the rooms in his house to someone else for a period of one year.

It is ordered that no one must go into the area known as Le Holme and take rushes to place on their roof or their floor.

Four villagers have been fined for carrying away the door of a waste house. This consisted of the wood, a socket stone, iron hanging post, a key, padlock, hinges and a latch.

Alice Kaa broke down the doors and windows and took away lamps and oil.

Philip Hogyns must repair the kitchen in his building. 99

SOURCE 5 Written by John Gower, a poet who lived in the fourteenth century

66 Labourers were not able to eat wheat bread; their bread was of beans and coarser corn, and they drank water alone. Cheese and milk were a feast to them. 99

SOURCE 6 Medieval peasants in their leisure time

SOURCE 7 From Chaucer's poem *The Canterbury Tales*, written in the fourteenth century

66 Once, long ago, there dwelt a poor old widow
in a small cottage, by a little meadow.
Sooty her hall, her kitchen dismal,
and there she ate many a slender meal
of milk and brown bread, in which she found no lack.
She had a yard that was enclosed about
by a stockade and a dry ditch without. 99

SOURCE 8 From the poem *Piers Plowman* by William Langland, a fourteenth-century priest. He was very critical of the social conditions of the time

66 I have no penny to buy pullets,
nor geese nor pigs, but [I have] two green cheeses,
a few curds of cream, a cake of oatmeal,
two loaves of beans and bran, baked for my children;
but I have parsley and pot herbs and plenty of cabbages,
and a cow and a calf.
This is the little we must live on till the Lammas season.
Poor folk in hovels,
charged with children and overcharged by landlords,
what they may save by spinning they spend on rent,
on milk, or on meal to make porridge. 99

5. Do Sources 3–8, from the Middle Ages, support what Sources 1 and 2 told you about:
   - the homes of the poor
   - the diet of the poor?
6. What do Sources 3–8 tell us that Sources 1 and 2 do not?
7. Which two sources may not be much use in showing us how poor people lived for most of the time?

The rich

What was life like for the rich? Source 9 gives us some clues. It is taken from a record of the daily expenses of the household of Eleanor, Countess of Leicester, during a seven-month period in 1265. Eleanor was the wife of the Earl of Leicester, who for several years was the most important baron in the country.

Study Sources 10–16.
1. What new information do they give that is not given in Source 9?
2. What information do they give which supports the information in Source 9?
3. What information do they give which disagrees with the information in Source 9?
4. How reliable is Source 9 for finding out how the rich generally lived?

SOURCE 9

■ *Eleanor received over 50 important visitors, including royal officials, church people and important women. Many visitors brought servants with them. When her husband arrived at their castle in March, hay was needed for 334 horses.*

■ *Much white bread was eaten.*

■ *Large amounts of meat and fish were bought. The meat included oxen, pork, sheep and geese. 'Stockfish' were popular. These were cod without their heads, gutted and dried in the sun. Other fish included 32 conger eels, 500 hake, a porpoise and a whale.*

■ *Dinner was eaten between ten and eleven o'clock in the morning. A light supper was then taken about five o'clock.*

■ *Much beer and wine was drunk. Much of the beer was flavoured with spices. Milk was mainly used for cooking, and water was rarely drunk as it was too polluted.*

■ *Vegetables and fresh fruit were rarely eaten.*

■ *Many eggs were used.*

■ *In the cooking, fish was often salted or smoked, baked or made into pies. Meat was preferred fried. All foods were heavily spiced.*

■ *Most of the lights were candles.*

■ *Eleanor took two baths in seven months.*

■ *Both men and women wore plain tunics. The men wore leg bandages. Shoes were shaped to the foot. Both men and women wore gloves. Women often hid their hair and wore leather leggings in winter. The men often had a beard or moustache. Dyes to colour the clothes were brought from abroad.*

SOURCE 10 Written by Alexander Neckham, who died in 1217

In the bedchamber let a curtain go around the walls for the avoiding of flies and spiders. On the bed there should be a feather mattress to which a bolster is attached. A quilted pad of striped cloth should cover it, on which a cushion for the head should be placed. Then sheets of muslin, ordinary cotton or at least pure linen should be laid. Next a coverlet with a fur lining of badger, cat or beaver.

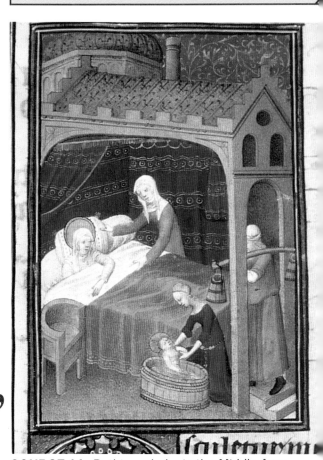

SOURCE 11 Bathing a baby in the Middle Ages

How typical was Eleanor? Sources 10–16 provide further evidence of the lives led by rich people.

SOURCE 12 A modern drawing of a medieval kitchen scene

SOURCE 13 Sir Geoffrey Luttrell and his family entertaining two Dominican friars

SOURCE 14 Hunting

SOURCE 15 Written by Peter of Blois about the food at the King's court in 1160

> *The beer is horrid to taste and filthy to look at. Meat is sold whether it be fresh or not. The fish one buys is four days old, yet the fact it stinks does not lessen the price. The servants care nothing whatever whether the unlucky guests become ill or die provided they load their master's table with food which is often rotten.*

SOURCE 16 A fifteenth-century recipe

> *Make a broth by simmering calves' feet and shins in white wine until they are soft. Strain the broth and pour over pork ribs and young chickens. Simmer until the meat is firm and skim off the fat. Add pepper, saffron and vinegar. allow to set and cover with almonds, a few curls of ginger and cloves.*
>
> *Chicken should be stuffed with a mix of parsley, suet, mashed boiled egg yolks, pepper, cinnamon, saffron, a little pork and cloves.*

Activity

a) In groups, decide what headings would be useful to help you compare the lives of the rich and the poor. For example, one heading might be 'food'.

b) Design a display that compares the lives of the rich and the poor, under the headings you have chosen.

Did people travel much in the Middle Ages?

ONE recent history book said this about the people in the Middle Ages:

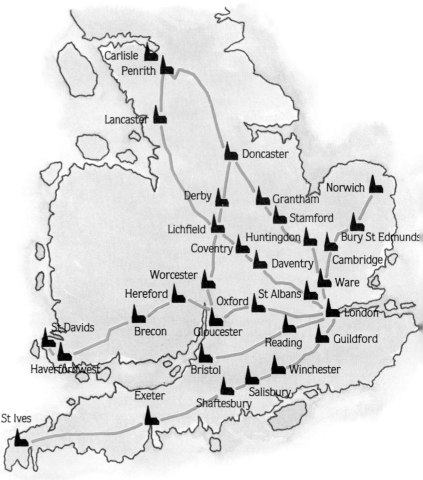

We are going to investigate whether the evidence actually agrees or disagrees with this statement. Did peasants really travel as rarely as the writer of Source 1 suggests?

Were there many roads in medieval England?

One way of finding out about medieval roads would be to look for ARCHAEOLOGICAL evidence. But this is not easy (see Source 2).

SOURCE 2 From a recent book on archaeology

"Medieval roads were not carefully laid like Roman roads, with stone and cement, so little is left of them today — just tracks and bridges — and we do not always know which tracks go back to the medieval period. New medieval roads were not constructed, they were just routes which, if used a lot, became tracks."

We can find out about the routes of medieval roads by using maps from the period (Source 3).

▲ **SOURCE 3** The Gough map. Drawn in about 1360, it shows 2940 miles of roads, but only the main carrier routes are shown here. We do not know who drew the map. Some of the routes are on the same lines as the old Roman roads

The third way we can find out about medieval roads is to use documentary evidence. For example, documentary evidence can confirm that the old Roman roads were still used in the Middle Ages.

Documents tell us, for instance, that:
- Three Roman roads, Watling Street, Ermine Street and Fosse Way, were royal roads under the King's protection.
- Roads had to be wide enough for two wagons to pass.
- Anyone attacking travellers on the roads would be fined 100 shillings.
- Messengers of Richard I rode from Scotland to the south coast using only the Roman roads.

1. Why do you think the King's messengers used the old Roman roads?

One document from Titchfield Abbey near Southampton lists all the regular journeys made by the monks to other abbeys in the country. From this document it is possible to construct a map of their journeys, like the one in Source 4.

2. Did the monks use any of the same routes as on Source 3?
3. Why do you think they used them?
4. Why did they sometimes use different routes?

Many other local routes are mentioned in people's letters and in the accounts of traders. From the records of the manor of Elton in Cambridgeshire, we see that regular journeys were made by manor officials to all the places marked on the map in Source 5 to buy things the manor needed.

▲ **SOURCE 4** Journeys by monks from Titchfield Abbey

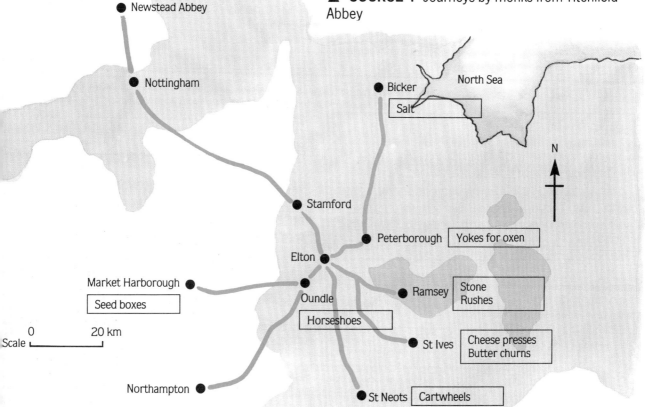

SOURCE 5 Map of routes used by people from Elton and the products they bought

5. 'Medieval England had very few roads.' Does the evidence we have looked at so far support or contradict this statement?
6. What difficulties face the historian trying to find out where medieval roads were?

What problems did travellers face?

As you have seen, there were a few main roads in medieval England. However, there were also many small local tracks joining villages to the local market town, and to other villages.

History books often disagree about what the roads were like, as we can see in Sources 6 and 7.

> **SOURCE 6**
>
> 66 *The means of communication were fairly good, and the main roads, even in winter, were kept in good condition.* 99

> **SOURCE 7**
>
> 66 *The roads were very bad indeed, because no one mended them. Farmers ploughed some of them, and in bad weather most of the roads became impossible to use.* 99

Now let's look at some evidence from the Middle Ages, and see which of the statements in Sources 6 and 7 they support.

> **SOURCE 8** From fifteenth-century town records
>
> 66 *At Aylesbury, the local miller dug clay out of the road, creating a pit so large that a glove seller passing through the town fell into it and was drowned. The local jury did not punish the miller because there was nowhere else he could get the clay he needed.* 99

> **SOURCE 9** A description of the roads written in 1406
>
> 66 *This year has been remarkable for terrible floods and rains. The roads between London and Greenwich were broken. The cartway between Whitney Bridge and Hereford was nearly swept away. In the Isle of Ely, around Cambridge, roads and bridges were wrecked and washed away. The sheriffs sent their men to request money from abbots and landowners, and indulgences were freely offered by the bishops to all who helped in repairing the damage.* 99

> **SOURCE 10** From the records of Parliament. An account of a journey from Northamptonshire to London in 1450
>
> 66 *160 persons and more, all dressed in the form of war with light helmets, long swords and other weapons, hid under a large hedge next to the highway and lay in wait for William Tresham from midnight to the hour of six, at which time William appeared. They attacked him and smote him through the body and foot and more. He died. And they gave him many more deadly wounds and cut his throat.* 9

> **SOURCE 11** A traveller's description of the roads in 1400
>
> 66 *Travellers often lose their way and go ways which are unknown. Therefore knots are often made in the branches of trees and bushes to mark the highway.* 9

1. According to Sources 8–11, what problems did travellers face?
2. Does the evidence so far suggest that roads were in good or bad condition?

A good way of discovering what condition the roads were in is to look at how people tried to improve the roads and make travel easier (see Sources 12–14).

> **SOURCE 12** In 1285, the King and Parliament passed the Statute of Winchester
>
> 66 *Highways leading from one market town to another shall be widened where there are bushes or ditches, so that there will be no bushes or ditches for a man to hide to do hurt within 200 feet of the road.* 9

Methods of transport

SOURCE 13 From the Records of the Borough of Nottingham, 1370

"The King allows the mayors of Nottingham to start a ferry service across the River Trent, on condition that all the profits shall be used on the repairing of the bridge, which has been broken for over 70 years."

SOURCE 14 A letter from King Edward I to the Prior and people of Dunstable in 1285

"Because we have learnt that the high roads which stretch through Dunstable are so broken up by the frequent passage of carts, that dangerous injuries threaten those using these roads, we command each one of you according to his means to fill in and mend the roads."

SOURCE 15 Packhorses carrying woolpacks, drawn in the thirteenth century

SOURCE 16 A harvest waggon drawn in the early fourteenth century. Notice the spiked wheels

3. Read Sources 12–14. Why do you think a) the King, and b) lords of the manor, wanted to keep the roads in good condition?
4. Do Sources 12–14 prove that the roads were looked after and kept in good condition?
5. Why do you think the historians in Sources 6 and 7 disagree about the condition of medieval roads?

1. How are these two methods of transporting goods different?
2. Which method do you think is the best?

DID PEOPLE TRAVEL MUCH IN THE MIDDLE AGES?

SOURCE 17 River routes in England

SOURCE 18 Unloading grain from a barge. Drawn in the late fifteenth century

---

1. What would be a) the advantages, and b) the disadvantages, of transporting goods by water?

Activity

You have to transport wool clippings from Carlisle to London (see the map in Source 17). Plan your journey, using the evidence in this section to help you work out:
a) what method of transport you are going to use
b) what places you will travel through
c) what problems you face.
Your teacher will give you an extract from a novel, *The Woolpack*, by Cynthia Harnett.

Why different people travelled

1. Study Sources 19–25. Draw up a table of all the different types of people who travelled. For each person say what their reason for travelling was.

SOURCE 19 Written by the Mayor of Exeter about a business trip to London in 1448

66 *On Wednesday at seven in the morning I rode out of Exeter to London [170 miles]. The next Saturday at seven in the morning I came to London.*

SOURCE 20 A recent account of the journeys of the Lestrange family from their home in Hunstanton to their home in London in the fifteenth century

66 *On their frequent journeys to London, the Lestranges usually halted at Castleacre, Brandon, Newmarket, Babraham, Barkway, Ware and Waltham. Most of these are on or near a river crossing, and they are spaced out at intervals of twelve to eighteen miles. These places were recognised stages where they called for refreshments, beds or fresh horses. They usually stopped at Newmarket the first night, at Ware the second, and reached London after two and a half days' travel.*

SOURCE 21 From a recent book on medieval towns

66 *The area served by a market town was governed by how far someone could walk to and from the town, and do their business, in a day. This was usually about ten miles each way.*

Within that area, the market town had to provide everything people needed which they could not provide themselves.

The small town of Stratford-upon-Avon had the following traders: weavers, fullers, dyers, tanners, shoemakers, glovemakers, tailors, carpenters, tilers, coopers, smiths, locksmiths, millers, a wheelwright, an oil-maker, a rope-maker, a butcher, a dairy, a baker and a cook.

SOURCE 22 From a recent book on the fourteenth century

Many landowners were lords of two or three manors. It was important for them to visit each from time to time if they didn't want to lose the respect of the tenants.

When a great lord moved from one of his houses to another, his servants and family went with him, and so did a great deal of his furniture, his valuables and the fittings of his chapel. Early in the fourteenth century many great lords were moving about every two weeks.

SOURCE 23 One reason why people travelled was to go on PILGRIMAGES. Many people went on pilgrimages to famous SHRINES such as Canterbury. (There is more about this later in this unit, on page 115.) This picture shows pilgrims from Chaucer's poem *The Canterbury Tales*. They included a merchant from Suffolk, a reeve (who was a villein) from Norfolk, and a wife from Bath, as well as a nun and a ploughman

SOURCE 24 Musicians. They travelled all over the country entertaining rich and poor people

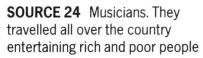

oniam dominus ipſe
e fecit nos ꞇ non ipſi nos.
us ꞇ oues paſcue eius
tas eius in confeſſione
i ẏmpnis confitemini illi.
omen eius quoniam

SOURCE 25 From fifteenth-century records

In 1484 William Naynow, an Exeter carrier, said he had been travelling between London and Exeter for over 35 years. He carried letters, pewter vessels and money, in fact anything that people wanted to send.

Activity

You are a French person visiting England in the Middle Ages. Using what you have learned from Sources 1–25, write a letter home saying how much English people travel. Remember to explain:
a) whether there were many roads
b) whether only the rich travelled
c) whether people travelled often
d) whether people made long journeys
e) why people travelled
f) whether there is enough evidence to give a definite answer to these questions.

The growth of towns

SOURCE 1 A general account of the typical development of towns during the Middle Ages, from a recent history book

❝*Most medieval towns did not exist at the time when the Domesday Book was written. They grew up for several reasons. Some were built near a good site to cross a river or where it was easy to defend against attackers.*

Towns were often established by a lord who wanted the town to grow because he would receive more rents and taxes. Often the towns were planned, with neat street patterns.

Towns often held regular markets and fairs and this attracted merchants and craftsmen. This made the towns prosperous and led to the building of grand buildings, such as merchants' houses and churches. But most of the houses were small and close together and usually built of wood. Fires were frequent.

Eventually, many of the inhabitants of the towns tired of paying taxes to the lord. Many towns bought Charters from the King so that they could run their own affairs. Towns prospered in the fourteenth century but declined in the fifteenth century.❞

THE rest of the evidence on these two pages is about the town of Ludlow. As you study it, you will see how far Ludlow fits this general pattern.

Ludlow

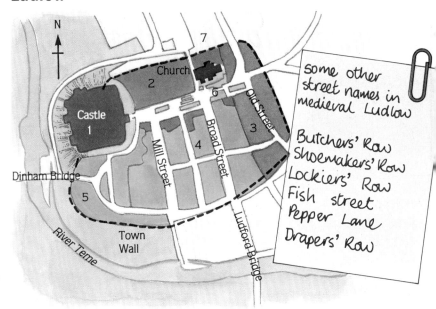

some other street names in medieval Ludlow

Butchers' Row
Shoemakers' Row
Lockiers' Row
Fish street
Pepper Lane
Drapers' Row

SOURCE 2 Plan of Ludlow, showing stages of growth and medieval street names. It was granted a Charter by the King in 1459

SOURCE 3 From a recent guidebook to Ludlow

❝*The town's economy was based on wool. In the thirteenth century Ludlow became a major collecting and distributing centre, and had an important cloth industry. The River Teme drops sharply through the gorge west of the town and was the major source of power. At one time there were eleven mills along its length. The Ludlow tradesmen still farmed the open fields outside the town. Their right to use the common land for grazing and brushwood was confirmed in 1221.*❞

▼ **SOURCE 4** A seventeenth-century picture of Ludlow Castle. It also shows the church, which was begun in 1199. It is still the largest church in Shropshire

SOURCE 5 From a modern history of Ludlow

No mention is made of Ludlow in Domesday Book. One of William's knights, Walter de Lacy, was given the manor of Stanton (two miles from the present-day Ludlow). Between 1086 and 1094 his son Roger began to build a castle. The site he chose was protected on three sides by cliffs over 100 feet high, commanded the crossing of the River Teme and had extensive views of the surrounding countryside.

A planned settlement grew up under the protection of the castle. The new town was laid out in the twelfth century. The town was laid out with 'burgage plots', which were long narrow strips with a building at one end, stretching back to a small lane at the back. The standard width of these plots was 33 feet.

SOURCE 7 The Bull Inn, built by a wealthy businessman in the fifteenth century

SOURCE 6 Extract from a history of Ludlow

The Guild of Palmers (people who had been on a pilgrimage to the Holy Land) was set up in Ludlow around 1250. By 1550 it owned 241 properties in Ludlow. It had its own street and college. Members paid fees and made gifts, in return for which priests employed by the guild said prayers and masses on their behalf when they were alive and after they were dead. In 1284 the Guild employed three priests. In the fifteenth century the number was over eight.

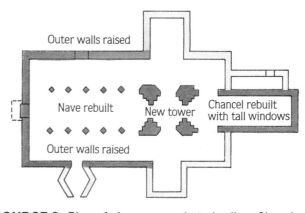

Outer walls raised

Nave rebuilt

New tower

Chancel rebuilt with tall windows

Outer walls raised

SOURCE 8 Plan of changes made to Ludlow Church in the fifteenth century

1. In what ways did Ludlow change during the Middle Ages?
2. Does the evidence support these statements?
   ■ 'Ludlow grew up where it did because it was a good place to cross the river.'
   ■ 'Ludlow's development was carefully planned.'
   ■ 'The local lord was very important in the development of Ludlow.'
   ■ 'Ludlow did well before 1400 but then fell into decline.'
3. How far does the evidence show that Ludlow's development followed the typical pattern described in Source 1? Your teacher will give you a worksheet to record your ideas.

THE GROWTH OF TOWNS

Market towns

Medieval manors did sometimes produce a surplus (more than they needed). They also needed to buy many things which could not be grown or made in the village.

Look back at Source 9 on page 100. Which of the items used by Eleanor would not have been produced on the manor? The manor needed somewhere to buy and sell goods – a market.

In the Middle Ages you needed the permission of the King to hold a market. But as there was a lot of money to be made from markets lords were very keen to do so, and more and more markets were set up. In Suffolk, for example, there were 12 markets in 1100, but 74 by 1350.

As a market grew, so the town around it usually grew as well. Such towns would often try to become independent of the lord. They did this by getting a CHARTER from the King. This set the townspeople free to run their own affairs.

The town officials would raise money from market tolls paid by tradesmen. In Lincoln, for example, the city fixed the toll so that a trader paid one penny to the city for every horse bought or sold. The more trade that went on in the market, the more money the towns earned from tolls.

Towns used some of their money to pay officials to make sure that prices were fair, that customers were not being cheated, and that anything sold in the market was good quality.

SOURCE 9 From London Court Records, 1327

❝John Bird the baker did skilfully cause a hole to be made upon a table in his bakehouse. And when his neighbours and others, who were wont to bake their bread at his oven, came with their dough, John put the dough on the table. John had a servant sitting in secret beneath the table. The servant carefully opened the hole and bit by bit withdrew some of the dough.

All those bakers beneath whose tables holes had been found should be put on the pillory, with dough hung from their necks, and those bakers whose tables did not have holes shall be put on the pillory, but without dough round their necks.❞

---

1. Did all the bakers have holes in their tables?
2. Why do you think the court decided to punish every baker?

Each trade was also controlled by its own GUILD. Source 10 lists the regulations of the Weavers' Guild in Shrewsbury.

SOURCE 10

❝If a member of the guild lived in adultery, none of the other members of the guild were to have anything to do with him.

No outsiders were allowed to sell cloth within the town.

No member could take more than one apprentice at a time.

A widow of a member could continue the craft of her husband for no longer than three months, when the stock would run out.❞

---

3. Why do you think the Weavers' Guild made each of these rules?

▶ **SOURCE 11** A medieval shoe shop

Traders began to use the front ground floor of their homes as shops and workshops (see Source 11). The front shutter could fold down into the roadway for use as a counter during opening hours.

▶ **SOURCE 12** A medieval market

▼ **SOURCE 13** A guild master and his apprentices

Conditions in medieval towns

SOURCE 14 From court records, 1321

66 *The jury decided that the lane called Ebbegate which runs between the houses of Master John de Pulteneye and Master Thomas at Wytte used to be a right of way until it was closed up by them. They built latrines which project out from the walls of the houses. From these latrines human filth falls on to the heads of the passers by.* 99

SOURCE 15 From medieval court records

66 *That no one shall have any pig in the town, penalty 4d a pig. Four men are elected to put pigs in the common pinfold.* 99

SOURCE 16 Written by a foreign visitor in the early sixteenth century

66 *The floors of the houses are of clay, strewed with rushes, under which lies undisturbed an ancient collection of beer, grease, bones, excrements of animals and men.* 99

1. Using Sources 1–16, compare life in the town with what you already know of life in the village. Divide into groups. Each group should choose one of the following headings: jobs, standard of living, danger of catching disease, personal freedom.

2. Villeins sometimes went to towns to escape from the control of their lords. Can you see why villagers might prefer life in a town?

3. Where would you rather have lived, in an English medieval town, or in Rome at the height of the Empire?

How religious were people in the Middle Ages?

RELIGION played a very important part in every aspect of people's lives in the Middle Ages. It was something which was with them every minute of the day. People thought God and the saints controlled every part of their lives, like illnesses, the weather and good fortune in business.

Every village had a church. It was usually right in the centre of the village. All around the village there would be SHRINES to particular saints, and holy crosses. Everybody had to go to church on Sundays and other holy days. The church also played an essential role in the most important stages in a person's life – with special services for birth, marriage and death.

Even the calendar was shaped by religion. The main feasts in every village were on special holy days, such as Candlemas (2 February), Palm Sunday, Easter and Christmas. Rents were paid on Lady Day (25 March) and Michaelmas (29 September).

Most people could not read the Bible for themselves. One way they learned about the life and teachings of Christ was from the paintings which could be found on the walls of most churches. As the services were carried out in a language (Latin) which they did not understand, all they could do was look at the paintings.

The painting in Source 1 shows a ladder going from Earth, through Hell, and finally reaching Heaven. The souls of dead men and women are trying to climb the ladder to get to Heaven. People were desperate to keep out of Hell, where they would stay in agony for the rest of time!

SOURCE 1 A medieval wall painting from a church in Surrey

How to get to Heaven

To get to Heaven people had to be free of sin. Since most people were committing sins all the time this was very difficult. They had to confess these sins and be genuinely sorry for committing them. This was done in various ways.

The priests

The men who were meant to help the people live good lives and get to Heaven were the PRIESTS. They were meant to be special people, different from everyone else. They were not allowed to marry, as they had to devote their lives to God, and they had special powers like being able to forgive people their sins.

England was divided into about 9000 parishes. In most cases a parish covered the same area as a MANOR. There was a priest in control of every parish.

Sources 2 and 3 are two stories told by priests to show people how they should live.

1. Here is a list of things happening in Hell. Match these up with the figures in the painting.
   - murderers being put into a pot of boiling water
   - a money lender burning on flames, still counting his gold
   - a bridge of spikes for dishonest tradesmen (can you see which tradesmen are shown?)
   - demons pulling people off the ladder
   - a woman having her hand bitten by a dog. She is confessing to pampering her own dogs with meat when poor people were going hungry
   - a drunken pilgrim drinking from a wine bottle.
2. Here is a list of things happening in Heaven. Match these up with the figures in the painting.
   - Christ defeating the Devil, who has his hands tied
   - St Michael weighing people's goodness to see if they should go to Heaven or Hell. (What do you think the demon on the left is doing?)
   - angels helping people up the ladder.

SOURCE 2

66 I find in the chronicles that there was once a worthy woman who had hated a poor woman for more than seven years. When the worthy woman went to church, the priest told her to forgive her enemy. She said she had forgiven her.

When the church service was over, the neighbours went to her house with presents to cheer her and to thank God. But then the woman said, 'Do you think I forgave her with my heart as I did with my mouth. No!' Then the Devil came down and strangled her there in front of everybody. So make sure that when you make promises you make them with the heart, without any deceit. 99

SOURCE 3

66 A woman lived with a priest and bore him four sons. After the priest died, the sons tried to persuade their mother to ask forgiveness for her deadly sin, but she refused.

The mother died soon after and for three nights the sons sat by her body. On the first night, at midnight, to their terror, the bier began to shake. On the second night it shook again and suddenly a devil appeared, seized the corpse, and dragged it towards the door. The sons fought to win the body back and tied it to the bier to keep it safe. On the third night at midnight a whole host of devils invaded the house and took the body, no one knows where, without end forevermore. 99

1. Why do you think priests told stories like these?
2. What do the wall painting and these two stories tell you about people's religious beliefs at that time?
3. How do you think you would have felt if you had been a medieval peasant in church looking at Source 1, and listening to stories like Sources 2 and 3? Would you have been terrified, amused, worried or bored?
4. Do you think this picture was trying to show that it is easy to get to Heaven or very difficult?

HOW RELIGIOUS WERE PEOPLE IN THE MIDDLE AGES?

The priest was obviously very important to the villagers, but he was not always popular. One reason for this was the payments that the villagers had to make to the priest.

The villagers had to give the priest a tithe (one tenth of everything they produced on their land). So if they harvested ten sheaves of corn they would give the priest one sheaf. Source 4 tells us what the villagers of Foxton in Cambridgeshire tried to do with the sheaves they were paying to the priest:

SOURCE 6 A medieval drawing of the priest from the *Canterbury Tales*

> **SOURCE 4** From court records
>
> "Ten of the tenants were each fined 2d because they made their sheaves much smaller, when they ought to have made them of the same size as they did when working for the Lady of the Manor."

The priest also received someone's second best working animal when they died, and kept collections made in the church at special services, e.g. at Christmas and Easter.

This extract from Chaucer's *Canterbury Tales* gives us one view of a priest in the Middle Ages.

However, not all parishes were lucky enough to have a priest like Chaucer's. Many priests did not live in their parishes. They often had more than one parish, and as they could not live in all of them they appointed deputies to do their work.

These deputies were often from ordinary village families and poorly educated. They were badly paid by the priest, who kept most of the money for himself. The deputies stumbled through the services, hardly understanding them, and very rarely gave sermons or told stories. They were farmers like the other villagers and looking after their strips of land and their animals took up most of their time.

> **SOURCE 5**
>
> "He truly knew Christ's gospel and would preach it
> devoutly to parishioners . . .
> . . . He preferred beyond a doubt
> giving to poor parishioners round about
> both from church offering and his property;
> he could in little find sufficiency.
> Wide was his parish, with houses far asunder,
> yet he neglected not, in rain or thunder,
> in sickness or in grief, to pay a call
> on the remotest, whether great or small.
> The true example that a priest should give
> is one of cleanness, how his sheep should live.
> He did not set his parish to hire
> and leave his sheep in the mire,
> or run to London to earn easy bread.
> His business was to show a fair behaviour
> and draw men thus to Heaven and their saviour."

> **SOURCE 7** From the records of the Bishop of Hereford in 1397. He took evidence from villagers about the parishes under his control
>
> "They say the vicar puts his horses and sheep to pasture in the churchyard.
>   They say the vicar was away for six weeks and made no arrangements for a substitute.
>   Sir John (the priest) spends his time in taverns, and there his tongue is loosed to the great scandal of everyone. He is living with a woman, Margaret, and he cannot read or write and so cannot look after his parishioners' souls."

> **SOURCE 8** Written by Edmund of Eynsham, a holy man and great critic of the Church in the 1190s
>
> "The acts of the priests have deeply offended God. Priests are polluted by every kind of sin. They never think of using the money of the church to help the poor, but stuff their own money bags."

1. Make a list of all the ways this priest helped his parishioners (the people living in his parish).

2. Read Sources 3, 7 and 8. How is what they say about medieval priests different from what Chaucer says?
3. Sources 3, 7 and 8 all seem to disagree with Chaucer about how good medieval priests were. Try to decide which view might be correct, taking into account the following information about each source:

Source 5: This comes from a poem Chaucer wrote about a group of pilgrims travelling to Canterbury. The priest is one of the pilgrims. Chaucer is not writing about a real priest, but is trying to say what a priest should be like.

Source 3: This comes from a story told by a priest in his sermon. It does tell us something about priests, but do you believe it?

Source 7: This comes from the records the Bishop of Hereford made as he visited parishes. However, he depended on his evidence from the villagers. Can they be trusted in what they say about their priest?

Source 8: This comes from a vision, or a dream, of a holy man who was a great critic of the Church because he regarded it as very corrupt. Can we trust what he says about the priests?

The parish church

The most important thing to do to get to Heaven was to attend the church service called the Mass every Sunday. People also confessed their sins to the priest, and he forgave them. This meant they were free of sin.

Source 9 comes from a medieval instruction book for priests. It lists some of the questions priests should ask during confession.

> **SOURCE 9**
>
> "*Do you believe in Father and Son and Holy Ghost?*
> *Have you done any sorcery to get women to lie with you?*
> *Have you spent Sunday going to the ale house?*
> *Have you been glad in your heart when your neighbour came to harm?*"

Travellers were often worried that they might die on their journey before they had been to a Mass, and so some churches had Morrow Mass. Priests held a Mass at about three o'clock in the morning for merchants and other travellers before they set out on their journey.

Pilgrimages

Another way of showing you were sorry for your sins was to go on a PILGRIMAGE to the SHRINE of a great saint. These saints could help you get to Heaven. You can see in Source 10 some of the most popular places for pilgrimages.

SOURCE 10 The main places of pilgrimage in England and abroad

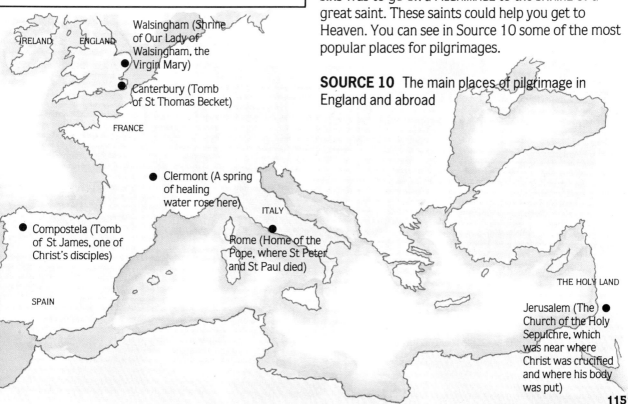

Walsingham (Shrine of Our Lady of Walsingham, the Virgin Mary)

IRELAND ENGLAND

Canterbury (Tomb of St Thomas Becket)

FRANCE

Clermont (A spring of healing water rose here)

ITALY

Compostela (Tomb of St James, one of Christ's disciples)

Rome (Home of the Pope, where St Peter and St Paul died)

SPAIN

THE HOLY LAND

Jerusalem (The Church of the Holy Sepulchre, which was near where Christ was crucified and where his body was put)

In Chaucer's poem about pilgrims, the Wife of Bath had been to Rome, to Compostela and to Jerusalem three times. Guide books were even written for the travellers, as journeys were long and could be dangerous.

> **SOURCE 11** Royal licences granted to ships' captains to take people on pilgrimages. All these licences were granted in just two months in 1434
>
> *John Widerous, master of the* Christopher *– 80 passengers*
> *Roger Brok, master of the* John *– 60 passengers*
> *John Nicoll, master of the* Cok John *– 50 passengers*
> *Thomas Marshall, master of the* Katherine *– 30 passengers.*

For those who could not afford overseas trips, there were shrines all over England. The most popular were the shrine of Our Lady at Walsingham, where there was a special statue of Mary and the baby Jesus (see Source 12), and the shrine of St Thomas at Canterbury (see page 130).

When a manor official called at the village of Snailwell to collect the rents in the fifteenth century, he found that 'nearly everybody in the village had gone on pilgrimage to Canterbury'.

> **SOURCE 12** An account by a visitor to England in the late fifteenth century
>
> *The Virgin Mary is very famous all over England. You can find hardly anybody in that island who thinks he can do well unless he makes some present to that Lady every year.*

Buying your way to Heaven

If you had enough money you could try to buy your way to Heaven.

One of the pilgrims in Chaucer's *Canterbury Tales* was the Pardoner (see Source 13). He sold pardons, which not only freed people from their sins, but also meant they would go straight to Heaven.

> **SOURCE 13** The description of the Pardoner from Chaucer's *Canterbury Tales*
>
> *He'd sewed a holy relic on his cap;*
> *his wallet lay before him on his lap,*
> *brimful of pardons come from Rome.*
> *In his trunk he had a pillow case*
> *which he claimed was Our Lady's veil.*

People believed that nearly everyone went to Purgatory when they died. This was not quite as awful as Hell. To move from Purgatory to Heaven you had to be sorry for your sins, and get people who were still alive to pray for you.

People often left money for prayers to be said for them after they were dead. Rich people paid for colleges to be set up, where priests did nothing but pray for their soul and perhaps for other dead members of their family. The less well-off paid to join GUILDS, which would arrange for masses for their souls after they died. There were over 100 of these guilds in Northamptonshire alone.

> **SOURCE 14** Extracts from medieval wills
>
> *To the Rood Loft 6s 7d*
> *to the bells 12d*
> *to the torches 12d*
> *I will that 30 masses be said for my soul and all Christian souls after my death.*

Nunneries

Some people in the Middle Ages decided to devote their whole life to God and became monks or nuns. In England there were about 130 nunneries, and many more monasteries. Most of the nunneries were small. Only four had over 30 nuns, and many had less than ten. Although the nunneries were not rich, most nuns came from rich families. For many of these women it was the only alternative to marriage and some women became nuns after they were widowed. It was very rare for peasant women to go into a nunnery. They were needed so badly in the fields.

The nuns' daily life was a strict one. Source 15 shows the timetable followed by nuns.

2 a.m. Religious services until dawn, when returned to bed and slept for three hours
6 a.m. Got up; services followed until 12 noon
12 noon until 5 p.m. Working on the farm, e.g. haymaking and digging
5 p.m. until 7 p.m. More services; then straight to bed.

The nuns had three meals a day. In the morning they had bread and ale, and for dinner at midday they had beef, pork or bacon. The Bible was read to them while they ate their dinner. Supper in the evening was usually a light meal of fish. The nuns had to remain silent nearly all the time and communicated by sign language.

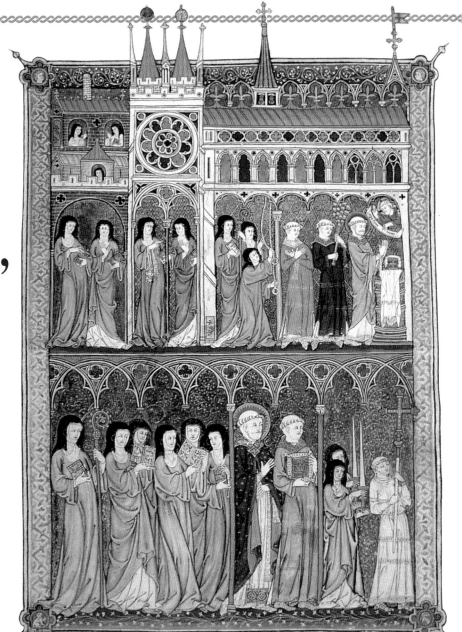

SOURCE 16 Inside a nunnery

1. Look at Source 16. See if you can identify:
   - the abbess, holding her staff and a book
   - the sacristan who rings the bell
   - the cellaress with her keys
   - the novice nuns carrying the candles.
2. Why did only rich women become nuns?
3. Do you think the women who became nuns led a better life than those who did not?

1. Sources 9–16 make it clear that the poor and the rich sometimes used different methods to make sure they got to Heaven. Make two lists:
   a) the methods used by both rich and poor
   b) the methods only used by the rich.
2. Look at Sources 1–16. Choose the two sources which show best of all how important religion was to people in the Middle Ages.
3. Explain whether you agree with this statement:
   - 'In the Middle Ages, religion was more important to most people than it is today.'

Activity

You are a priest giving a sermon to tell your parishioners how to get to Heaven. Using all the evidence on pages 112–116, write down what you are going to say.

How tolerant were people in the Middle Ages?

The Jews in medieval England

'WHY do you treat us like dogs?' This question was put by a Jew to the Abbot of Westminster Abbey in the 1090s.

Jews had settled in England soon after the Norman Conquest. They had helped William raise money for the Conquest.

For the next 200 years they contributed much to English life, including supplying much of the money needed to build cathedrals and fight wars. Jews were forbidden to hold land or enter a trade, but they were allowed to lend money at interest. Christians were not allowed to do this.

Some Jews did very well from their business and at first the Jews were protected by the English kings, who made a lot of money by taxing them. But this protection did not last. There were some terrible massacres of Jews and in 1290 they were thrown out of the country.

As you look at the evidence on this page, see if you can work out why things changed.

> **SOURCE 1** Extracts from the records of Richard of Anestey for 1158
>
> **"**Easter: Borrowed 60 shillings from Vives the Jew of Cambridge for six months, and paid 24 shillings interest.
> Whitsun: Borrowed £2 from Deuleeresse the Jew. Kept it two months and paid 5 shillings and 4 pence interest.
> November: Borrowed £3 10 shillings from Jacob of Newport. Kept it eight months and paid 37 shillings and 4 pence interest.
> I still owe the money and all the interest. **"**

> **SOURCE 2** Written by William of Newburgh – a Christian priest – in 1196
>
> **"**To that treacherous nation and enemy of the Christians, the Jews, King Henry II gave unfair help because of the profits he received from their money lending. He did this to such an extent that they showed themselves insolent towards Christians, and inflicted great injuries upon them. **"**

1. Do Sources 1 and 2 show that at first the Jews did well in England?
2. Is there any evidence here that people were beginning to hate the Jews? Explain your answer.

In 1144 a Christian boy called William disappeared. He was found dead in Thorpe Wood near Norwich. Rumours quickly spread that he had been crucified by the Jews. His tomb in Norwich Cathedral became a great attraction for pilgrims. In the following years the Jews were blamed for other unexplained deaths of young boys all over Europe.

SOURCE 3 A medieval engraving. It shows a Christian boy being crucified by Jews

3. There was no evidence that any Jews had anything to do with William's death, so why do you think people believed the rumours? Discuss this in the class. Source 4 will help.

> **SOURCE 4** From a recent history book
>
> **"**The Jews were obviously different from everyone else in England. They spoke a different language and often lived apart from Christians. They did not believe that Christ was the son of God. The Christian religion taught that the Jews had crucified [killed] Christ. In 1189 Richard I was preparing for a Crusade against the Muslims. But why go all the way to the Holy Land when you could kill non-Christians in England?

Things began to come to a head in 1189 when Richard I was preparing to go on CRUSADE. Sources 5, 6 and 7 – which were all written by medieval writers – describe the terrible violence of 1189–90.

SOURCE 5 Events at King Richard I's coronation in 1189

The leaders of the Jews arrived, against the orders of the King. The King's men seized the Jews, stripped them and flogged them and threw them out. Some they killed. Others they let go half dead.

However, the people of London, hearing this, turned on the Jews of the city and robbed them and killed many of both sexes. They set light to their houses and razed them to ashes.

SOURCE 6 Events in 1190

Throughout England many of those preparing to join the Crusade to Jerusalem decided they would first rise up against the Jews. And so, on 6 February in Norwich, all those Jews found in their homes were slaughtered. On 18 April, Palm Sunday, they say that 57 were massacred at Bury St Edmunds.

In March of 1190 there was a bloody massacre in York (see Source 7). The writer of Source 7 first of all explains that a mob had trapped some Jews in York Castle. The leaders of the mob owed the Jews a lot of money. They gave the Jews a choice: to become Christians, to be massacred, or to kill themselves. This is what happened next.

SOURCE 7 Written by William of Newburgh, a Christian, six years after the events he describes

The Jews burnt their own most precious possessions. Then they prepared their throats for the sacrifice. Joce cut the throats of Anna, his wife, and his sons. All of them died together.

At daybreak, crowds of people stormed the castle. Those Jews who were left threw down the bodies. Many of our men were horrified, but the leaders of the crowd persuaded the remaining Jews to come out. They then butchered them.

Things did not get better for the Jews. In 1253 a law was passed that 'No Christian shall eat with a Jew, and every Jew shall wear on his breast a large badge'.

In the thirteenth century the English kings taxed the Jews so heavily that most of them became poor. Then, in 1290, Edward I threw all the Jews out of the country.

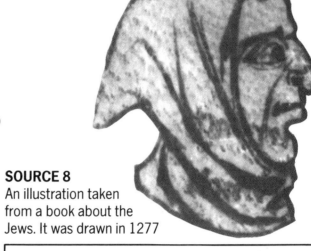

SOURCE 8
An illustration taken from a book about the Jews. It was drawn in 1277

---

4. What impression is the artist trying to give of the Jews in Source 8?
5. Draw up a timeline between the dates 1066 and 1290. Mark on it the events in the history of the Jews in England described on these two pages.
6. Do you agree that the Jews in England were treated more and more badly as the Middle Ages went on?
7. Why did a) the kings' attitude, and b) the ordinary people's attitude change?

Could you get justice in the Middle Ages?

MANY history books claim that violent crimes were common in the Middle Ages, that the courts were not fair, especially to the poor, and that punishments were cruel.

In this section we shall be examining whether these claims are true. You should also be looking to see what changes occurred during the Middle Ages.

The manorial court

The lord's manorial court was the court that ordinary people had most contact with. Everybody had a part to play. It was held several times a year, and everybody in the village had to attend or else pay a fine.

The lord's STEWARD was in charge of the court. It usually met in the hall of the manor house, which would become crowded, noisy and very smelly. In warm weather the court met outside.

The court heard two types of cases:
■ the lord's business – collecting money from the villagers and making sure they did the work they owed the lord
■ sorting out arguments and keeping law and order in the village.

The JURY was made up of twelve villeins, chosen by the whole village. Being on the jury was hard work and not popular, and many people tried to get out of it. One way of avoiding it was to claim that you were a freeman.

The jury collected all the evidence, presented it to the court and then decided whether someone was guilty and how to punish them.

The hue and cry

This made sure everyone helped to track down people who broke the law. For example, if a villager was attacked she would raise the hue and cry. Everybody within earshot had to come to the rescue and help hunt for the guilty person. If the villagers did not help they were all fined!

Tithings

All the men over the age of twelve were placed in groups of ten called tithings. Each member of the tithing had to make sure that the other members did not break the law. If one of them did get into trouble, the others had to make sure he went to court. They often had to promise that they would pay his fine or that he would behave himself in the future. If he did not, all the members of the tithing were fined.

SOURCE 1   A boy stealing cherries

SOURCE 2   A woman beating a man

1. Describe how the ordinary villagers helped to keep law and order.
2. Why do you think everybody was required to help keep law and order?
3. Do you think the system of tithings would work today, e.g. in your school?
4. You are members of a manor court. Reconstruct a meeting to try the two people shown committing crimes in Sources 1 and 2.

SOURCE 3 From Elton manorial court records

a) Maud struck Emma and Emma raised the hue and cry upon her. And the hue and cry was not carried out.

b) John Joce let Peter, a stranger, stay at his house without the lord's permission.

c) Robert's oxen wandered into the lord's land and damaged the barley growing there.

d) Alex, Gilbert and Henry badly beat Reynald.

e) John Lane assaulted Alice his stepmother in her own house and hit her with a stick, breaking her right hand.

f) Allota brewed ale at a penny and sometimes half a penny and sold it before it was tasted by the ale tasters, and sometimes made the ale weak.

g) Henry Godswein refused to work at the second boon-work of the autumn, and he ordered everyone to go home early.

h) Agnes, who is poor, gave birth to a child when she was not married.

i) Nicholas ploughed the lord's land very badly.

j) Hugh dug holes in the road opposite his house.

k) William Bunstede and Emma his wife took the corn of Joan. Joan raised the hue and cry but it was not carried out.

l) Robert owned a dog which ate a foal.

Look at Source 3, which shows crimes from the manorial court in Elton.

1. a) Which of these crimes are to do with the business of the lord of the manor?

   b) Which of these crimes are to do with the morals of the villagers?

2. What excuses do you think the accused would have for crimes e), g), i) and j)?

3. Which of these are likely to be still regarded as crimes today?

4. Why do you think those which are no longer crimes were seen as crimes in the Middle Ages?

5. What punishments do you think the people received?

6. When your teacher has told you the punishments, decide which of the following words best describes them: barbaric, fair, or soft. Give reasons for your answer.

More serious cases were not dealt with in the manorial court. Instead, they went to one of the King's courts. As you will see, the methods used gradually changed during the Middle Ages.

Trial by ordeal – God decides

One way of reaching a verdict in the King's courts was to use trial by ordeal. This was a way of asking for God's judgement.

The method usually used for women was ordeal by hot iron. The woman picked up a piece of hot iron. If after three days in bandages the burns on her hand had healed, it was a sign that she was innocent.

For men, the usual method was ordeal by cold water. The water was first blessed by priests:

SOURCE 4

It is said: 'Let this water be to thee now a trial.' The accused is undressed and cast, thumbs and toes tied together, into the water. And it is said: 'O thou water, in the name of God, do not receive this man if he be guilty, but make him swim upon thee.'

If the man floated on the surface he was guilty and had one foot and his right hand chopped off.

1. Would you rather undergo trial by hot iron or trial by cold water?
2. Why were these methods used?

Both ordeal by hot iron and ordeal by cold water were used in England before the Normans arrived. The Normans did, however, introduce a new way of asking for God's judgement: trial by battle. This method was used in 1249 in Hampshire, for some robbers (see Sources 5–8).

SOURCE 5 Written by Matthew Paris, a monk, in the thirteenth century

The suspected persons were arrested but were freed by a jury made up of local men. Many people in the area were involved, and no one would accuse anyone else. The King's advisers told him that robbery was a frequent occurrence throughout England.

At last one of the thieves, Walter Bloweberme, admitted his guilt and then became an informer (see Source 6).

SOURCE 6 From Hampshire Court Records of 1249

> *Walter accuses Hamo Stare that they were at the house of Edeline Cross at Winchester and there stole clothes and other goods. Hamo had as his share two coats. Walter offers to prove by his body that Hamo was guilty. Hamo comes and denies everything and says that he is willing to defend himself by his body. So it is decided that there be battle between. The battle takes place and Hamo has given in.*

SOURCE 7 From Hampshire Court Records of 1249. Walter Bloweberme and Hamo Stare in the trial by battle. Walter is the one on the right. In the background you can see what happened to Hamo after the battle

SOURCE 8 The bill for the equipment for the battle between Walter and Hamo

> *Purchase of:*
> | | |
> |---|---|
> | 2 shields | 13s 4d |
> | 2 wooden staves | 3s |
> | white leather, felt and linen cloth for tunics | 8s 3d |

SOURCE 10 Another drawing of trial by battle

SOURCE 9 A medieval account of a different trial by battle

> *They were dressed in white leather and had wooden staves with iron heads on the ends. They had neither meat nor drink before the battle and if they needed any drink they had to take their own piss. Jamys lunged at Thomas, breaking his weapon in so doing. Thomas fought on until the officials disarmed him. Then they fought on unarmed. They bit with their teeth so that the leather and their flesh was torn in many places. Jamys grabbed Thomas by the nose with his teeth and put his thumb in his eye. Thomas called for mercy and the judge stopped the fight. Thomas admitted he had wrongly accused Jamys and was hanged.*

1. Study Source 5. Did trial by battle have any advantages over the jury system?
2. Study Sources 6–10 carefully. Was the result of the battle left entirely for God to decide?
3. How are the two pictures of trial by battle (Sources 7 and 10) different?
4. Which of the two pictures do you think is the more accurate? It will help if you read Sources 6, 8 and 9 again.

By the thirteenth century trial by ordeal was gradually disappearing. The Church was against it, and in 1215 it was abolished. Trial by battle was still used, but not very often. These methods were gradually replaced by trial by jury.

Villein or freeman? The jury decides

SOURCE 11 The King's court

In 1225 Richard, a peasant in the village of Ashill in Norfolk, was seized by Peter de Nereford, the lord of the manor, and forced to pay Peter money. Richard prosecuted Peter in the King's court.

> SOURCE 12 From court records
>
> **Peter** defended the taking and holding of Richard. He said that Richard was a villein who had not performed his villein services and so he had seized his cattle to make him perform his services.
>
> **Richard** said that he was a freeman.
>
> **The court** said to Peter that he should prove Richard to be a villein and to Richard that he should prove himself to be free. The sheriff was ordered to make Richard's relatives and six free and lawful men from the same village come to the court to say what services Richard and his family did for the lord.
>
> **Richard** brings one of his relatives, Reginald, who says that his mother was the sister of Richard's father, and that he is a freeman. He also brings forward other cousins on his father's side and they all come and say they are freemen.
>
> **Peter** brings forward Ordgar and Simon Grim, who are both related to Richard on his mother's side and who say they are villeins. And Peter, asked if he has any of Richard's relatives on his father's side, says no because Thurkill, Richard's father, was not born on his estate.
>
> **Richard** agrees that all those are his relatives on his mother's and are villeins. However, he says that Thurkill his father was a freeman, and he occupied a freeman's holding which his wife, Cristina (Richard's mother), had inherited from her father, who received it from Gore Stiward.
>
> **Peter** says that Gore held his land as a villein's holding and was a villein. He asks for the court's verdict because Richard agrees that his relatives on his mother's side are villeins, and the holding came to Richard from that side of the family.

1. Read Source 12.
   a) Who brought the case to the court?
   b) Where did the court get the evidence from?
   c) Was this a fair way of getting evidence?
   d) Why was there no written evidence?
2. Use the evidence in Source 12 to argue that Richard was a freeman.
3. Use the evidence in Source 12 to argue that Richard was a villein.
4. If you were on the jury which argument would you agree with?
5. Is trial by jury a better method than trial by ordeal or battle?

Now that you have studied this section on justice answer the following questions:
1. Were most cases about violent crimes?
2. Were punishments harsh?
3. Which aspects of medieval courts changed, and which stayed the same?

Was the Black Death a disaster?

PEOPLE in medieval England always faced famine and disease, but in the middle of the fourteenth century they had to survive the Black Death. It spread from Asia to Europe and then to England, where nearly half the population died. At that time doctors did not know about germs causing diseases, but they did have their own ideas about the Black Death.

---

1. What does Source 1 tell you about the attitudes of medieval people towards the Black Death?

Some historians think that there were two different plagues at this time:

Bubonic plague

The germ is carried in the bloodstream of rats. The fleas which bite the rats become infected and when they leave the rats for more food they often bite humans and pass on the plague. These fleas multiply in warm weather but die off in cold weather, so bubonic plague does not spread very widely in the winter. Sufferers have a fever and buboes (swellings) in the groin and on the armpit. About 70% of patients die. It takes between four and seven days for them to die. Their blood is usually not infected enough to infect more fleas.

Pneumonic plague

This plague is caught through breathing. It attacks the lungs. Patients cough blood and spray out germs every time they breathe out. It kills everyone infected within two days and is not affected by the weather or climate.

▶ **SOURCE 1** A medieval picture showing the Black Death as a rider on horseback

SOURCE 2 Medieval descriptions of the Plague

"a) *Apostumes and carbuncles on the armpits and the groin. From this, one died in five days.*

b) *Continuous fever and spitting of blood. Men suffer in their lungs and breathing, and whoever has been corrupted cannot live beyond two days or three days.*

c) *The emergence of certain tumours in the groin or armpits, some of which grew as large as a common apple. Black spots appeared on the arm or the thigh.*

d) *Anyone who is infected by it dies, all who see him in his sickness, quickly follow thither.*"

---

2. Which type of plague does each extract in Source 2 describe? Make sure you give reasons for your answers.
3. From what you know about living conditions in villages and towns, do you think diseases like the Plague would have spread very easily?

▶ **SOURCE 3** Map showing the spread of the Plague

4. Match each of the extracts in Source 4 with the correct place number on the map in Source 3. An atlas will help you do this. Then write an account entitled 'The spread of the Plague'.

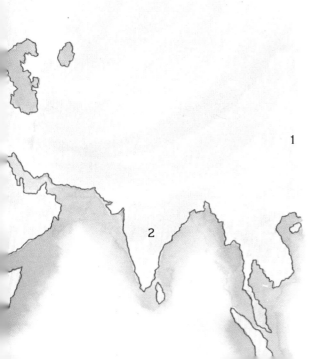

1

2

SOURCE 4 Medieval descriptions of the spread of the Plague

"a) *In 1347 twelve galleys entered the harbour of Messina (Sicily). In their bones the sailors bore so virulent a disease that anyone who only spoke to them was seized by a deadly illness.*

b) *In 1348 that memorable mortality happened here in Florence. It was sent upon us by the just anger of God. The city was cleansed of much filth, and sickly persons were banned from entering, but nothing prevented it.*

c) *Jews were burned in Strasbourg in 1349. It was believed that the Jews had caused the plague by poisoning drinking water.*

d) *In 1345, in China and India, fire fell from heaven and stinking smoke, which slew all that were left of men and beasts. By these winds the whole province was infected.*

e) *Flagellants whipped themselves in Germany early in 1349. They believed that the plague was sent by God as a punishment for human sin. They were punishing themselves for these sins.*

f) *1349. To the Lord Mayor of London. Order to cause the human dung and other filth lying in the streets to be removed. The city is so foul with the filth from out of the houses that the air is infected and the city poisoned.*

g) *In June 1348, in Melcombe, in the county of Dorset, two ships came alongside. One of the sailors had brought with him from Gascony the seeds of the terrible pestilence and, through him, the men of that town were the first in England to be infected.*"

5. Some people at the time thought that the Black Death was caused by bad air. Which of the extracts in Source 4 takes that view?

6. What other beliefs are there in these extracts about causes of the Plague?

7. Use everything you know about medieval people and their beliefs to explain why you think they believed in these causes.

8. Would any of the actions described in Source 4 help to protect people from the Plague?

Did the Black Death change medieval villages?

In the period before the Black Death the population of England rose sharply and there was not enough land for everyone. People were keen to have land, and this meant the lord of the manor would put rents up and increase labour services. Anyone who failed to look after their land was likely to have it taken from them.

Many history books tell the following story about the effects of the Black Death.

> **SOURCE 5**
>
> ❝The Black Death, 1348–1350, killed so many villeins that the lord of the manor could not get enough people to live and work on his estates. Some villages were deserted. In other places many villeins stopped doing their labour services for the lord and paid low rents instead. The villeins became free and their lives improved. Because of the shortage of villeins on their estates the lords had to employ labourers on their estates and pay them high wages.❞

You should by now have a good idea of what medieval villages were like. Study Sources 6–15 and judge for yourself whether villages changed much after the Black Death.

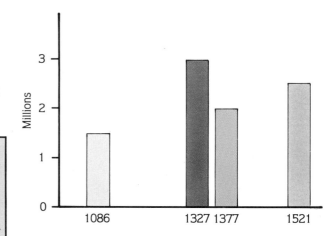

SOURCE 7 Population of England

Sources 8–11 describe some of the immediate effects of the Black Death.

> **SOURCE 8** Written by one of the King's advisers in 1350
>
> ❝The King ordered that reapers and other labourers should not be paid more than they used to receive.
>
> But if anyone wished to hire the labourers he had to pay them what they wanted.
>
> Many small villages were completely deserted; there was not one house left in them, and all those who had lived in them were dead. The lords had to reduce their tenants' rents, and those who received day work from their tenants, as is usual from villeins, had to release them. Land everywhere remained completely uncultivated.❞

Key

• Deserted village

▨ Land over 245 metres

SOURCE 6 Deserted medieval villages

SOURCE 9 From a modern history book

For peasants who survived the Black Death these were good times. Prices were low and wages were high. They were not afraid to stand up for themselves against the barons and lords, the Church, even the King. Perhaps the disaster had something to do with this: so many had died that those who were left felt special in some way. Once they had faced death and escaped it, why should they be frightened of anything?

SOURCE 10 From the manorial accounts of Elton

1349 Rent lacking from eleven cottages by reason of the mortality of the previous year
From the fulling mill nothing because it is broken and useless
1350 6d from the smithy because it fell down after All Saints and from then on was empty
40 workmen hired to reap and bind the lord's corn for lack of tenants.

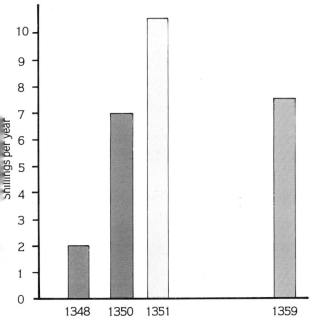

SOURCE 11 Ploughman's wages in Cuxham, Oxfordshire

1. What changes took place in villages at the time of the Black Death?
2. Did everybody benefit from these changes?

As Sources 12–15 show you, however, there are also signs that things had been changing in English villages before the Black Death, and continued to change long after it.

SOURCE 12 From a recent history book

On the estates of Durham Priory things were changing before the Black Death. The lord was already renting out his lands to people who would pay him a rent instead of doing services. One possible reason is that the lord realised he was not getting the best out of people doing week-work because they were having to do the work for no reward to themselves. Also many officials were dishonest and were stealing things from the lord's land. The lord decided he could make more money from rents.

SOURCE 13 Events in the Middle Ages

1258 Famine — so many died that bodies were left unburied around the streets
1315–1317 Famine — people starved to death, rumours of cannibalism
1349–1350 THE BLACK DEATH
1361–1471 Eight more outbreaks of Plague

SOURCE 14 From Elton manorial court records

1279 Henry Godswein fined 12d because he came late to reap the lord's land in the autumn.
Henry Achard, Ralph the shoemaker all the same.
1286 16 of the 48 villeins had their week-work changed to rents.

SOURCE 15 From a recent history book

In Warwickshire, 6 villages were deserted by 1400, 90 had disappeared by 1485, and 24 more after that date.

Look at all the sources on these two pages.
3. Which sources suggest that the changes in medieval villages were caused only by the Black Death?
4. Which sources suggest that there were other causes for these changes?

The problems facing medieval kings

The Empire

BY THE time of King Henry II, English kings ruled over an enormous EMPIRE stretching from the border with Scotland to the border with Spain. The vast distances involved made it difficult for English kings to rule this Empire, especially because travel was difficult and slow. Another problem was the threat from neighbouring kings, who were determined to conquer parts of the Empire. For more than 100 years English kings had to fight expensive wars to defend the Empire, until they were left with just the area around Calais.

1. Look at Source 1. How far is it from York to Bordeaux?
2. It was important for the King to visit all parts of the Empire. How long would it take Henry II to travel from York to Bordeaux? (He would be travelling on horseback and covering about 50 km a day at the most.)

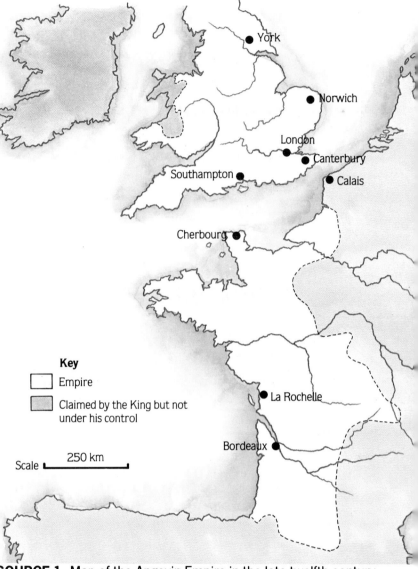

Key

☐ Empire

▨ Claimed by the King but not under his control

Scale ⊢ 250 km ⊣

SOURCE 1 Map of the Angevin Empire in the late twelfth century

The succession to the throne

Today there are rules about who will be the next monarch when a King or Queen dies. Their eldest son or daughter takes over. This has not always been the case. Sometimes the King chose his successor, sometimes he had no children, and sometimes the BARONS wanted to choose the next King. Disputes over who should rule England led to monarchs being murdered and to several civil wars during the Middle Ages.

SOURCE 2 The King dreaming

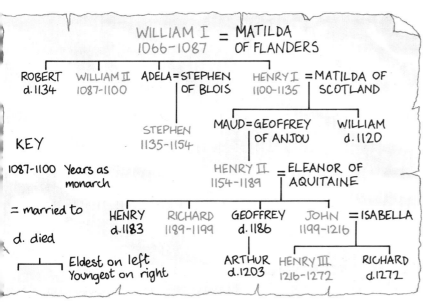

WILLIAM I = MATILDA
1066-1087   OF FLANDERS

ROBERT   WILLIAM II   ADELA=STEPHEN   HENRY I = MATILDA OF
d.1134   1087-1100   OF BLOIS   1100-1135   SCOTLAND

                         STEPHEN   MAUD=GEOFFREY   WILLIAM
KEY   1135-1154   OF ANJOU   d.1120

1087-1100 Years as   HENRY II = ELEANOR OF
           monarch   1154-1189   AQUITAINE

= married to   HENRY   RICHARD   GEOFFREY   JOHN = ISABELLA
                 d.1183   1189-1199 d.1186   1199-1216
d. died

   ⌐──┐   Eldest on left   ARTHUR HENRY III   RICHARD
         Youngest on right   d.1203 1216-1272   d.1272

SOURCE 3 Family tree of English kings from 1066 to 1272

---

1. Look at Source 3. How many children did William I have?
2. If modern ideas about SUCCESSION to the throne had been used, who would have become King after William?
3. In 1135 both Stephen and Henry II claimed the throne. What were their claims?
4. Which King first inherited the throne according to modern ideas?

The barons

English kings could not rule the country properly without the co-operation of the BARONS. These landowners controlled large parts of England, and were powerful enough to demand special privileges from the King.
King John was one of several kings who had to deal with revolts by the barons.

The Church

English kings were not complete masters in their lands for another reason – the Roman Catholic Church. This was under the control of the Pope in Rome. You have already seen how important religion was to everybody at this time. This gave the Church a lot of influence over people. Disputes broke out between the King and the Church over who was more important. The dispute between Henry II and Thomas Becket, the Archbishop of Canterbury, led to Thomas being murdered.

The peasants

As you have seen, the vast majority of people in England were peasants working on the land. Their lives were hard, and famine and starvation were never far away. This meant there was always the danger of uprisings. In 1381 the peasants rose up in a rebellion which almost overthrew King Richard II.

Scotland and Wales

English kings could never really feel secure while the Welsh princes threatened the western borders and the Scottish King threatened the northern borders. Northern England was constantly invaded by Scotland. Various attempts to conquer Wales and Scotland were only partly successful and caused English kings many problems.

---

1. Look at Source 2. The King is dreaming of problems he faces. Which of his problems are shown in each section of the picture?

Activity

You are a medieval King of England writing to your son. Explain what problems you face in governing the country.

The murder of an Archbishop

1. Becket and Henry are friends

2. Henry appoints his friend Becket as Archbishop of Canterbury

3. Becket and Henry quarrel over who controls the church

4. Becket flees abroad but Henry asks him to come home

5. Becket and Henry quarrel again

YOU have already seen how important the Church was in everybody's lives. You have also seen that the head of the Church was not the King but the Pope in Rome. This meant that disputes broke out between the Pope's BISHOPS and the King about who should control the Church in England. These disputes came to a head in Henry II's reign:

■ Kings often appointed their friends and officials as bishops. These men had no interest in the Church. Often, they kept working for the King's government and neglected their Church duties. For example, they did nothing about PRIESTS who were not doing their jobs properly. Having his men as bishops helped Henry to control the Church in England. The Pope claimed Henry had no right to appoint bishops.

■ The Pope said that the CLERGY should be tried in Church courts rather than in the King's courts. Church courts rarely handed out severe punishments to clergy. Henry wanted everyone to come under the power of his courts. He had a list of over 100 murders committed by churchmen who had escaped the King's courts.

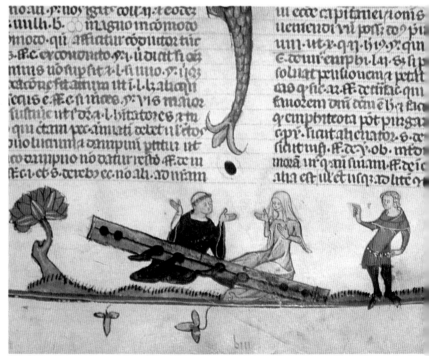

SOURCE 1 When clergy committed crimes they were often given light punishments like a short spell in the stocks

Why did Henry and Becket quarrel?

SOURCE 2 Written in the 1180s by Gerald of Wales, a bishop

Henry was a man of reddish, freckled complexion, with a large round head and grey eyes which glowed fiercely and grew bloodshot in anger.

SOURCE 3 A recent description of Becket

Becket was a vain, obstinate and ambitious man, who sought always to keep himself in the public eye; he was above all a man of extremes, a man who knew no half measures.

In 1162 Henry II made his close friend Thomas Becket Archbishop of Canterbury. Becket was already Chancellor, and for a number of years he had been running the government for Henry. This looked like a clever move by Henry, as it would surely put the Church under his control. But he soon discovered that he had made a mistake, as Sources 4–10 will show you. Very soon, Becket and Henry found themselves arguing.

SOURCE 4 From a recent history book

Becket refused to allow a priest who had killed a man and raped the daughter to be tried in the King's court. He put him in a bishop's prison for protection against the King's men.

SOURCE 5 Written by Becket to the King

It is certain that kings receive their power from the Church. You have not the power to give orders to bishops, nor to drag priests before your courts.

There were attempts to patch up the quarrel, but as Sources 6–8 show you, they were not successful.

SOURCE 6 Written by Henry to Becket

My Lord Archbishop, let us return to our old friendship, and help each other as best we can, forgetting our hatred completely.

SOURCE 7 Written by William of Newburgh, not long after the events he is describing

The Archbishop returned to England with the permission of the King. But unknown to the King he carried with him letters directed against a number of bishops. As soon as he was in England he excommunicated them.

SOURCE 8 What Henry is reported to have said

What miserable traitors I have nourished and promoted in my household, who let their lord be treated with such shameful contempt by a low-born priest.

SOURCE 9 From a nineteenth-century children's history book

Becket wanted to be as great a man as the King, and tried to stop the judges punishing wicked clergy. For this reason there were sad quarrels between the King and Becket.

SOURCE 10 From a twentieth-century children's history book

Henry was a strong King. He tried to force the clergy to obey his rules, and in a fit of temper made some of his knights kill Becket.

1. What kind of men do Henry and Becket seem to be? Do any of these words describe them well: stubborn, weak, unreasonable, bad-tempered, fair, deceitful?
2. Henry and Becket were once great friends. Why did they end up as enemies? Use evidence from Sources 2–8 to support your answer.
3. Look at Sources 9 and 10. Who do the writers blame for the quarrel? Use the evidence on this page to explain why these historians disagree.

THE MURDER OF AN ARCHBISHOP

How was Becket murdered?

In 1170, Becket and Henry seemed to have settled their arguments. Becket returned to England. But as soon as he arrived at Canterbury he expelled all the bishops who supported the King from the Church.

Henry was still in Normandy, and when he heard this news some reports say he shouted out, 'Is there no one who will rid me of this troublesome priest?' Other writers say simply that Henry showed his deep anger by his face and gestures.

Whichever is true, four knights decided that they should kill Becket, and they sailed for England. They arrived in Canterbury on the afternoon of 29 December 1170.

SOURCE 11 This account is by William Fitzstephen. He was Becket's clerk and friend

"One of the knights struck him with the flat of his sword between the shoulders, saying, 'Fly, you are a dead man.' The knights tried to drag him out of the church. But the monks held him back.

Edward Grim, one of the monks, putting his arm up, received the first stroke of the sword and was severely wounded. By this same stroke the Archbishop was wounded in the head.

As he knelt down clasping and stretching his hands out to God, a second stroke was dealt him on the head, at which he fell by the altar.

While he lay there Richard Brito struck him with such force that the sword was broken against his head. Four wounds in all did the saintly Archbishop receive.

The whole of the crown of his head was lopped off. But he didn't try to avoid or parry the blows. He accepted death from a desire to be with God.

Hugh of Horsea extracted the blood and brains from the hollow of his head with the point of a sword."

SOURCE 12 This account is by Edward Grim, a priest, who was with Becket at the time of his death

"The murderers came in full armour, with swords and axes. The monks cried out to the Archbishop to flee to the church. But he had long since yearned for martyrdom and dreaded that it would be delayed if he fled to the church. But the monks pulled, dragged and pushed him into the church. The four knights followed with rapid strides. The Archbishop ordered the doors of the church to be kept open.

In a spirit of mad fury the knights called out, 'Where is Thomas Becket, traitor to the King and the country?' At this he quite unafraid came down the steps and answered, 'Here I am, no traitor to the King, but a priest.'

Having said this he stood by a pillar.

'You shall die this instant,' they cried.

They pulled and dragged him violently trying to get him outside the church. But they could not get him away from the pillar. Then he inclined his head as one in prayer and joined his hands together and uplifted them.
The wicked knight leapt suddenly upon him and wounded him in the head.

Next he received a second blow on the head, but still he stood firm.

At the third blow he fell on his knees and elbows, saying in a low voice, 'For the name of Jesus I am ready to die.'

The next blow separated the crown of his head and the blood white with the brain and the brain red with the blood stained the floor.

The fourth knight warded off any who sought to interfere.
A fifth man placed his foot on the neck of the holy priest and scattered the brains and blood about the pavement."

SOURCE 13 A painting of Becket's death, made in the thirteenth century

1. How do the accounts of Becket's death in Sources 11 and 12 differ?
2. What evidence is there in their accounts that both these writers were sympathetic to Becket?
3. Does the fact that they are both on Becket's side mean they cannot be trusted?
4. Is there any evidence that Becket wanted to die?
5. How reliable do you think Source 13 is?
6. Which gives you the best idea of what happened, the written accounts or the painting?
7. Who do you think was to blame for Becket's death: Henry, Becket or the knights who killed him? Explain your answer.

Who won?

- Becket was made a saint in 1173 by the Pope.
- One year after Becket's death Henry came to Canterbury and was flogged by the monks as a punishment.
- Pilgrims flocked to Becket's tomb at Canterbury, and still do.
- The monarch kept the power to appoint bishops.
- 80 churches and two hospitals were named after Becket.
- The CLERGY were still tried in Church courts.

1. Some of these results are short-term ones and some are long-term.
a) Who do you think won in the short term?
b) Who do you think won in the long term? Explain your answers.

King John – an evil King?

IN 1199, 10 years after Henry's death, his son John became King. Most people would agree with the view of King John in Source 1.

> **SOURCE 1** From a recent history book
>
> 66 John was a thoroughly bad lot. He was cruel and beastly. He made many enemies and killed people with his bare hands. He was the worst king ever to have sat on the English throne.

Where does this view come from? Most people's view of John has been influenced by J.R. Green's best-selling *Short History of the English People*, published in 1875 (see Source 2).

> **SOURCE 2** Written by J. R. Green
>
> 66 His punishments were cruel: the starvation of children, the crushing of old men under copes of lead. His court was a brothel where no woman was safe from the royal lust. He scoffed at priests. Foul as it is, Hell itself is defiled by the fouler presence of King John.

Green based his account on the medieval chronicles of Roger of Wendover and Matthew Paris (see Sources 3–5). These are almost the only contemporary accounts of John that we have. But both Wendover and Paris were monks – and John treated monks very badly and came into conflict with the Church. They were also both supporters of the BARONS, who fought against John.

> **SOURCE 3** Written by Matthew Paris. He got most of his information from Roger of Wendover
>
> 66 John was a tyrant, a destroyer, crushing his own people. He lost the duchy of Normandy and many other territories. He hated his wife and she him. He gave orders that her lovers were to be throttled on her bed.

Can we trust Source 4? Most of it is very vague: why does Roger not say where it happened? Why are we not told the name of the sheriff? But then at the end Roger claims to know exactly what John said! Government records from this time show that John had ordered that anyone killing a priest should be hung from the nearest oak tree.

> **SOURCE 4** Written by Roger of Wendover
>
> 66 The servants of a certain sheriff somewhere in Wales brought to the royal court a robber. He had robbed and murdered a priest. John said, 'He has killed an enemy of mine, let him go.'

Source 5 is another extract from Roger of Wendover's account.

> **SOURCE 5** Written by Roger of Wendover
>
> 66 In 1209, Geoffrey, a priest, said it was not safe for priests to work for the King any longer. John heard of this and, in a fury, had Geoffrey imprisoned in chains, clad in a cope of lead, and starved. He died an agonising death.

When we check the records, we find that Geoffrey was still alive in 1225 and had been appointed Bishop of Ely by John!

1. Study Sources 1–5.
a) Find three opinions in these sources about what kind of man John was.
b) Do the sources contain any facts?
2. Is there evidence in Source 2 that Green did use Roger of Wendover's account?
3. Do you think Roger of Wendover and Matthew Paris can be trusted?

Sources 6–9 give a variety of information about John.

SOURCE 6 From a recent history book

66 John tried hard to be a good king. He visited all parts of England and was merciful to helpless people – the poor, widows and children. But he was untrustworthy and a poor soldier who lost the war with France. 99

SOURCE 7 A medieval picture of John feeding his dogs

SOURCE 8 Written by a contemporary monk who is normally regarded as reliable

66 The King ordered the few monks who remained at Canterbury, the blind and the crippled, to be thrown out, and the monks to be regarded as public enemies.

After John had captured Arthur [his young nephew] and kept him in prison for some time, he became drunk and possessed with the devil and murdered him with his own hand; and tying a heavy stone to the body cast it into a river. 99

SOURCE 9 John's orders to an English city

66 We commit the Jews dwelling in your city to your charge; if anyone attempts to harm them always protect and assist them. 99

4. Study Source 7. Does John look evil?
5. Study Sources 6, 8 and 9. Which gives the most balanced account of John?
6. Why do you think people have been so ready to believe that John was an evil King?
7. Is it possible to prove whether or not John was an evil King?

Was the Magna Carta a failure?

JOHN had become King of England at a very difficult time.

His brother, King Richard, had spent nearly all his reign fighting the CRUSADES and had neglected England. He had also left John with no money.

John's nephew Arthur also claimed the throne. Some historians believe John murdered him (see Source 8 on the previous page).

To add to John's problems, there was also a powerful new King of France, who was planning to conquer England's French lands. By 1206 John had lost most of the lands in France. He tried to win them back in 1214 but was unsuccessful.

To fight these wars he had to tax the BARONS heavily, even though many of them had lost their lands in France as well. John also increased the many FEUDAL payments from the barons. For example, it was normal for a baron to pay the King about £100 when he inherited his father's lands, but John charged as much as £600. The barons also resented the payment called scutage. Normally they paid this to the King instead of sending him knights for his army. John turned it into a tax which they paid every year.

John also ran into trouble with the Church. He quarrelled with the Pope about who should be the new Archbishop of Canterbury. The Pope closed all the churches in England for the rest of John's reign.

There were no marriages and no one could be buried in holy ground. In return John seized the lands of a number of monasteries.

John's reign was not all failure:
- He had victories against the Welsh and the Scots. One contemporary writer said, 'Ireland, Scotland and Wales all bowed to his nod.'
- He successfully reformed and strengthened the English navy.
- He made sure his law courts brought law and order and justice to everyone (he often delayed trials to make sure he could be present).
- He introduced a new money system, which helped government finances.

However, by 1215 the barons had had enough and they rebelled. This was nothing unusual. Every King since William I had faced barons' revolts.

---

1. Give three reasons why the barons rebelled in 1215.

In 1215 the barons forced John to sign the Magna Carta (the Great CHARTER).

SOURCE 1 A nineteenth-century picture of John signing the Magna Carta, now hanging in the Houses of Parliament

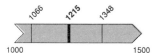

2. What impression does Source 1 give you of John?

The Magna Carta is often seen as the document that laid down for the first time the rights and freedoms of the English people and made sure that we still have these freedoms today. See what you think.

When the barons put this Charter together their aims were:

- to stop their civil war with the King
- to stop John taking too much money from them
- to make sure they received a fair trial from John's courts.

In other words, they were looking after themselves. They were not trying to set down the rights of all English people. They included the rights of other groups, like MERCHANTS and the Church, but only to win as much support as possible.

Much of the Charter was concerned with the rights of the barons – but there were only just over 100 barons. The rights in the Charter were restricted to FREEMEN – but most people at that time were not free, they were VILLEINS.

3. Look at the points from the Charter in Source 2. Which group of people would benefit from each of these points? Which group of people would be no better off?

John only signed the Charter to gain some time and stop the barons rebelling. He had no intention of keeping to it. Only months later, fighting broke out again between the barons and the King, so the Charter could be said to be a failure.

However, it was in the centuries after John's reign that the Charter became more important. The kings after John did give the barons the rights laid down in the Charter. What's more, after the Black Death, as more and more villeins became free, the rights in the Charter also applied to them. Most people, not just the barons, began to pay regular taxes, and so their permission was needed before taxes could be set by the King.

Two of the points in the Charter are still very important to everybody in Britain today:

- We cannot be punished without a fair trial.
- We cannot be taxed without our representatives (Members of Parliament) agreeing.

SOURCE 2 Some of the main points in the Magna Carta

a) *We grant to all freemen all the liberties written below.*

b) *A baron's heir shall inherit his lands on payment of £100 to the King.*

c) *No scutage [tax] shall be imposed on the barons except with the common counsel of the realm.*

d) *To obtain the common counsel of the realm we will summon bishops, earls and barons.*

e) *No freemen shall be arrested or imprisoned without a proper trial and according to the law of the land.*

f) *The English Church shall be free to make its own appointments.*

g) *All merchants shall have safety, in staying and travelling in England, for buying and selling goods free from evil tolls.*

SOURCE 3 Written by a twentieth-century historian

“*The Magna Carta made it clear that the King was subject to laws which would protect the rights of the people. It was an immediate success.*”

SOURCE 4 A seventeenth-century revolutionary describes the Magna Carta's results

“*The clergy and gentry have got their freedom, but the common people are still slaves.*”

4. Which of Sources 3 and 4 do you agree with?

5. Why do you think the writer of Source 4 claims the Magna Carta was a failure?

6. Why could the Charter be said to be a long-term success?

Why did Parliament develop?

Stage 1:

The barons give the King advice when he asks for it

IF KINGS were sensible, they ruled the country with the advice of their most powerful subjects, the barons and BISHOPS. These men controlled large parts of the country. If the King wanted to stay in power, raise armies, keep law and order and collect taxes, he needed the support of these men. Several kings in the Middle Ages lost their thrones because they lost the support of their barons, and the barons rebelled against them.

Saxon kings had realised that they needed to consult the bishops and nobles. They took advice from a group of bishops and nobles called the Witan, which is shown in Source 1.

William I (1066–1087) continued this system. His tenants-in-chief (the barons he had given land to) formed his Great Council. Kings held these meetings because they were sensible. The barons did not have a right to be there. If a king wanted to risk it, he could govern without the barons, or he could invite some barons to meetings but not invite others.

SOURCE 1 The Anglo-Saxon Witan

▶ **SOURCE 2** Parliament in Edward I's reign (1272–1307)

SOURCE 3 The modern Parliament

Stage 2:

Kings have to meet with the barons

You have already seen that in King John's reign there was an important development. The barons forced John to sign the Magna Carta in 1215. Look back at Source 2 on the previous page. Points c) and d) mean that the King needed the barons' permission before he could set a tax. In other words, the King now *had* to call meetings of his barons.

John did not do this (and we have already seen the trouble he got into as a result). But the kings who followed him did. This gave the barons more power. If the King asked them for taxes, they could demand things in return.

Stage 3:
The Commons are sometimes invited

You have probably noticed that the most important difference between the Great Council and the Parliament we have today is that only bishops and barons were invited to the Great Council.

This changed after 1264, when the barons rebelled again and defeated and captured King Henry III. The barons were led by Simon de Montfort, who ruled the country for a time. Simon did not have the support of all the barons, so to try and get more people on his side he called a Parliament which included not just the nobles but also some of the ordinary people. Two KNIGHTS from each county and two representatives from each of the large towns were chosen by rich property owners.

Henry's supporters defeated and killed Simon at the battle of Evesham in 1265, but from this time Parliaments often contained representatives of the ordinary people, or Commons, as well as lords and bishops.

Stage 4:
The Commons become more powerful

For much of the time between 1337 and 1453 England was at war with France. This was known as the Hundred Years' War. As you can imagine, 100 years of war was very expensive. The only way to pay for the war was to tax everybody in the country. But before the kings could tax anybody, representatives from the counties and the towns had to come to Parliament and agree to the taxes.

The Lords and the Commons met in two separate groups. Before they would agree to any taxes, the Commons began to ask the King for reforms. Sometimes these were about local matters, like the right to build a new bridge, but sometimes the Commons had views on how the country should be governed.

However, this was still a long way from Parliament as we know it. Kings still tried to stop the Commons from discussing important matters like foreign policy. It is also important to remember that Parliament only met for a few weeks every year. For most of the time the King ruled with the help of his advisers from the Lords.

---

1. Look at Sources 1–3. What are the main differences between these three Parliaments?
2. Draw a timeline from 1066 to 1500, and mark on it the important developments in the history of Parliament.
3. Here are a number of reasons that caused Parliament to develop at various stages:
   - the Kings' need to keep the barons on their side
   - the rebellion by the barons against John
   - the rebellion led by Simon de Montfort
   - Simon de Montfort's need to get as much support as possible from ordinary people
   - the need to pay for the Hundred Years' War against France.

   Discuss in the class how each of these reasons helped the development of Parliament.
4. Which of these reasons was the most important? Why?
5. For each statement below, say whether it describes:
   a) Parliament in the thirteenth century
   b) Parliament today
   c) Parliament at both times.
   - 'Parliament meets for a few weeks every year. The monarch rules the country with the Council for the rest of the time.'
   - 'Parliament consists of Lords and Commons.'
   - 'The Commons are elected by people around the country.'
   - 'Only the rich are allowed to vote.'
   - 'Parliament is not allowed to discuss certain subjects, like foreign policy.'
   - 'The House of Lords is more important than the House of Commons.'
   - 'Parliament has to agree before people can be taxed.'
   - 'The Prime Minister comes from the House of Commons and is more powerful than the King or Queen.'

The Peasants' Revolt

What happened?

SOURCE 2
London and
the south east
in 1381

SOURCE 1 Written by a monk in York in 1399

"At Brampton in Essex, Thomas Brampton
demanded a new payment of taxes from the
people, who said they would not pay a penny
more. Thomas ordered the men to be arrested.
Then the commons said they had already paid the
tax, and rose up against him and tried to kill
Thomas. They then went from place to place to
stir up other folk.

And at this moment [30 May 1381] a tax
collector was sent to Kent, but he was turned
back by the commons. And after this the
commons of Kent gathered together in great
numbers without a head or chieftain and on the
Friday [4 June] came to Dartford. On the next
Friday they came to Rochester. They then took
their way to Maidstone, where they made Wat
Tyler their chief. And on the Monday next they
came to Canterbury. After cutting off the heads of
three traitors, they took 500 men of the town
with them to London, but left the rest to guard
the town.

At this time the commons had as their adviser
an evil priest named Sir John Ball. A fit reward he
got later, when he was hung, drawn and
quartered. The commons went to many places
and gathered 60,000 men. On their way to
London they burned the manors of the Duke of
Lancaster to the ground, because they hated him.
When the King [Richard II] heard of these doings,
he sent his messengers to them, asking why they
were doing this. And they answered that they had
risen to rescue him from traitors. The King
agreed to meet them at Blackheath the next day.

The commons of Kent came to Blackheath and
the commons of Essex came to the other side of
the water. The King was on his way, but turned
back when his advisers warned him not to trust
the commons. The commons sent a message
asking for the heads of the Duke of Lancaster and
the other fifteen lords who ran the government.
The commons of Kent came to Southwark, and at
the same time the commons of Essex came to
Lambeth, where they ransacked the buildings of
the Archbishop of Canterbury.

The commons of Kent went on to London
Bridge to pass into the city. The commons of
Southwark rose with them, and forced the guards
to lower the drawbridge. The commons from
Essex entered through Ald Gate. They came at the
Duke of Lancaster's palace, broke open the gates
and burnt all the buildings within the gates.

The next day the commons from Kent and
Essex met the King at Mile End. They asked that
no men should be villeins. The King proclaimed
that they should be free and pardoned them. The
commons from Essex went home, but Wat Tyler
with some men then made their way to the
Tower, where they cut the Archbishop's head off
and paraded it through the streets, on wooden
poles. That night they murdered some 140
people, and there were hideous cries and horrible
tumult all through the night.

The King told all the commons to meet him at
Smithfield the next day.

---

1. Using your own copy of the map (Source 2), plot the movements of the rebels with dates.
2. Write your own account of the main events in no more than 100 words.
3. Do you think the account in Source 1 is fair, or is it biased?

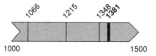
Why did the peasants revolt?

WE HAVE seen that, because of the Black Death, lords did not have enough people to work their land. This meant wages went up, and in some places PEASANTS were able to pay money instead of doing labour services. It seems that the peasants were better off than they had ever been. Why did the peasants of England rebel in 1381? Sources 3–8 will give you some clues.

SOURCE 3 A government decree in the 1350s

Because a large number of people, especially labourers and servants, have lately died of Plague, many refuse to work unless they are paid excessive wages. Therefore every man and woman, free or villein, not already working, shall be bound to serve him who shall require their labour, and receive only the wages traditionally paid. And if any workman in a man's service leaves the service without permission, he shall be imprisoned.

SOURCE 4 A sermon by the peasants' leader, John Ball

The rich have wines, spices, and fine bread, while we have only rye and water. It is by our labour that they can live so well. We are called slaves, and if we do not perform our services we are beaten. Let us go to the King, he is young, and from him we may receive a favourable answer.

SOURCE 5 From a recent history book

The spark that ignited the flames was a check by government officials on who had not paid the Poll Tax of 1380 (12d a head). This tax had to be paid by everyone. This was the third such tax in three years. Those who did not pay were imprisoned. The tax was needed to pay for the war against France, but was seen as an attempt by the rich to make the labouring classes pay more as they had been better off since the Black Death.

SOURCE 6 Written by Sir John Froissart, who lived at the time of the Peasants' Revolt, but did not see what happened. He once worked for the royal family

The lower orders are bound by law to plough the lands of the gentry, to harvest their grain, to thrash and winnow it. In the counties of Kent, Essex, Sussex and Bedford these services are more oppressive than in other parts of the kingdom.

SOURCE 7 From a recent history book

The peasants knew who they blamed for bad government:
■ *John of Gaunt (the King's uncle)*
■ *the Chancellor, Archbishop Sudbury*
■ *the Treasurer, Sir Robert Hales*
and they later executed the last two.

SOURCE 8 John Ball talking to the peasants

1. Events like the Peasants' Revolt usually have many different causes. Use evidence from Sources 3–8 to explain how each of the following helped cause the Peasants' Revolt:
   ■ money
   ■ hatred of particular people
   ■ causes beyond anyone's control
   ■ desire for freedom and equality.
2. Which of these do you think is most important? Give reasons for your answer.

Death at Smithfield – you be Richard's judge

SOURCE 9 A version of events in June 1381

PEASANTS BETRAYED!

London, 15 June 1381

Today King Richard proved what a coward and trickster he is. Hiding behind bodyguards, Richard played his treacherous part in the bloody murder of peasant leader Wat Tyler. Tyler agreed to the meeting because he believed the King was going to help put right the evils which made life a misery for so many ordinary people. But Richard went back on all the promises he had made to help the people.

In good faith Wat rode across to speak with the King, but was immediately surrounded by soldiers. Out of sight of the peasants, the bloodthirsty Mayor of London hacked down Tyler as he spat out some of the drink he had been given. It is not clear whether the drink had been tampered with.

The King rode up to the peasants. He told them to follow him, and he would see they got home safely, but they soon found themselves surrounded by soldiers.

SOURCE 10 A version of events in June 1381

BRAVE KING BEATS REBELS!

London, 15 June 1381

Today saw great celebrations after brave fourteen-year-old King Richard led his men to a brilliant victory over the peasant rebels who had brought death and destruction to the city.

With courage and majesty, the King rode to Smithfield with his trusted followers to meet an army of 20,000 angry rebels. Tyler advanced to the King, dagger in hand, and spat at him. He then stabbed the Mayor of London in the stomach. The Mayor bravely struck back with his sword and Tyler fell to the ground, screaming for revenge. King Richard calmly strode forward to the peasants and ordered them to obey him. Surprised, they followed him to nearby fields, where they surrendered. The King then let them go home safely.

SOURCE 11 This picture was painted about 60 years after the revolt. It shows Richard twice. On the left hand side he is raising his hand as Wat Tyler is struck down. On the right he is speaking with the rebels

On 15 June, one day after the King's meeting with the rebels at Mile End, he agreed to meet them again at Smithfield. He had already agreed to many of their demands.

Sources 9 and 10 are two very different versions of how Richard and his advisers behaved at this meeting.

1. Read Sources 9 and 10, the two newspaper accounts of events at Smithfield.
a) What do they agree about?
b) What do they disagree about?

SOURCE 12 Written by Sir John Froissart

Tyler still kept up the conversation with the Mayor. The Mayor replied, 'I will not live a day unless you pay for your insolence.' Upon saying which, he drew his sword and struck Tyler such a blow on the head as felled him. As soon as the rebel was down, he was surrounded on all sides so his own men might not see him.

SOURCE 13 Written by a monk in York in 1399

The commons were arrayed in battle formation in great numbers. Tyler dismounted, carrying his dagger. He called for some water and rinsed his mouth in a very rude disgusting fashion in front of the King.

Tyler then made to strike the King's valet with his dagger. The Mayor of London tried to arrest him, and because of this Wat stabbed the Mayor with his dagger in the stomach. But the Mayor, as it pleased God, was wearing armour, and drew his cutlass and gave Wat a deep cut on the neck, and then a great cut on the head.

SOURCE 14 Written by a monk in York in 1399

The King and important men in the city met with Sir Robert Knolles [an army commander] about how they could get rid of the rebels.

SOURCE 15 From a recent history book

The King's advisers knew that the death of a rebel leader in France had stopped a revolt in 1358.

SOURCE 16 King Richard speaking to the peasants after the revolt

You wretched men, who seek equality with the lords, are not worthy to live. You will remain in bondage, not as before but harsher.

SOURCE 17 Written by a monk in York in 1399

When the commons saw Wat Tyler was dead they cried out to the King for mercy. The King kindly granted them mercy and ordered two knights to lead the peasants out of London safely so they could go home.

SOURCE 18 From a recent history book

Once the rebels were safely dispersed, the King broke all the promises he had made. All over Essex and Kent, rebel leaders were rounded up and hanged.

SOURCE 19 Written by Sir John Froissart

Later John Ball was found hiding in an old ruin. The King had his [John Ball's] head cut off, as was that of Wat Tyler's, and fixed on London Bridge.

2. Look at Sources 11–19. Which could be used to support Source 9's version of the events, and which to support Source 10's version?
3. Was Richard a coward or was he brave? What do you think about his behaviour?
4. Why do historians today still disagree about what happened at Smithfield?

Scotland victorious, Wales conquered

IN UNIT 1 of this book, you saw how the Romans succeeded in conquering Wales, but not Scotland.

A thousand years later, history repeated itself: Wales was conquered by the English during the Middle Ages, but Scotland remained independent. To understand why the Scots succeeded where the Welsh failed, it is necessary to look at:
- the different ways the two countries developed after 1066
- events during the reigns of Edward I and Edward II.

SOURCE 1 Map of England, Wales and Scotland

Scotland united

Scotland was able to develop peacefully after the Norman conquest of England.

England's kings were not very interested in conquering Scotland. At the time of the Normans it was a poor country, and it was difficult to get to. Some Norman barons were given land in Scotland, but they fitted in well with Scottish landowners, supported the Scottish King and soon became Scottish. Their ability to build strong castles helped to strengthen the Scottish monarchy. The last violent struggle over the Scottish throne was in 1097, and the Scottish kings took control of the whole of Scotland. For a while, during the reign of England's Henry II, the kings of Scotland recognised him as their overlord. But by the time Edward I became King of England in 1272, Scotland was richer and more united than in 1066, and was independent of English control.

Scotland defeats England

In 1286, the Scottish King died without an heir, Edward I of England was asked to decide between the different claims. He expected the king he chose to support him. This did not happen, so in 1296 Edward invaded Scotland, with immediate success. His cavalry seemed to be unbeatable. But although he was able to conquer Scotland, it was difficult to keep it. It was a long way from London, and the mountain area of the Highlands was difficult to keep under control.

The Scots were determined not to be ruled by the English, and led by two great leaders they fought back. The first of these leaders was William Wallace. He was eventually caught by the English, and in 1305 was dragged through the streets of London and then hung, drawn and quartered. His head was stuck on a pike on London Bridge, and his arms and legs were sent to Newcastle, Berwick, Perth and Aberdeen for all to see. However, in the following year the Scots crowned Robert Bruce as their new King and the struggle continued.

An important turning point came in 1307, when Edward I died. His son Edward II was a poor soldier and had no interest in wars with Scotland.

Bruce realised that new tactics were needed and began a brilliant guerrilla campaign. He avoided large battles. Small groups of Scots ambushed English soldiers. Castles and crops were destroyed to stop the English using them. The English were forced to withdraw. Edward II at last realised what was happening and sent an army of 25,000 men, including longbowmen, and 3000 heavily armed cavalry. The Scots had only 7000 men and few cavalry, but they were all volunteers and were determined to fight to keep the English out. The two sides met at the Battle of Bannockburn.

In this battle, Bruce again used new tactics, this time to deal with the English cavalry. Scottish foot-soldiers were armed with long pikes and organised into circles, with wooden stakes hammered into the ground in front of them. The heavily-armed English cavalry could not break through, became trapped on boggy ground and were cut down. Meanwhile, the English bowmen were dealt with by the fast-moving and lightly-armed Scottish cavalry.

There was a dreadful slaughter, with the Bannock Burn full of English corpses, which were used by the retreating English as bridges.

The English had to recognise Robert Bruce as the rightful King of Scotland.

▶ **SOURCE 2** Diagram of the battle

STIRLING CASTLE

River Forth

English archers

Lightly armed troops rush forward to help during the battle

Scottish cavalry

Scots army moves forward to attack

Gillies Hill

Coxet Hill

Lightly armed troops hidden at first

Bannock Burn

"Pots" or traps

▼ **SOURCE 3** Painting of the Battle of Bannockburn, from a fifteenth-century manuscript

1. Which of Sources 2 and 3 gives you a better idea of what happened at Bannockburn?
2. Is there anything that the written account of the battle tells you that Sources 2 and 3 do not?

Wales is gradually conquered

In the years after 1066 Wales was not united. It consisted of three kingdoms, which were constantly fought over by warring princes. There was no one to unite the country.

Wales is much closer to London than Scotland is, and William I was keen to guard the border with Wales. He gave the borderlands (called the 'Marches') to some of his barons. Over the next 200 years these barons gradually conquered parts of Wales for themselves and strengthened their hold on the country by building castles. They were helped by the arguments between the Welsh princes. Source 4 shows how much of Wales the English controlled by 1150.

However, the Welsh did fight back. Llywelyn the Great, the Prince of Gwynedd, managed to unite the Welsh, and in 1267 his grandson Llywelyn was recognised by the English as 'Prince of Wales'. Even so, by the time Edward I became King of England in 1272, all but the north and west of Wales was under the control of the English barons.

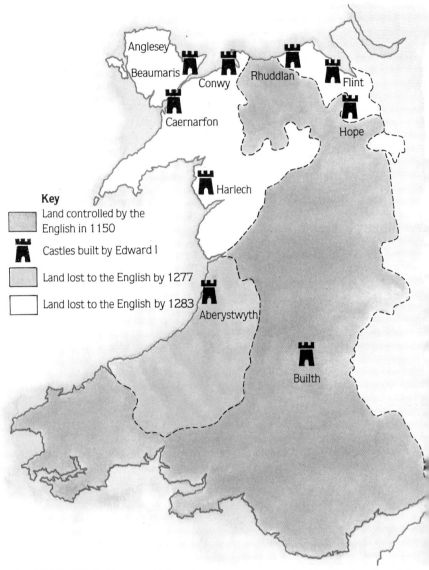

Key
Land controlled by the English in 1150

Castles built by Edward I

Land lost to the English by 1277

Land lost to the English by 1283

▲ **SOURCE 4** Map of Wales showing areas controlled by the English by 1150

SOURCE 5 Edward I's parliament. Llywelyn, the Prince of Wales, is shown sitting on the right of the King, and Alexander, King of Scotland, on the left

The final conquest of Wales by Edward I

The defeat of the Welsh was partly caused by mistakes by their leader Llywelyn. When Edward I became King of England, Llywelyn refused to support him. Edward decided to conquer Wales, and showed his great military skill and his determination in the conquest.

Llywelyn was let down by the other Welsh leaders and was left to fight by himself, while Edward advanced with three armies, building roads, camps and castles as he went. His navy cut Llywelyn off from his food supplies, which came from the island of Anglesey. Soon Llywelyn was isolated in the north-west corner of Wales and had to surrender.

Llywelyn was allowed to keep his title of 'Prince of Wales' and some of his lands. Then, in 1282, he was persuaded by his brother David to rebel again. They took Edward by surprise, but he gathered together a large well equipped army, which again cut off the Welsh army in the north-west corner of Wales.

Llywelyn and David would probably have been safe from attack there, in their winter stronghold, but Llywelyn took the risk of going south to raise more support. This was a mistake. He was killed while attacking Builth Castle. David was captured in the spring of 1283 and Welsh resistance crumbled.

This time Edward took control of a large part of Wales and made his son Prince of Wales. Wales was divided into counties, like England, and English courts were set up. New castles were also built, to help keep Wales under control, but it wasn't until 300 years later, in 1536, that England and Wales were finally united by the Act of Union.

1. By the time of Edward I large parts of Wales had been conquered, but Scotland had not.
a) How important were particular people in deciding the different outcomes? Get into groups to compare the part played by Robert Bruce in Scotland with that of Llywelyn in Wales. Who was the better leader?
b) Was it important that the Welsh had to fight Edward I, whereas the Scots fought Edward II?

▼ **SOURCE 6** Harlech Castle, one of the Welsh castles built by Edward I

England – part of Europe?

FOR much of the Middle Ages, England was part of a large Empire. Medieval kings regarded England as only one part, not always the most important, of this Empire.

William I had united Normandy and England in 1066. Henry II (1154–89), a Frenchman, was already Count of Anjou and Duke of Aquitaine before he became King of England in 1154. For a while he even forced the Scottish and Irish kings to recognise him as their overlord. His Empire covered a vast area (see Source 1).

Anjou, not England, was the centre of the Empire and French, not English, was the language used by the King and his nobles. Regular ferry services ran across the Channel between Portsmouth and Southampton in England and Dieppe and Barfleur in Normandy.

Henry and his son Richard I spent nearly all their reigns outside England. Richard spent much of his time, along with the French King, leading armies from all over Europe in a Crusade to win back Jerusalem (see Unit C pages 194–207).

As the Middle Ages went on, it was more and more difficult to hold the Empire together. The French kings were determined to conquer those parts of the Empire that had borders with France.

Things came to head during King John's reign. It was much easier for the French kings to concentrate on this struggle than it was for King John. He had big problems in England to worry about, and he found it very difficult to get supplies and orders to his armies across the Channel. By the end of John's reign (1217) only Gascony was left under English control.

Gascony had an important trade with England. Gascony sold wine to England, which in return sold cloth and corn to Gascony. English kings were determined to keep control of Gascony. They also hoped to become kings of France, although it was unlikely they would succeed. It was these two aims that kept the Hundred Years' War with France going from 1337 to 1453.

By 1453 England's only possession on the European mainland was Calais.

---

1. Draw a timeline to show the main stages in England's relationship with France.

SOURCE 1 The Empire in 1154, 1224 and 1453

1154

1224

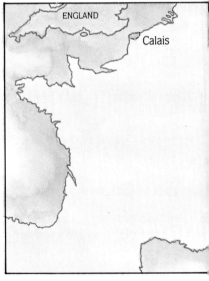

1453

Europe's influence on England

In the twelfth century, William of Malmesbury wrote, 'You might see churches rise in every village and town, built in a style unknown before.' Most Saxon churches had been small and simple (see Source 2). Sources 3 and 4 show how church architecture was changed by European styles.

1. Describe the main similarities and differences between these three churches. For example, you could comment on the size of the building, the size of the windows, and the building materials used.

SOURCE 2 The Saxon church at Bradford-on-Avon, built in the tenth century

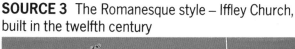

SOURCE 3 The Romanesque style – Iffley Church, built in the twelfth century

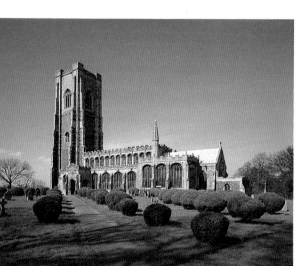

SOURCE 4 The Gothic style – Lavenham Church, built in the fifteenth century

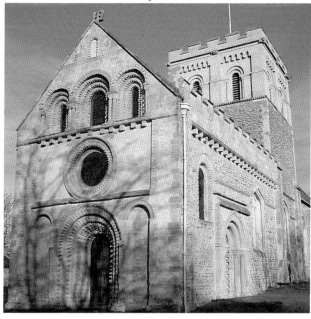

The effects on architecture were obvious for all to see, but involvement in Europe did have other less obvious effects. For example:

■ The heavy taxes needed to pay for the wars with France increased the power of Parliament in England (see page 139).

■ The Poll Tax – also raised to pay for wars in France – helped to trigger the Peasants' Revolt (see page 140).

■ When England finally lost its French lands in 1453, Henry VI became so unpopular in England that he was overthrown. A long struggle for the throne followed between the rival families of Lancaster and York (the 'Wars of the Roses', 1455–1487).

ENGLAND – PART OF EUROPE?

Trade

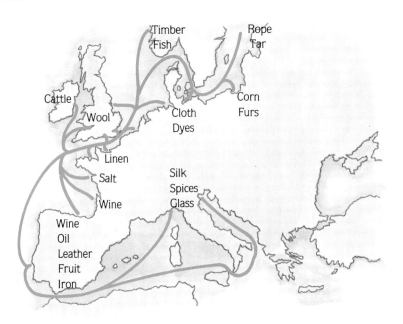

Timber
Fish
Rope
Tar
Cattle
Wool
Corn
Furs
Cloth
Dyes
Linen
Salt
Silk
Spices
Glass
Wine
Wine
Oil
Leather
Fruit
Iron

SOURCE 5 England's main trade routes in the Middle Ages

Contact with Europe affected what the English drank and ate. Early in the Middle Ages ale (beer) was the most popular drink for both rich and poor people, but later the rich drank wine from Gascony, one of England's French lands.

England's involvement in the CRUSADES led to the introduction of many new foods and spices such as pepper, cloves, ginger, almonds, rice, dates, oranges, apricots and melons.

Trade with Europe made a lot of money for the government from customs duties. For example, in 1306, the government had an income of £17,000 from the Gascony wine trade.

The English language

European influences also changed the English language.

Before the Norman Conquest, English was already a mixture of Anglo-Saxon, LATIN, CELTIC and Danish. This mixture can be seen in many English place names.

Place names

The Rivers Avon and Stour have Celtic names (both words simply mean water), while River Cam means crooked.

York and Leeds also have Celtic names, while the Latin 'chester' (meaning fort) was often added to the Celtic to produce names like Manchester and Winchester.

Most place names are either Saxon or Danish. Danish names are common in the north of England, where the Danes settled. Danish endings for place names include '–by' meaning village, '–beck' meaning brook, '–mel' (sand dune), and '–rigg' (ridge).

Saxon endings, found more in the south, include '–burgh' (fort), '–ton' (a village), '–ham' (a farm) and '–mouth' (river mouth), '–ley' (field), and '–stead' (town).

1. Look at a map of your local area. Are Saxon or Danish place names more common?

After 1066 different languages were used for different purposes.
- Most English people – the peasants – carried on using English, although how they spoke it varied between different regions of England.
- Latin was still used in law courts and official documents (such as the Magna Carta) and for services in monasteries and parish churches, as it had been before the Norman Conquest.
- The influence of the Normans meant that French became the language of the lords and the landowners. Some French words gradually became part of the English language.

Words to do with government, such as parliament, justice, court, prison, rent, money, crown, state, council and nation are French; titles, such as prince, duke and baron, are also French.

House is an English word, while manor and palace are French.

Oxen is English, while beef is French.

Many of the older crafts have English names, like baker, miller and shepherd, but newer jobs like mason and tailor are French.

2. How can you tell that the French language was used more by the rich than by the poor?

After the Norman conquest French first names became popular. Names such as Robert, Roger, Maud, Alice and William spread down through society to the peasants. First names from the Bible also became very popular after the Norman Conquest. John was the favourite, but Thomas also became very popular after Becket's murder.

Manorial records from the twelfth century show that only a handful of people had surnames – but 100 years later nearly everyone had one.

They came from parents' christian names (e.g. Nicholson = son of Nicholas), a person's occupation or status (e.g. Thatcher), the place where they lived (e.g. Bridge), or what they were like (e.g. Short).

3. Look at this list of medieval surnames. Decide which come from:
   - parents' names
   - job, occupation or status
   - names of towns or village landmarks
   - appearance or personality.

```
MILLER        CARTER
LANE          GATES
FRAUNCEYS     YORK
FREEMAN       REEVE
STAFFORD      ATWELL
ROBERTSON     SMITHSON
SMITH         GREY
```

4. Do the same with some of the surnames of people in your class.

Early in the Middle Ages, English was spoken very differently in different areas and hardly written down at all. But slowly through the centuries an agreed spelling and grammar for English developed as it was used more and more in writing (see Sources 6–8).

Chaucer's *Canterbury Tales* was one of the first great poems to be written in English, in the late 1300s. By the fifteenth century English was replacing both French and Latin as the language of books.

As the Middle Ages went on, more and more people learned to read and write. By the fifteenth century about 30% of the population could do so.

Books became easier to get hold of after the invention of printing in Europe. This spread to England in the 1470s. Caxton, the first English printer, specialised in printing books in English.

5. Sources 6, 7 and 8 show the way written English changed during the Middle Ages. See if you can write any of the three extracts into modern English. Then put the extracts into the correct chronological order.

SOURCE 6

66*She will in no wise receive nor keep your ring with her, and yet I told her that she should not be anything bound thereby; but that I knew by your heart of old that I wist well ye would be glad to forbear the levest thing that ye had in the world, which might be daily in her presence, that should cause her once a day to remember you.*99

SOURCE 7

66*He wæs swyþe spedig man on þæm æhtum þe heora speda on beoþ, þæt is, on wildrum.*
He hæfde þagyt, tamra deora unbebohtra syx hund.
*He wæs mid þæm fyrstum mannum on þæm lande: næfde he þeah ma þonne twentig hryþera, and twentig sceapa, and twentig swyna.*99

SOURCE 8

66*Withoute bake mete was nevere his hous of fissh and flessh, and that so plentevous, it snewed in his hous of mete and drynke, of all deyntees that men koude thynke. After the sondry sesons of the yeer, so chaunged he his mete and his soper. Ful many a breem and many a luce in stuwe.*99

1. Did England benefit from its contacts with Europe? Draw a line down the centre of your page. On one side write all the advantages of being closely involved in Europe, and on the other side all the disadvantages.

Change and continuity

Which century would you choose to live in?

HERE are some things historians have found out about the different centuries in the Middle Ages.

The fourteenth century (1300–1400)
- Bad famine early in the century
- Heavy taxes for many people
- Peasants' Revolt
- Plague kills many people, but those who survive are better off
- Villages deserted
- Peasants do fewer services for lord of the manor
- Wages go up, and landowners find it difficult to keep workers
- Less trade with Europe because of war.

The twelfth century (1100–1200)
- Landlords in trouble – they have to reduce the labour services of villeins
- Many new churches built
- At end of century, population growing, new land being farmed
- Some towns prosper. Many markets and fairs
- Overseas trade growing
- Prices go up sharply
- Henry II improves system of justice.

The fifteenth century (1400–1500)
- Much waste land
- Towns do not grow. No new towns
- Population carries on falling
- Landowners receive low rents
- Prices for farm products very low
- Villages deserted
- A quarter of harvests fail
- Much destruction because of civil wars
- Expensive wars with France, heavy taxes, little trade with Europe
- Ransoms and loot captured from France in wars
- Some signs of things getting better towards end of century, but some towns still in bad state
- Some landowners get rich from sheep farming
- People can afford to eat more meat.

The thirteenth century (1200–1300)
- Expansion and prosperity in countryside and towns. Many new towns
- Much trade
- Landowners making money from rents
- Prices stay about the same
- Many beautiful buildings built
- Long periods of civil war
- England not well governed in Henry III's reign.

Activity

Divide into three groups:
Group 1 – peasants
Group 2 – lords and ladies of the manor
Group 3 – town shopkeepers and merchants.
Using the information on this page, and what you have learned from the rest of this unit on the Middle Ages, decide which century your group would most like to live in and which century you would least like to live in.

1. Now that you have studied the Middle Ages, which of the descriptions you wrote on page 65 seems most accurate? (You may decide it is a combination of both descriptions.) Give at least five reasons for your answer.

ISLAMIC
CIVILISATIONS

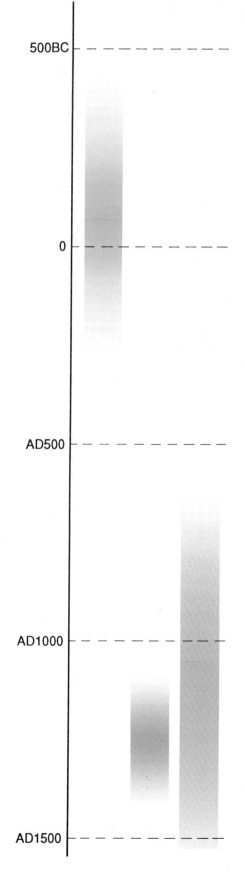

500BC

0

AD500

AD1000

AD1500

Connecting empires

SOURCE 1

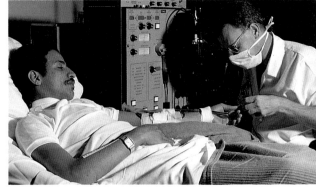

SOURCE 2

Sources 1–4 are four recent pictures of Saudi Arabia.

1. With a partner, write down everything Sources 1–4 tell you about Saudi Arabia. Make four separate lists – one for each picture.
2. Are there any things in your lists that you can't be sure about? Underline anything in your lists that you *are* sure about. Don't underline things that are guesses.
3. Now write a paragraph summing up your impressions of Saudi Arabia.

SOURCE 3

SOURCE 4

ONE thousand four hundred years ago, Arabia was where the religion of ISLAM began. It became the heart of a new EMPIRE.

Source 5 compares the Islamic Empire with the Roman Empire, which you studied in Unit A.

▶ **SOURCE 5** The Roman Empire and the Islamic Empire

4. Which Empire covered the greatest area?
5. Which Empire controlled Britain at one time?
6. Some countries were part of the Roman Empire and then, centuries later, were part of the Islamic Empire. Which countries are these?

Atlantic Ocean EUROPE

● Rome

Mediterranean Sea

AFRICA

Roman Empire
Approximate area in AD100:
9.3 million km^2
Population: 50–60 million
Main language: Latin

Borrowed words . . .

As you can see in Source 5, the Islamic Empire included some parts of Europe, but it did not stretch as far north as France or Britain. Even so, Islam's influence can be clearly seen in both countries. For example, the English and French languages both have words which come from Arabic, the language of the Islamic Empire. Here are a few:

English	French	English	French
alcohol	alcool	camel	chameau
cheque	chèque	admiral	amiral
sofa	sofa	ginger	gingembre
assassin	assassin	orange	orange
blouse	blouse	sugar	sucre
guitar	guitare	checkmate	échec et mat
algebra	algèbre	racket	raquette
coffee	café	giraffe	girafe
safari	safari	cotton	coton
zero	zéro	apricot	abricot
satin	satin		

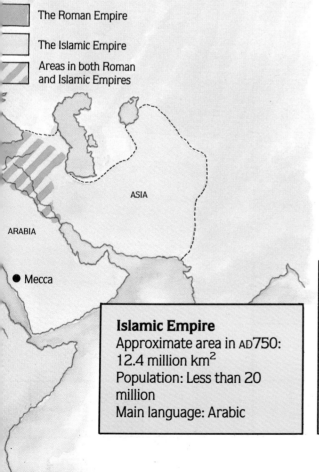

Key

- The Roman Empire
- The Islamic Empire
- Areas in both Roman and Islamic Empires

ASIA

ARABIA

● Mecca

Islamic Empire
Approximate area in AD750:
12.4 million km^2
Population: Less than 20 million
Main language: Arabic

---

1. Why do you think we have borrowed these words to use in English and French?
2. By looking at the kinds of words that have been borrowed from Arabic, we can begin to see the type of connections that existed between Islamic and Western European countries.

    Working in groups, sort the words into the following categories:
    - war and fighting
    - travel and trade
    - clothes and textiles
    - food and drink
    - animals and birds
    - religion
    - furniture
    - games, sports and pastimes
    - mathematics.

You'll probably have found that some categories have no words in them. When you've finished studying this unit you'll be able to say why.

. . . Borrowed numbers

Source 6 shows numbers used by the Romans and numbers used by the Arabs, compared to the numbers we use today in Britain.

TODAY	ROMAN	ARABIC
1	I	1
2	II	2
3	III	3
4	IV	4
5	V	9
6	VI	6
7	VII	7
8	VIII	8
9	IX	9
10	X	0
50	L	90
100	C	100
1000	M	1000
1998	MCMXCVIII	1998

SOURCE 6

1. Which numbers, the Roman or the Arabic ones, are most like the numbers we use today?
2. You'll see that the Arabic number 1998 is very similar to the one we use today. Now try to write out the number 1998 in Roman numbers.
3. a) Try to do this sum: CLVIII plus XLI.
    b) What problems did you face? Is it easier to use Arabic numbers or Roman numbers?

Arabia before Islam

ONE THING in Arabia is much the same today as it was 1400 years ago: the desert. Look at Sources 1 and 2.

SOURCE 1 A modern photograph of the Arabian desert near Mecca

---

SOURCE 2 Two poets of sixth-century Arabia describe the hard conditions in the desert

"a) *The thorns prick the camel's hooves.*
The summer winds swell and swirl about me
in scorching blasts

b) *And many's the morning I've shielded myself*
from the wind and cold,
when its reins lay in the fingers of the bitter
north"

In Arabia today there are no permanent rivers or lakes. Desert areas can go without rain for years and then suddenly have torrential rainstorms.

SOURCE 3 From the holy book of Islam, the Quran (Sura 16.9)

"*It is God who sends down water from the sky, which provides you with your drink and brings forth the pasture on which your cattle feed. With it He brings up corn, olives, dates and grapes and fruits of every kind.*"

---

1. In what ways do Sources 1 and 2 agree about the Arabian desert?
2. What can you learn about the desert from Sources 2 and 3 that you can't from Source 1?
3. What would be the difficulties of living in the desert?

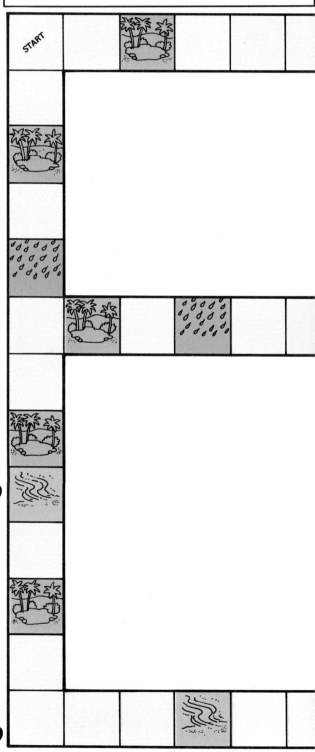

Survival

Could you survive in the desert? Play the Survival Game and find out.

Get into groups of four players. You'll need dice and a record sheet, which your teacher will give you.

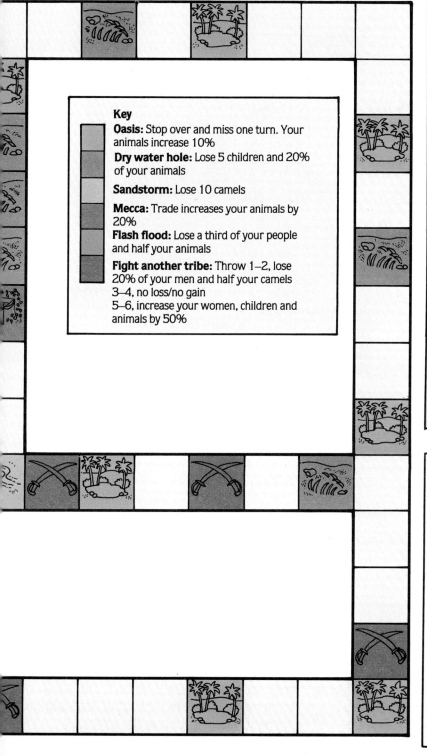

Key

	Oasis: Stop over and miss one turn. Your animals increase 10%
	Dry water hole: Lose 5 children and 20% of your animals
	Sandstorm: Lose 10 camels
	Mecca: Trade increases your animals by 20%
	Flash flood: Lose a third of your people and half your animals
	Fight another tribe: Throw 1–2, lose 20% of your men and half your camels 3–4, no loss/no gain 5–6, increase your women, children and animals by 50%

Rules

1. Your TRIBE starts with 100 people (30 men, 30 women, 40 children), 50 camels and 100 stock (sheep and goats).
2. Men can only fight if they have a camel to ride. If you have fewer camels than men the extra men must leave the tribe.
3. You must have at least 1 stock animal for every 2 adults and every 4 children. If your number of stock animals drops below this, then you lose the number of adults shown on the dice every time you make a throw (1 child = half an adult). This goes on either until you have lost enough people, or until you get some more stock, and the numbers balance again.
4. Move around the board by throwing the dice. Do what the board tells you.
5. See if you can survive twenty throws

1. Who survived best? Why was it difficult to survive?
2. Would you expect Arabia to have a small or large population for its size? Give reasons.
3. Where would you expect to find the most people: in an oasis, in a trading city, or in the desert?
4. What would decide how rich someone living in a country like this would be?
5. Why do you think Arabs felt they were living at the mercy of nature?

ARABIA BEFORE ISLAM

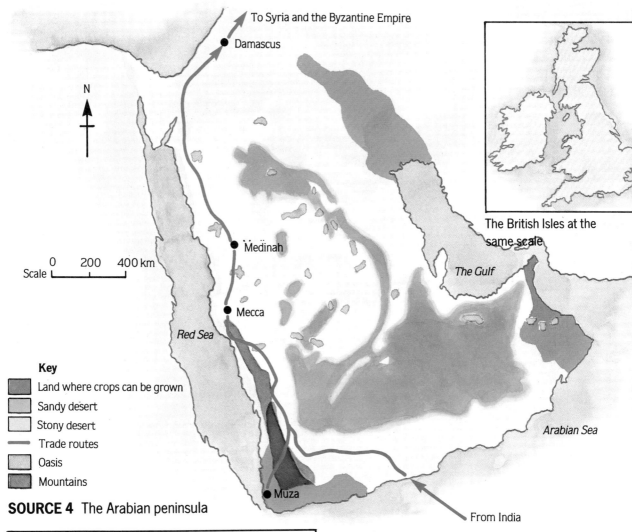

SOURCE 4 The Arabian peninsula

Labels on map:
- To Syria and the Byzantine Empire
- Damascus
- N
- Medinah
- The Gulf
- The British Isles at the same scale
- Mecca
- Red Sea
- Muza
- Arabian Sea
- From India
- Scale 0 200 400 km

Key
- Land where crops can be grown
- Sandy desert
- Stony desert
- Trade routes
- Oasis
- Mountains

Use the key to the map in Source 4 to answer these questions:

1. Is Arabia a good place for growing food?
2. Where does the main trade route through Arabia go to?
3. Would travel in Arabia be easy or difficult? Explain your answer.
4. How many kilometres is it from Damascus in Syria to the Arabian seaport of Muza? A camel train travels at an average of twenty kilometres a day depending on travel conditions: how quickly could it make that journey?

In the Survival Game you found out about the lives of the desert people. Three aspects of their lives are particularly important in explaining why these people were soon going to build a great Empire.

The cities

By the early 600s, the main cities of Arabia were Medinah and Mecca. These were important trading centres where the desert tribes came to trade. They exchanged wool, meat, milk or hides for the things they couldn't grow or make themselves, such as spices or weapons. In Mecca, this trade took place at a religious SHRINE called the Kaabah.

Religion

Arabia was already influenced by a number of religions. Trade had brought many Jews and Christians to Arabia. Some ARABS had converted to these religions. But most followed other gods. They could all be worshipped at the Kaabah, which at that time contained hundreds of IDOLS. The people of Mecca made a lot of money out of Arab pilgrims coming to worship idols at the Kaabah.

The tribes

Everyone belonged to a clan – a kind of extended family. A number of clans together made up a tribe. Loyalty to your tribe was fierce and disputes between tribes were often settled by fighting.

Some tribes, such as the Quraysh, which you will come across later, were city-dwellers and MERCHANTS. They were beginning to be more powerful than the other tribes, who were desert NOMADS. The desert tribes were skilful travellers, who followed the stars to cross featureless deserts, moving from oasis to oasis.

Could someone make use of the skills and loyalty of the desert tribes and turn them into a powerful army?

---

1. Imagine you are a traveller in ancient Arabia. Write three sentences of good advice for someone thinking of making the same journey.
2. Here is a list of statements which sum up the situation described on pages 156–159. As a class, try to sort the statements into two groups:
   a) things which would make Arabia backward and less united
   b) things which suggest that changes might take place in Arabia: people becoming richer or the country becoming more united.

   ■ The nomads' main loyalty was to their tribe. These tribes were constantly fighting one another.
   ■ The nomads worshipped different gods.
   ■ These gods could all be worshipped at the Kaabah.
   ■ There was no system of law and order to settle disputes between the tribes, or to punish tribes that attacked traders.
   ■ Only a small population could live in the harsh desert area.
   ■ The nomads' lifestyle meant they weren't interested in building up great wealth.
   ■ The Meccans were gradually becoming rich from the profits of trade and PILGRIMAGE. Meccans had enough wealth to pay tribes not to attack traders.

How do we know?

What are the problems of finding out what Arabia was like 1400 years ago, just before the Islamic religion began?

■ Because the desert tribes were nomadic, they didn't build permanent homes, or have many belongings.
■ Most Arabs could not read or write 1400 years ago. There was no need to. However, each tribe recorded its history and achievements in long poems. Because poetry is easy to memorise these poems could be passed on word for word from generation to generation. Collections of the best poems were later gathered together and written down. Source 2 on the previous page shows poems of this period.
■ The harshness of the environment meant very few outsiders ever visited Arabia. The few who did have left very incomplete impressions of what Arabia was like (see Source 5).

SOURCE 5 Written by a Greek sailor in the first century

66 *The country inland is peopled by rascally men who live in villages and nomadic camps, by whom those sailing off course are plundered and those surviving shipwrecks are taken for slaves.*

Muza (a seaport) is crowded with Arab shipowners and seafaring men, and busy with the affairs of commerce. 99

---

1. What problems are there for ARCHAEOLOGISTS trying to find out about life in Arabia before Islam?
2. What problems face historians using written evidence to find out about Arabia before Islam?
3. Despite the problems, we can learn some things abouts Arabia before Islam. Use the information on pages 156–159 to write a paragraph about it.

Muhammad* and Islam: the role of the individual

On pages 156–159, you found out something about the world that Muhammad*, the great PROPHET of ISLAM, was born into. Muhammad's* life was going to lead to great changes in Arabia as the faith of Islam took root – and eventually to changes throughout the world. But as the timeline at the bottom of the page shows, it began in hardship and suffering.

> * You may have noticed one unexplained feature in this book – the * after Muhammad's* name. When Muslims speak or write the name of Muhammad* they add 'Peace be upon him'. In this unit we have shown this by a *.

SOURCE 1 Route from Mecca to Medinah

The Muslim calendar

So far in this book we have been giving dates in the familiar way you will know from your study of medieval England. MUSLIMS, however, do not use this time system. Their calendar begins at what they consider to be the major turning point in the history of the world (just as the Christian calendar begins in the year that people think Jesus Christ was born).

> **1.** Look at the events shown on the timeline. From that evidence decide when you might expect the Muslim calendar to begin. Which of the events shown might Muhammad's* followers consider the most important turning point?

The life of Muhammad*: turning points

610 Muhammad's* first vision
Muhammad* kept his messages to himself to start with.

He feared he was possessed by devils. Once he said that these messages 'strike straight to my heart like a ringing bell'. Another time he described being seized by violent shuddering as he received the messages.

Many of his messages appealed directly to Jews and Christians. He said Islam was the true religion that Abraham and Jesus had been preparing the world for.

613 Muhammad* begins to preach in public
Muhammad* was unhappy about what he saw as the injustice of the Meccans, and by the plight of the poor and the slaves in the city. Many of the early messages of the QURAN are seen as direct criticisms of the people of Mecca.

Other things made the Meccans angry as well. 'There are some among the Meccans who speak ill of you concerning the distribution of alms' (Quran, 9.57).

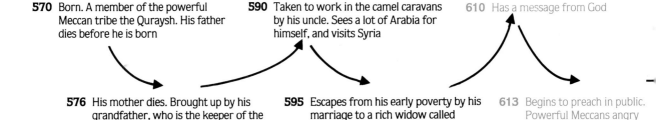

570 Born. A member of the powerful Meccan tribe the Quraysh. His father dies before he is born

590 Taken to work in the camel caravans by his uncle. Sees a lot of Arabia for himself, and visits Syria

610 Has a message from God

576 His mother dies. Brought up by his grandfather, who is the keeper of the KAABAH in Mecca

595 Escapes from his early poverty by his marriage to a rich widow called Khadijah

613 Begins to preach in public. Powerful Meccans angry

Your teacher will tell you when the Muslim calendar does in fact begin.

Historians think that the new calendar was in use only ten years after Muhammad's* death.

From now on in this book, dates will be given according to both the Christian and Muslim calendars.

To convert dates from one calendar to the other, you need to know that the Muslim year is eleven days shorter than the Christian year. A Muslim century equals 97 years in the Christian calendar. There are some easy and useful correspondences to remember: AD1300 is the same as 700AH; 1400AH began in November 1979. (AH stands for after the HIJRA.)

SOURCE 2 Modern drawing of the prophet's home in Medinah

2. Calculate the year of your birth in AH.

622 The first Muslim community
Opposition increased so much that Muhammad* and his followers fled 200 miles across the desert to Medinah. Muhammad's* house in Medinah became the centre of the first community of MUSLIMS (see Source 2).

He specially concentrated on convincing the many Jews in Medinah that Islam was the true religion.

630 Muslims take control of Mecca
Muhammad* came to Mecca with a few lightly armed forces. In his earlier battles Muhammad's* forces had beaten much larger armies. He reached a peaceful agreement with the Meccans, who allowed him to clear the IDOLS out of the Kaabah. He dedicated the Kaabah to the faith of Islam. Many Arab tribes, as well as people in Mecca, accepted his leadership.

619 His wife (and financial supporter) Khadijah dies. So does Abu Talib, his uncle and head of his family. Opposition to Muhammad* increases with the head of his family out of the way

624 Muslims defeat a larger army of Meccans at Badr, then embark on a series of wars and raids on other tribes who are opposing Islam

630 Muslims take control of Mecca

622 The HIJRA (migration). Muhammad* moves to Medinah as leader of the first community of MUSLIMS

627 Muslims survive Meccan siege of Medinah. A truce is agreed between Muslims and Meccans

632 Muhammad* dies. By this time nearly all of Arabia has been converted to the Islamic religion

MUHAMMAD* AND ISLAM: THE ROLE OF THE INDIVIDUAL

The messages of God to Muhammad* were collected together in the QURAN.

Here are some statements from the Quran that tell us things about Muhammad* – what he was like as a person and how people reacted to him.

SOURCE 3 From the Quran

66 *Did God not find you [Muhammad*] an orphan and give you shelter? (Sura 93.6)*

It was thanks to God's mercy that you [Muhammad] dealt so leniently with [some deserters]. Had you been cruel they would surely have deserted you. (Sura 3.159)*

[Muhammad] frowned and turned his back when the blind man came towards him. But to the wealthy man he was all attention. This is a criticism. (Sura 80.1)*

When they are blessed with good fortune they say 'This is from God'. But when evil befalls them they say 'It was Muhammad's fault'. (Sura 4.79)*

Remember how the unbelievers plotted against you [Muhammad]. They sought to take you captive or have you slain or banished. (Sura 8.30)*

When [Muhammad] rose to pray, they pressed around him in multitudes. (Sura 72.19)*

The spoils taken from the town-dwellers and given by God to his apostle [Muhammad] shall belong to God, to the apostle and his family, to orphans, to the poor and to the travellers in need; they shall not become the property of the rich among you. (Sura 59.7)*

On entering the house of the Prophet [Muhammad] . . . Do not engage in familiar talk, as this would annoy the Prophet and he would be ashamed to bid you go. (Sura 33.53)*

It shall be unlawful for you [Muhammad] to take more wives – or to change your present wives for other women. (Sura 33.52)*

Your own city (Mecca) has cast you [Muhammad] out. (Sura 47.13)*

Remember when you [Muhammad] left your people early in the morning to lead the Muslims to their battle positions? (Sura 3.122)* 99

---

1. Write two paragraphs about Muhammad*, using the evidence in Source 3.

Islam

What was the new religion of Islam about? Its followers will tell you it is not a complicated religion. The word Islam means 'submitting', and at the heart of Muhammad's* message were five basic rules for every Muslim – called the five Pillars of Islam.

1. Using the evidence in Source 4 – taken from the Quran – can you work out what these five rules are?

SOURCE 4 From the Quran

66 a) *In the month of Ramadan the Quran was revealed,*
a book of guidance distinguishing right from wrong.
Therefore whoever of you is present in that month, let him fast [go without food and drink]. (Sura 2.184)

b) *The righteous man is he who:*
believes in God
and the last day [of judgement],
in the Angels
and the Book
and the Prophets . . .

c) *Who, though he loves it dearly, gives away his wealth*
to relatives,
to orphans,
to the helpless,
to the traveller in need,
and to the beggars,
and for the ransom of slaves . . .

d) *Who attends to his prayers*
and renders the alms [charity] levy. (Sura 2.177)

e) *Make the pilgrimage and visit the sacred house [at Mecca] for his sake.*
If you cannot, send such offerings as you can afford. (Sura 2.196)

In addition, Islam teaches that it is an important duty of Muslims:

■ to be willing to fight for other Muslims if they are attacked.

■ to obey the many other rules laid down in the Quran and the HADITH (things the prophet is supposed to have said) concerning practical day-to-day matters such as family life, business, not drinking alcohol, and not eating pork.

► **SOURCE 5** Front page of an Islamic atlas showing the direction to Mecca from various Islamic cities. (The square in the centre is the Kaabah.) Until AD624/2AH the Muslims prayed towards Jerusalem. Ever since then they have prayed towards Mecca

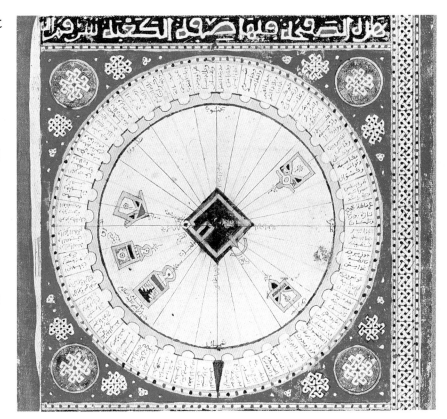

▼ **SOURCE 6** The flag of modern-day Saudi Arabia, the only country to have a religious declaration on its flag. The writing says 'I witness that there is no god but God, and Muhammad is the prophet of God'

2. Source 6 includes what is said to be the most important part of Islamic belief. Which of the five pillars of Islam (Source 4) is this?

Activity

You are a young member of a rich Meccan MERCHANT family who have just become Muslims. Use all the evidence on pages 160–163 to describe a few of the changes that this new religion has brought about in the way you live your life.

Heaven and Hell

Like Christianity, Islam presents its followers with vivid descriptions of Heaven and Hell.

> **SOURCE 7** Description of Heaven and Hell from the Quran (Sura 88.2)
>
> *On the Day of Judgement many faces will be downcast,*
> *toiling, weary,*
> *scorched by burning fire,*
> *drinking from a boiling spring.*
> *No food for them save bitter thorn-fruit, which does not feed or satisfy.*
> *On that day other faces will be calm, glad for their past effort,*
> *in a high garden,*
> *where they hear no foolish chatter, where there is a gushing spring,*
> *where there are couches to lie on,*
> *and glasses (to drink from) set to hand,*
> *and cushions piled up,*
> *and silk carpets spread out.*

1. Use Sources 7, 8 and 9 to describe what Heaven and Hell are like.
2. In what ways do these visions of Heaven and Hell reflect the best and the worst things about life in a desert environment?
3. Compare Sources 7, 8 and 9 with a Christian vision of Heaven and Hell on page 112 (the Chaldon Mural). What similarities and differences are there?
4. Look at Sources 4–9 again. How do you get to Heaven if you are a Muslim?
5. How does this differ from the way people in medieval England thought Christians got to Heaven?

SOURCES 8 and 9 A vision of Heaven and a vision of Hell from the *Miraj Namah*, a book illustrated by an Iranian Muslim in the fifteenth century AD/ninth century AH

Why did people follow Muhammad*?

Above are some of the reasons people had for deciding to follow
Muhammad* and Islam.

Some of these reasons show the importance of Muhammad* as an
individual — others show different factors.

Look at the reasons people had
for following Muhammad*.

1. Which reasons show the
importance of what
Muhammad* had to *say*?
2. Which reasons show the
importance of what
Muhammad* *did*?
3. Why do you think many
people believed that
Muhammad's* message
came from God?

Activity

a) Imagine you are a
Meccan slave in AD630/
8AH. Explain why you
have decided to become
a Muslim.
b) Imagine you are a Meccan
merchant in 630/8. Explain
whether or not you have
decided to become a
Muslim. Give your reasons.

How did Islam survive the death of Muhammad*?

IT IS 633 or 11AH – one year after Muhammad's* death. On the Arabian border, a thousand miles from Mecca, some Persian chiefs are gathered to discuss an important letter (see Source 1).

> **SOURCE 1** Letter to the Persian border chiefs
>
> " In the name of God, the merciful and the compassionate. From Khalid ibn al-Walid to the border chiefs of Persia.
> Become Muslim and be saved. If not, accept protection from us and pay the poll tax. Otherwise, I shall come against you with men who love death as you love to drink wine. "

Scenes like this were happening again and again all over the Middle East. One region after another came under the control of Islamic forces. How did the Muslims manage this, when their leader Muhammad* was dead?

Muhammad's* death was a crucial moment for Islam. During his lifetime, Muhammad* had seen all Arabia accept his leadership. His death came as a terrible shock. People asked whether this signalled the end of the Islamic faith. Or would it simply be the beginning of a new phase?

Muhammad's* followers had two particular problems to solve:

■ Who should succeed Muhammad*? He had not named the next leader. Should anyone succeed him at all? Muhammad* was, after all, the last PROPHET of God. A new leader might be thought to be claiming a similar position.

■ Some tribes said that they had sworn to obey Muhammad*. Now that he was dead they said they were released from their oath and were free to give up Islam. A military campaign against the tribes might bring them back under control.

Discuss with a partner how you would advise the Muslims to solve these problems.

1. Should they choose a new leader?
2. If so, who should they choose: Muhammad's* closest adviser and friend, the best soldier, the oldest Muslim, or someone else?
3. How could they convince the desert tribes that Islam was alive and well even though Muhammad* had died?

The Muslims finally elected Abu Bakr, one of Muhammad's* closest followers.

> **SOURCE 2** The early Muslims swear loyalty to their new leader, Abu Bakr
>
> " You are the worthiest of those who travelled with the Prophet to Medinah, and the second of the two who were in the cave, and heard the messages from God. You are the deputy (khalifa) of the Prophet of God in prayer, and prayer is the noblest part of the religion of the Muslims. Stretch out your hand so that we may swear allegiance to you.

> **SOURCE 3** Abu Bakr probably made this speech when he became leader
>
> " O people, I have been appointed to rule over you, though I am not the best among you. If I do well help me, and if I do ill correct me. Truth is loyalty and falsehood is treachery. . . If any people holds back from fighting the holy war for God, God strikes them down. If weakness spreads among a people, God brings disaster upon all of them. Obey me as long as I obey his Prophet. And If I disobey God and his Prophet you do not owe me obedience. Come to prayer, and may God have mercy on you.

---

4. Read Sources 2 and 3. Why do you think people at that time thought Abu Bakr would make a good leader?

Abu Bakr was actually called *khalifa* or Caliph – which means deputy or successor, not leader. From this time on, the leaders of Islam (see Source 4) were thought of as Muhammad's* deputies.

Abu Bakr led a very successful military campaign against some of the desert tribes who had abandoned Islam when Muhammad* died. The tribes quickly returned to Islam and recognised Abu Bakr as leader. Then the campaign spread into neighbouring countries. Islam was about to begin an expansion which would be more rapid and far reaching than even the growth of the Roman Empire.

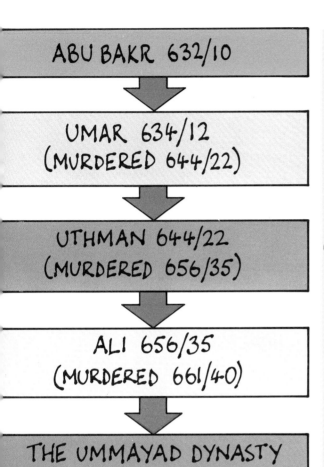

ABU BAKR 632/10

UMAR 634/12 (MURDERED 644/22)

UTHMAN 644/22 (MURDERED 656/35)

ALI 656/35 (MURDERED 661/40)

THE UMMAYAD DYNASTY ESTABLISHED

SOURCE 4 The first caliphs of Islam

No pictures

Unlike the Romans, who made statues of their emperors, or people in medieval Britain, who painted pictures of their kings, the Muslims made very few pictures of Islamic places, people or events. Source 5 explains one reason why.

SOURCE 5 A saying (*hadith*) of Muhammad*

Those who will be most clearly punished on the Day of Judgement are one who murders a prophet, one who has been put to death by a prophet, one who leads men astray, and the maker of images and pictures.

1. What might be wrong with making images and pictures?

Instead of pictures, Islamic writers wrote detailed accounts of the birth of Islam and descriptions of early Islamic leaders.

One of the earliest Islamic histories which have come down to us is Al Tabari's. It was written almost 300 years after the birth of Muhammad*.

Source 6 gives descriptions of Umar, one of Muhammad's* first followers and the second Caliph (see Source 4).

SOURCE 6 Written by Al Tabari

I heard from Hannad, who heard from Waki, on the authority of Sufayan, on the authority of Asim, on the authority of Zirr, who said: 'Umar went forth on the festival day. He was ruddy, tall and ambidextrous [both right and left handed] and walked as if he were riding.'

Al Tabari gives other descriptions, explaining how each one came to him from different people.

SOURCE 7

'I saw Umar arrive at the festival, walking barefoot, ambidextrous, tucking up his sewn garment, standing taller than the people, as though he were mounted.'

'Umar used to dye his beard yellow and dress his head with henna.'

I heard the son of Umar describe Umar, saying, 'A pale man, with a touch of redness, tall, grey and bald.'

2. From the four descriptions what can you say is probably true about Umar?
3. Why does Al Tabari list the people he got his information from? Does this make you trust his account more than you would if he didn't tell you how he found out?
4. Why do you think he gives several different versions? Does this make you trust him more than if he only gave one version?
5. What Umar looked like might not seem to be such an important question to us – so why do you think Al Tabari was so concerned to get it right?

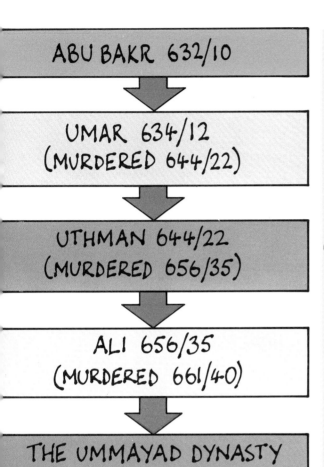

What made the Arabs so successful?

SOURCE 1 shows you what happened to the ARAB Muslims in the century following Muhammad's* death.

723/113
Western Europe
Advance into France, but defeated by Charles Martel near Tours

637/15 and 718/99
Central Europe
Fail to capture Constantinople despite a long siege. No progress into Central Europe

636/14
Yarmuk
Opponents: Byzantines
Muslims attack in the middle of a sandstorm, and destroy a mixed force, including Armenians and Syrians. Byzantine emperor escapes back to Constantinople and abandons Syria to the Arabs

642/20
Egypt
Capture Alexandria and its shipyards. This allows rapid expansion along north African coast and capture of Cyprus (648/33)

CENTRAL EUROPE

WESTERN EUROPE

Key
- The Islamic Empire in 632
- Area conquered by 634
- Area conquered by 644
- Area conquered by 656
- Area conquered by 750
- The Byzantine Empire
- The main lines of attack
- Battle

Scale 0   1000 km

Arab expansion from 636/14 to 751/133

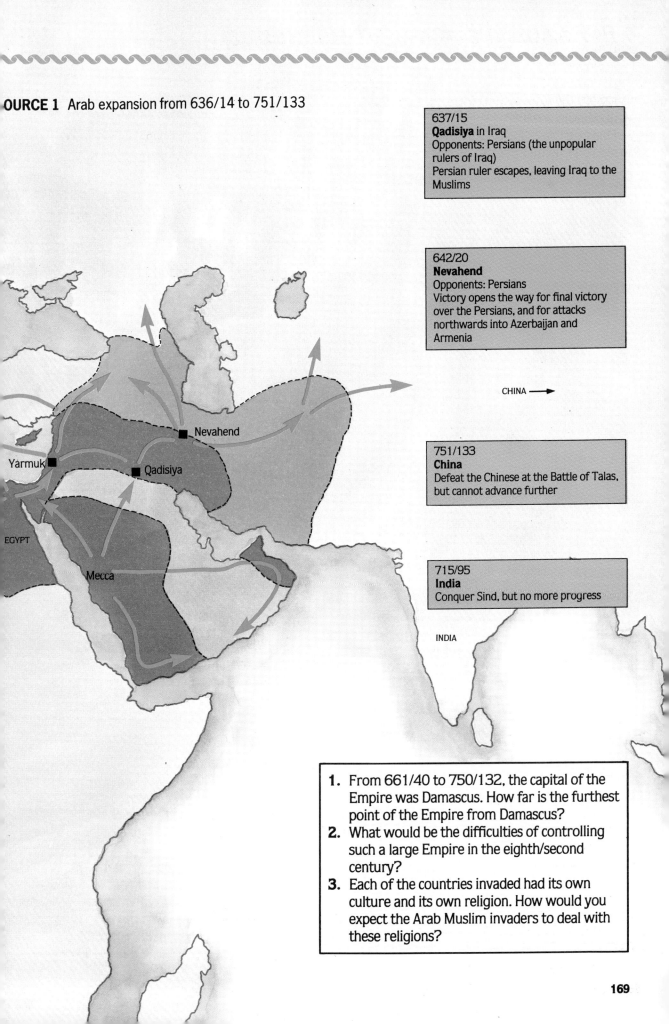

637/15
Qadisiya in Iraq
Opponents: Persians (the unpopular
rulers of Iraq)
Persian ruler escapes, leaving Iraq to the
Muslims

642/20
Nevahend
Opponents: Persians
Victory opens the way for final victory
over the Persians, and for attacks
northwards into Azerbaijan and
Armenia

CHINA →

751/133
China
Defeat the Chinese at the Battle of Talas,
but cannot advance further

715/95
India
Conquer Sind, but no more progress

INDIA

Nevahend

Yarmuk

Qadisiya

EGYPT

Mecca

1. From 661/40 to 750/132, the capital of the
   Empire was Damascus. How far is the furthest
   point of the Empire from Damascus?
2. What would be the difficulties of controlling
   such a large Empire in the eighth/second
   century?
3. Each of the countries invaded had its own
   culture and its own religion. How would you
   expect the Arab Muslim invaders to deal with
   these religions?

WHAT MADE THE ARABS SO SUCCESSFUL?

What are the explanations for the success of the Arab Muslim armies?

One possible reason is that they were brave, well armed and skilful fighters.

SOURCE 2 Arab soldiers in the seventh/first century, painted about 800 years later

SOURCE 3 A fragment from a tenth/fourth-century manuscript, showing Arab soldiers at that time

SOURCE 4 A modern historian describes Arab tactics

The Arabs made good use of their experience of desert warfare. They were mounted on camels – their opponents on horses. After attack they could therefore retreat back into the safety of the desert.

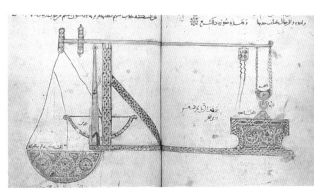

SOURCE 5 A catapult, drawn in the fourteenth/eighth century, but used by the Arabs from the eleventh/fifth century

SOURCE 6 Hand grenades – used by Muslim troops from the twelfth/sixth century

SOURCE 7 A ninth/third-century Persian writer describes Arab tactics and methods

The Persians said to the Arabs, 'You had only cane lances, tipped with ox-horn, and you used to ride your horses bareback in battle.

'The Arab lance used a solid shaft, but we know that a hollow one is lighter to carry and gives a more powerful thrust.

'You used to make war in separate, unorganised bands. You used not to fight at night, and you knew nothing of the ambush. Nor did you know anything of the instruments of war – the battering ram, the catapult, or throwing fire.'

1. What does Source 2 tell you about the way the early Arab soldiers were dressed and armed and the methods they used to fight?
2. Look at Sources 3, 4, 5 and 6, which are all about warfare in a later period. What changes have taken place in the Muslims' methods of fighting?
3. Do you think all these changes are improvements?
4. Read Source 7. What is the writer's view of the Arabs as fighters? Do you agree with his view?

Most historians agree that there were other reasons that the Arab Muslim armies were so successful. Here are some of them:

■ When the Arabs were divided, they were no threat to anyone. When they were united together they suddenly became a major new power.
■ The Arabs were transformed by Islam. The habit of disciplined prayer five times a day helped them to take orders and co-operate when fighting.
■ They believed that if they died fighting for Islam they would go straight to Heaven.
■ The neighbouring BYZANTINE and Persian Empires had been fighting each other from 603 to 629/7. By the time they had to face the Muslims they were already exhausted by war.
■ Many people whose countries had been taken over by the Byzantine and Persian Empires hated their rulers and welcomed the Muslim invaders as liberators.
■ The more lands the Muslims conquered, the more wealth they got to pay their armies and the more soldiers wanted to fight for them.

5. Try to link these reasons with what Sources 8–12 tell you about Arab warfare.

SOURCE 8 Two sayings of Muhammad*

a) Swords are the key to Paradise.
b) A day and night fighting on the frontier is better than a month of fasting and prayer.

SOURCE 9 Written by a modern historian

In Emesa in Syria, the townspeople – Jews and Christians – closed the city gates against their own Byzantine troops and sided with the Muslims.
In Spain, the Jewish communities rose up together in armed revolt against their rulers and in city after city the overstretched Muslims organised them into garrisons.

SOURCE 10 An Arab general offers terms for surrender in the seventh/first century

This is what we would grant the people of Damascus if we enter it: security for their lives, property and churches. So long as they pay the poll tax, nothing but good shall befall them.

SOURCE 11 A modern Muslim writer describes the spread of Islam

It has united all the different nations in one bond of love. This could only have been done by God.

SOURCE 12 Some rules of war laid down by Abu Bakr in the seventh/first century

Do not betray or steal any of the booty. Do not practise treachery or mutilation. Do not kill a young child, an old man or a woman.

Activity

Get into groups. You are going to produce a project or a display showing why the Arabs were so successful. First of all, put the reasons for their success in order of importance. Explain why you have chosen this order. Then add any other explanations that the sources suggest to you.

1. Some historians think the Arabs would never have won so many wars or conquered so many countries if they had not become Muslims. Do you agree?

What was life like in an Islamic city?

Where should the capital city be?

AT FIRST, the expanding Arab Empire was ruled from Medinah. But in 661/40 the UMMAYAD family took control and made Damascus the capital. Almost a hundred years later, in the 740s/120s, the ABBASSIDS defeated the Ummayads in a civil war. Should they have a different city as their capital?

1. You must advise the CALIPH on where to have the capital city. Source 1 shows three possible sites. Which of these sites would you choose, and why?

▼ **SOURCE 1** Cities in the Islamic Empire

Baghdad

■ At the moment only a village, but ready for development or planning an entirely new city
■ Fertile area, because of the annual flooding from the Tigris and Euphrates rivers
■ Rivers also provide trade links with the east and west of the Empire
■ Good water supply to town from these rivers.

Your teacher will tell you which city the Caliph chose, and why.

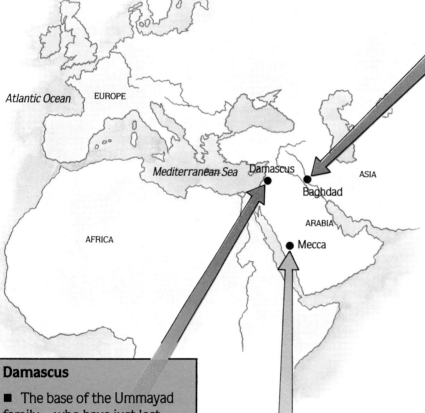

Damascus

■ The base of the Ummayad family – who have just lost power in a civil war
■ Has a magnificent and large MOSQUE
■ Ex-capital of Syria, and an important city of the BYZANTINE Empire
■ Has been an important city for 3000 years
■ In a fertile farming area
■ Well established capital with lots of expert government officials.

Mecca

■ The most holy city of Islam
■ The birthplace of Muhammad*
■ In a safe place if the frontiers of the Empire were ever attacked
■ In a desert – all food needs importing
■ Could only support a small population.

An Islamic city

Source 2 shows an Islamic city, Ankara in Turkey. As you can see it is very different from cities in the Roman Empire and in medieval England.

It is surprising how much you can find out about Islamic cities by looking at just one picture. Source 2 was painted in the eighteenth/twelfth century. (There are very few pictures of earlier cities.) We need to look at more evidence to find out if this was typical, and to try to reconstruct what an earlier Islamic city would have looked like. Were earlier cities such as Baghdad anything like this?

1. It is important to ask good questions about the topic you are studying. Write down five things you want to know about Islamic cities.

▼ **SOURCE 2** The Islamic city of Ankara, about 1000 years after Muhammad*

1. Trace the outline of Source 2 into your book. Then find the following, add them to your drawing and label them:
   - the MOSQUE, with its tower and dome
   - the merchants' booths (shops)
   - the inside of a house (what do you think the people in this house are doing?)
   - a jeweller weighing his precious stones
   - a family scene – people cooking, smoking and weaving
   - shearing sheep
   - a camel caravan setting off.
2. Describe the buildings and shops. What is being sold? Are the shops different from shops in medieval England?
3. Describe what the people are wearing. Are men and women dressed differently?
4. What other things do the people seem to be doing?

WHAT WAS LIFE LIKE IN AN ISLAMIC CITY?

What did the new capital look like?

The caliphs chose Baghdad as their capital. They built it as a round city. To the Muslims, a circle meant unity and power. Nothing remains of this original city, but many people visited it and wrote about it. From their descriptions it is possible to reconstruct what the city looked like (see Source 3).

Baghdad grew very quickly. It was founded in 762/144, and by 814/198 it was the world's largest city!

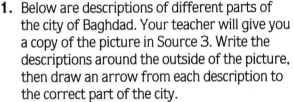

SOURCE 3 Reconstruction of the Round City at Baghdad

SOURCE 4 Map of Baghdad in 814/198

Key
- Roads
- Canals

1. Below are descriptions of different parts of the city of Baghdad. Your teacher will give you a copy of the picture in Source 3. Write the descriptions around the outside of the picture, then draw an arrow from each description to the correct part of the city.
   - The royal palace and the mosque were in the middle. The palace was placed so that when Muslims prayed towards Mecca they had to bow to the Caliph's palace as well.
   - Open spaces surrounded the palace.
   - The palace was protected by circular walls which separated the palace and its grounds from the rest of the city.
   - The city had four main gates. Over each of these gates was a gatehouse. When the Caliph made a speech to the people, he spoke from the roof of the gatehouse. Each gate had a guard of 1000 men.
   - Areas of the city could easily be sealed off in case of riots or other disturbances.
   - The whole of the Round City was surrounded by a dry moat, another wall and a ditch on the outside. Soldiers could be assembled in the moat in times of danger.

2. What do you think was the main aim of the person who designed Baghdad: to allow the Caliph to mix freely with the people or to make sure the Caliph was safe from attack?

3. Compare Source 4 with Source 3. Describe how Baghdad has grown.

   Your teacher will give you a worksheet which explores why Baghdad grew so quickly.

Life in Baghdad

Although it was founded by the Arab Muslims, Baghdad quickly became an international centre. People from Turkey, Persia, India and all over the Islamic world came there. The city mixed together elements of many different cultures.

What life was like in Baghdad, or any Islamic city, depended on who you were. In particular, it depended on whether you were rich or poor.

You have seen that the Caliph had his court in Baghdad. You have also seen that Baghdad was a major trading centre. Many MERCHANTS lived there. But Baghdad also had vast numbers of poor people.

> **SOURCE 5** Two eighth/second-century proverbs about buying a house in Baghdad
>
> a) *The neighbour is the first consideration, the house is the next.*
>
> b) *2000 dinars [gold coins] for the house. And another 2000 for the neighbourhood.*

> **SOURCE 6** From a description of ninth/third-century Baghdad
>
> *Areas where the poor lived: Auatin al-Kilab, Nahr Adanj*
> *Areas where the rich lived: Zhir, Shammasiya, Mamuniya*

1. Do Sources 5 and 6 suggest that rich and poor people lived together in the same parts of Baghdad?
2. Describe three differences between the houses of the rich and the poor in Sources 7 and 8. Are there any similarities?

SOURCE 7 A rich person's house

Rich people's houses had a courtyard in the centre. The rooms would be around the courtyard. The number of rooms depended on how rich the owner was. Very rich people had large fountains in the courtyard. Some houses had a garden, too. In the crowded cities a garden was almost as expensive as the house itself.

Most houses did not look very grand from the outside. People did not want the authorities to know how rich they were, because they didn't want to pay much tax.

Inside the house, the family (wives, children, servants and slaves) led a very private life. Most of the windows faced the inside, overlooking the courtyard. Windows facing the outside often had screens over them, so that the women could look out without being seen.

The rooms were divided into different sections by curtains. Floors were covered by rugs and carpets, but there was not much furniture – perhaps a few chairs and a couch. Rich people's houses had plenty of books for the children, who were often educated at home.

Meals were important events. The men would gather around large trays covered with bread, meat and fruit. The women and children ate separately. The food was cooked outside. Very few Islamic houses had kitchens. They didn't have bathrooms, either, although most houses had a toilet.

Most of the cooking and cleaning was done by the slaves. Slaves were often people who had been captured in war, or were the children of slaves. They had some rights – they had to be looked after and fed, and cared for when they were old.

To keep the occupants cool, houses would have a funnel to direct any wind down into the house. Some of the rich in Baghdad could pay for large blocks of ice to be placed in the roof – then a servant fanned it to blow the cold air into the house. This ice had to be transported hundreds of miles from the mountains of Syria or Iraq. In hot weather, people would often sleep on the roof of the house.

The poor could not normally afford even the cheapest rents inside the city. They built their own mud shelters or small houses on the edges of it (see Source 8).

SOURCE 8 A poor person's house

Life at court

Many of the people of Baghdad worked for the Caliph, including thousands of soldiers. Most of them were mercenaries who came from Turkey. The soldiers kept tight security around the Caliph, who lived in great luxury.

SOURCE 9 The bath-house attached to the Caliph's palace in Baghdad in the eighth/second century. The Caliph is seated in the centre having a haircut. (The painting was made in 1528/935)

1. How is the water being drawn up?
2. What else is happening apart from the haircut?

SOURCE 10 A small extract from a list of the Caliph's belongings in 809/193. It took four months just to make the list

"4000 embroidered robes
4000 silk cloaks
2000 pairs of trousers
4000 turbans
500,000 gold coins
5000 cushions
1000 washbasins
300 stoves
4000 pairs of socks
1000 Armenian carpets"

SOURCE 11 Some of the servants employed at the court in Baghdad

"Cheetah keepers
Dog keepers
Falconers
Archers
Runners
Elephant keepers"

▶ **SOURCE 12** Court activities. A carving made in the twelfth/sixth century

3. Use the evidence in Sources 9–12 to describe what life must have been like at the court.

How did people dress?

All men wore turbans. The wealthy owned several, often highly decorated. The poor used simple strips of cloth. Women did not wear the turban. But from about 100 years after Muhammad's* death women began to wear veils. This modest way of dressing was clearly encouraged in the Quran and the Hadith.

The length and colour of your robe showed your status in society. The more important you were, the longer your robe was. To wear black was a sign that you were in the service of the Caliph.

▲ SOURCE 13

◀ SOURCE 14

1. Look at Sources 13 and 14. One shows farmworkers and the other shows a father and daughter before a *Qadi* (a judge). Which is which? Give as many reasons as you can to support your answer.
2. The father and daughter are dressed in a very similar way.
a) How does this conflict with the information given above?
b) Can you explain why there might be these differences?
3. How do you think the Caliph's clothes were different from the farmworkers' clothes? Do you think there were any similarities?

What did people eat?

The favourite meal for both rich and poor people was called *harisa*. This was a tasty but cheap meal of boiled meat with chicken and herbs. It was cooked overnight and first thing in the morning the *harisa* shops in Baghdad would be very crowded. *Harisa* was always the first dish served at weddings.

But *harisa* was the exception. Usually the rich ate very differently from the poor, as Source 15 shows.

> **SOURCE 15** From ninth/third-century records
> a) Dinner for a poor family
>
> **"** *Cheap meat or small fish*
> *Rice bread [the rich ate wheat bread]*
> *Treacle, saffron, pickle, olive and vinegar, dates or oil cakes.* **"**
>
> b) Dinner at the court
>
> **"** *The Caliph ordered the number of main dishes prepared for each meal to be reduced to twelve, and the number of sweets to thirty.* **"**

> **1.** Look at Source 14 on the previous page. The farmworkers are being brought their midday meal. What are they going to eat?

Making a living

In the countryside around Baghdad most people were farmers. But in an Islamic city, just as in modern cities, there were many ways for both men and women to make a living. Keeping the cities going called for a wide range of skills, as you can see in Sources 16–22.

▶ **SOURCE 16** Gold coin (dinar) from eighth/second-century Baghdad, showing a transport worker leading a camel

> **SOURCE 17**
> a) Street names in Baghdad's Round City
>
> **"** *The Street of the Women*
> *The Street of the Dungeon*
> *The Street of the Water-carriers*
> *The Street of the Police*
> *The Street of the Guards* **"**
>
> b) Names in the suburbs
>
> **"** *Bridge of the Oil-merchants*
> *Soap-boilers' Quarter*
> *Road of the Painter*
> *Canal-diggers' Quarter*
> *The Place of the Tanners*
> *The Cookmen's Quarter* **"**

▼ **SOURCE 18** Tanning leather in modern Morocco, using exactly the same technology as 1000 years earlier in Baghdad. Tanning was a job done by poor people. The industry created many unpleasant smells and by-products

SOURCE 19 A chemist's shop in Baghdad in the fourteenth/eighth century

SOURCE 20 City laws in Islamic Spain

66 *The contractor of hotels should not be a woman* 99

SOURCE 21 Al Khatib's *History of Baghdad* includes biographies of 29 influential women

66 ■ *Twelve taught leading male scholars of the time.*
■ *All of them were highly educated.*
■ *Some were poets.*
■ *Many were religious teachers or saints.* 99

SOURCE 22 Jobs mentioned in ninth/third-century records for Iraq

66 *In Basra there were people who collected the waste (human sewage) from the privies and dried it in the sun to sell in the markets as fuel.*
    Water-carriers would use donkeys or their own backs to carry water to houses, shops, baths, mosques and public fountains.
    Other jobs: mosque attendants, carpet and cloth weavers, brick-makers, market stall holders, dock-workers, Quran readers, straw-merchants, butchers . . . 99

Activity

Baghdad is straining at the seams. The Caliph has called on everyone to prove that their job is essential to the working of the city.

Choose one of the jobs listed below and in a class debate argue why your job keeps the city going.
■ a dock-worker
■ a water-carrier
■ a palace guard
■ a privy cleaner
■ a mosque attendant
■ a market stall holder.

1. What evidence can you collect from pages 172–179 about the life and work of women in Islamic cities?

How important were trade and travel?

As you have seen in Units A and B, both the Romans and people in medieval England were great travellers. How about the Muslims?

For 500 years, from 750/132, the Muslims were the world's leading traders. Islam had spread to many countries. The original Islamic Empire, with its capital in Baghdad, had split up. There were several separate Islamic empires, with their own big cities and their own rulers.

As you can see from Source 6 opposite, a network of many trade routes had built up around the Islamic world. The Muslims were able to supply their cities with goods from all over the world.

SOURCE 2 Slave market in Yemen (from a thirteenth/seventh-century manuscript)

> **SOURCE 1** A ninth/third-century guide to imports to Baghdad
>
> 66 *From India: tigers, elephants, rubies, sandalwood and coconuts.*
>
> *From China: spices, silk, porcelain, paper, ink, spirited horses, saddles and rhubarb.*
>
> *From the Byzantines: silver and gold vessels, coins, medicines, cloth, slave-girls, experts in water engineering and farming.*
>
> *From Arabia: horses, pedigree she-camels, tanned hides.*
>
> *From North Africa: leopards and black falcons.*
>
> *From the Yemen: cloaks, giraffes, breastplates, indigo.*
>
> *From Egypt: donkeys, fine cloth.*
>
> *From Central Asia: slaves, armour, helmets, grapes, sugarcane.*
>
> *From Persia: plums, soft woollen coats, honey, fruit drinks, glass.* 99

1. Look at Source 2. Find the slaves, one customer choosing a slave to buy and another customer paying.

> **SOURCE 3** Market regulations in Islamic Spain
>
> 66 ■ *Shopkeepers are forbidden to reserve places in the forecourt of the great mosque. Instead, whoever comes first should take his place.*
> ■ *The market inspector must arrange the crafts in order, putting like with like.*
> ■ *The baking of bread must be supervised. Often the bakers take a small quantity of good dough and use it to cover up the front of the bread, which is made from bad flour.*
> ■ *The shopkeepers' weights for weighing food should always be inspected.*

Because it was a trading centre, Baghdad had many specialised markets. Here are some of them:
- fruit markets – one of them known as the Melon House
- poultry market
- flower market
- goldsmiths' market
- sheep markets
- booksellers' market
- market for Chinese goods
- market for hunting equipment.

Shops and markets became such an important part of life in Islamic cities that rules were made to make sure business was run fairly (see Source 3).

2. Look at Source 3. With a partner, choose one rule and decide why it might help the market to run fairly.

Key
- .... Desert routes: 30km per day
- ——— Land routes: 40km per day
- ——— Sea routes: 150km per day
- ▮ The Islamic world

3. Look at Source 4.
a) Describe this form of transport in as much detail as you can.
b) This form of transport did not change for centuries. Do you think this was because the Muslims were reluctant to use new methods or for other reasons?
4. Sources 4 and 5 show two different types of travel. For four of the trade routes shown on Source 6, say which type of travel would be used and which of the goods in Source 1 would be transported.

SOURCE 4 A thirteenth/seventh-century dish from Iran

SOURCE 5 A book illustration from the thirteenth/seventh century

Activity
Divide into groups. Each group has to organise either:
■ kitchen and food supplies for the Caliph to give a banquet for a visitor he wants to impress
■ supplies for a new division of the army – an élite bodyguard for the Caliph
Your teacher will give you a copy of Source 6, which shows you the distances between Baghdad and the different places the goods come from.
1. Decide which supplies you need and where you need to go to get them.
2. Plan the routes. Different people in your group could be responsible for getting different goods.
3. Estimate how long the journeys will take. Write brief descriptions of the journeys.

SOURCE 6 Baghdad's trade routes

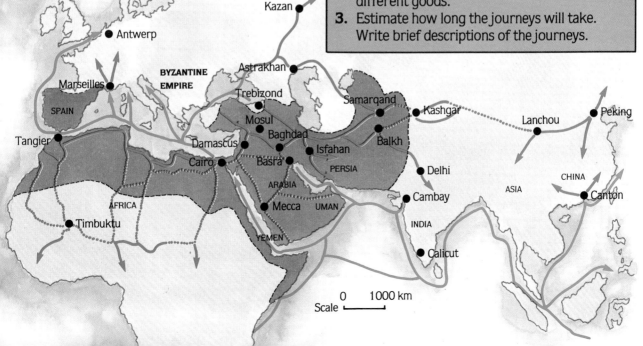

HOW IMPORTANT WERE TRADE AND TRAVEL?

Stopping at a caravanserai

Trade routes criss-crossed the whole of the Islamic world. Along the routes – about one day's journey from each other – were hostels called caravanserais. These provided food and somewhere to sleep for weary travellers. Many Muslim rulers let people use them free of charge. Hospitality was very important to Muslims, and still is today.

The travellers entered the caravanserai through a gatehouse into a large courtyard. Here they unloaded all their goods from the camels and locked them away in storerooms. The camels were taken off to the stables. The stables could only be approached through a narrow passage, which was heavily guarded. The MERCHANTS' business, and even their lives, depended on the camels, so they had to be well protected.

As you can see from Source 7, the courtyard would be alive with activity. You can also see where the travellers slept on the upper floor. They brought their own bedding with them. The rich had private rooms, but most people slept in dormitories. The caravanserai also had bathrooms and lavatories.

After settling in, the travellers would pray in the mosque. Sometimes, the flat roofs of the buildings were used for prayer. Afterwards, the merchants would go to the coffee shop. Here they exchanged stories about their journeys.

Some of the caravanserais were in towns. There would be markets in the town, and the merchants would sell some of their goods to the townspeople before moving on.

---

1. Source 7 shows many different merchants. You are one of them. Tell the story of your journey to the caravanserai. What are you transporting? Describe what it is like at the caravanserai.

SOURCE 7 Reconstruction of a caravanserai

The Haj

Trade was not the only reason why Muslims travelled so much. Muhammad* had said that every Muslim man and woman should make the PILGRIMAGE (or Haj) to Mecca once in a lifetime. Both powerful and ordinary people did so. Some of them journeyed to Mecca many times. Some pilgrims had to travel thousands of miles overland to get to Mecca.

Some rich pilgrims would carry many treasures and goods to give away along the way. Governments around the Islamic world organised official caravans which were protected from bandits by soldiers. Hundreds of caravanserais sprang up along the pilgrim routes to Mecca. They were paid for by gifts from rich Muslims.

SOURCE 8 A pilgrim caravan in the thirteenth/seventh century

SOURCE 9 A fourteenth/eighth-century pilgrim describes his travels through Egypt towards Mecca

66 *The governor of the city came to meet us. Seeing my clothes all soiled by the rain, he gave orders that they should be washed at his house, and in place of my old worn turban sent me one of fine Syrian cloth. Into this he had tied two gold dinars. This was the first alms I received on my journey.* 99

SOURCE 10 Description of the famous pilgrimage made by Jamila bint Nasir in 977/366

66 *Jamila brought with her, loaded on camels, fresh green vegetables contained in earthenware crocks. She brought 500 horses and camels for disabled pilgrims to ride on. She gave 10,000 dinars to the Kaabah. She freed 300 slaves and 200 slave-girls. She provided 50,000 fine robes for the ordinary people in Mecca.* 99

1. Look at Source 8. Why are there musicians with the pilgrims?
2. In what ways were pilgrims helped on their journey to Mecca?
3. How did pilgrims help others?

SOURCE 11 Ibn Battuta, a fourteenth/eighth-century Muslim traveller, describes what happened on two of the many pilgrimages he made to Mecca

66 *[1325] ... At the place where the prophet had put on the pilgrim dress I divested myself of my clothes, bathed and put on the pilgrim's garment ... [1326] ... my illness had made me weak, and I had to make the circuit of the Kaabah and the visits to Saafa and Maarwah riding on the amir's horse. We then camped at Mina.* 99

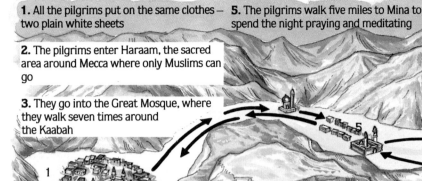

1. All the pilgrims put on the same clothes — two plain white sheets

2. The pilgrims enter Haraam, the sacred area around Mecca where only Muslims can go

3. They go into the Great Mosque, where they walk seven times around the Kaabah

5. The pilgrims walk five miles to Mina to spend the night praying and meditating

4. The pilgrims run seven times between Mecca and Maarwah. This reminds them of Hagar searching for water for her son. Then they drink at the Zamzam well

SOURCE 12 A modern chart showing the rituals performed by pilgrims today

1. Compare Sources 11 and 12. Do pilgrims today still do the same things as pilgrims in the fourteenth/ eighth century?

▼ **SOURCE 13** One of Al Idrisi's maps of the world, made in 1154/ 549

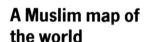

A Muslim map of the world

With so many Muslims on the move, on pilgrimages or trading journeys, their knowledge of the world increased a great deal. Travellers needed maps, and Islamic scholars began to gather this knowledge together. They produced some of the most advanced and detailed maps and geography books there had ever been.

When Roger II, the Christian King of Sicily, needed an accurate map of the world, he asked Al Idrisi, a Muslim scholar, to make one. Al Idrisi spent sixteen years researching what the world was like. He interviewed the captains of almost all the boats that docked at Sicily's main ports, to find out what they knew. The atlas he produced was probably the most accurate of its time.

▶ **SOURCE 14** Modern version of one of Al Idrisi's maps

6. Then they go to the plain of Arafat, where they pray and meditate from midday until sunset

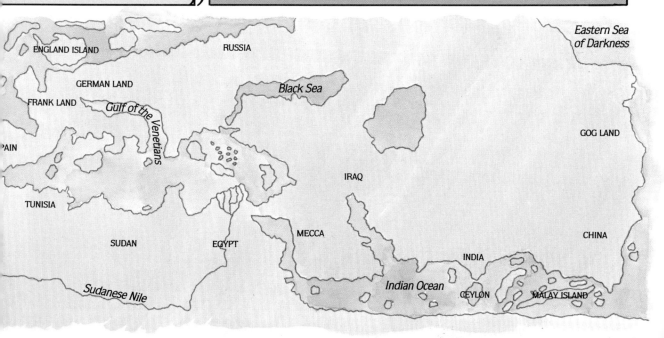

7. On the way back, they spend the night at Muzdaliffah. Then they go back to Mina, where they spend three nights stoning pillars (which are symbols of the devil)

SOURCE 15 From Al Idrisi's *Book of Roger*

[Britain] is set in the Sea of Darkness.

It is a considerable island, whose shape is that of the head of an ostrich, and where there are flourishing towns, high mountains, great rivers and plains.

This country is most fertile; its inhabitants are brave and active. But it is in the grip of endless winter. "

1. Compare Sources 13 and 14 with Source 2 on page 194. Is Al Idrisi's map a more accurate map of the world?
2. Is there information in Source 14 or Source 15 which is still not very accurate?
3. How did Al Idrisi gather his information?
4. From the evidence in Sources 13–15, what areas of the world had not been explored in detail by the people Al Idrisi spoke to?
5. Many maps produced up to 200 or 300 years later were not as accurate as Al Idrisi's map. Why do you think the makers of these maps did not learn from his knowledge?

Activity

Look at the following points.

■ Relationships between different Islamic countries were not always warm. Many Islamic rulers were worried about spies entering their countries. Border security was tight.
■ Sometimes people travelled abroad to escape paying taxes.
■ In many areas peasants were moving to the cities, leaving less people to grow food for the bigger population in the cities.
■ The pilgrimage and trade led to a massive increase in travel.

You are an adviser to a Muslim ruler. You are worried about the large numbers of people travelling through your country.
Using all the material on pages 180–185:

1. Write down for your master a list of the advantages and the disadvantages of allowing people to travel.
2. Draw up for him a set of six rules which travellers will have to obey. Use a whole page for these and illustrate the page with travel scenes.

Were people religious in the Islamic world?

SOURCE 1 Painting of the city of Istanbul

PEOPLE'S everyday lives in the Islamic world were ruled by their religion. Islam laid down laws about all aspects of life. Here are some examples:

Muslim men and women:
- had to pray towards Mecca five times a day. This meant work and mealtimes had to be organised around the prayer times
- had to fast (go without food and drink) during the month of Ramadan
- were not allowed to eat pork or drink alcohol
- had to go on PILGRIMAGE at least once in their lifetime.

Muslim children:
- had to obey their parents.

All Muslim men:
- had to go to the main MOSQUE every Friday (the Muslim holy day) for prayers
- had to wash themselves well before going to Friday prayers.

But there is sometimes a difference between what people are meant to do and what they actually do. Did Muslims always obey the religious laws?

---

1. Look at Source 1. The arrow marks one of the many mosques in the city. You can recognise the mosques by their tall, brightly-coloured towers, called minarets, or their domed roofs. How many mosques can you count?
2. Why should a city need so many mosques?

SOURCE 2 From a ninth/third-century joke book

Some people came to Al Rustumi's house on some business. When the time came for midday prayers they asked him, 'Which is the direction of Mecca in this house of yours?' He replied, 'I only moved in a month ago.' 99

SOURCE 3 Recorded in various histories of Baghdad

There was a running debate in ninth-century Baghdad as to whether the favourite drink — called nadibh — was or was not in fact alcoholic and therefore forbidden to Muslims. 99

SOURCE 4 Written in the tenth/fourth century about the activity of some religious groups in Baghdad who wanted Muslims to live much stricter lives

66 *They raided everyone's houses. If they found wine, they poured it away. If they found a singing girl, they broke her instruments. They looked for men who were going with women and took them to the chief of police. They caused uproar in Baghdad.* 99

SOURCE 5 By a ninth/third-century visitor to Baghdad

66 *The Friday [main] mosque in Baghdad could not hold all the people, and so roads around had to be closed to traffic and the surrounding area was used for prayer.* 99

SOURCE 6 Written by Ibn Battuta, a famous Muslim traveller, when he was on pilgrimage in 1326/726

66 *There were so many pilgrims they couldn't be counted. The earth surged with them like the sea, and the earth resembled the movement of a high piled cloud.*

Any person who left the caravan for a moment, and had no mark to guide him to his place, could not find it again because of the multitude of people. 99

---

3. Which sources support the view that people did obey the religious laws?
4. Which sources support the view that people did not obey these laws?
5. Which sources can be used to support both views?
6. What evidence is there here and on page 183 that Muslims followed Muhammad's* instruction to them to go on pilgrimage to Mecca?

How tolerant were Muslims?

At first, Islam was the religion only of the Arabs. As the Empire grew, people of different cultures and religions were conquered. Many of the people in these countries became Muslims, and Islam became the official religion of countries as far apart as Spain and India.

The Muslims wanted to run their Empire according to Islamic ideas and beliefs. But many people in the countries they took over chose to keep their own religion. Iraq, for instance, had one of the most important Jewish communities in the world when the Muslims took over the country. What should the Islamic rulers do about people who had different religions, especially Jews and Christians? Muhammad* had always respected these religions.

When you have read these two pages, decide for yourself whether you think Jews and Christians were treated well in the Islamic world. You can also think about whether Jews were treated better than in medieval England (see pages 118–119).

Muhammad* had said that Jews and Christians should be allowed to become Muslims, but that they should not be forced. If they wanted to stay as Jews and Christians they should be allowed to. As long as they paid their taxes, they would be protected.

In 630/8 Christians in Syria agreed to obey certain rules while they lived in the Islamic Empire (see Source 7). These rules became the basis for similar agreements between Muslims and Jews and Christians in all parts of the Islamic Empire.

> **SOURCE 7** The Pact of Umar – rules agreed by Syrian Christians in 630/8
>
> 66 We shall not build new churches in our cities.
> We shall not shelter any spy.
> We shall not hold our religious ceremonies in public.
> We shall not try to convert anyone.
> We shall not stop any of our people becoming Muslims.
> We shall rise from our seats when Muslims want to sit down.
> We shall not wear swords.
> We shall dress in our usual way and shall not dress like Muslims.
> We shall not display our crosses anywhere in Muslim streets or markets. 99

1. Which of these rules were designed to:
   a) keep Christians separate from Muslims
   b) make sure Christianity did not grow?
2. What are the remaining rules about?
3. Which rule do you think would be the most difficult to enforce?

In most cities, the kind of rules listed in Source 7 enabled Jews and Christians to live peacefully alongside Muslims. But they might live in separate parts of the city – in Baghdad there was a street called 'The Street of the Jews'.

Some Christians became rich and powerful in Syria and Iraq, while the Jews did very well in Islamic Spain.

> **SOURCE 8** Customs duties paid by different groups in the eighth/second century
>
> 66 Muslims: 2½% of the value of goods
> Jews and Christians: 5% of the value of goods
> Foreigners: 10% of the value of goods 99

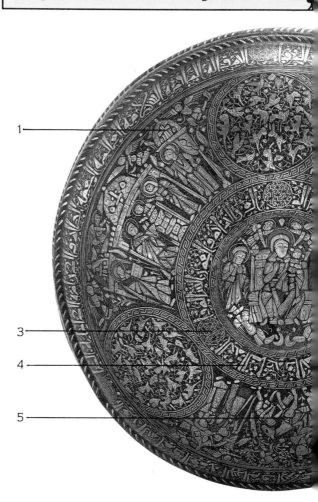

4. Look at Source 9. Match each of the descriptions below to the appropriate numbered feature on the water bottle:
- Illustration of the birth of Jesus
- Illustration of Jesus riding into Jerusalem on a donkey
- Islamic calligraphy (writing)
- A Christian cross
- An Islamic star.

5. What does this design tell you about relationships between Muslims and Christians?

SOURCE 9 A water bottle made in Syria, which combines Islamic and Christian designs

—2

SOURCE 10 Written by a Jewish philosopher in the ninth/third century

❝*One of the reasons why the Muslims respect the Christians is that many of them work for the King as officials and doctors, whereas the Jews are only tanners, butchers and tinkers.*

Jews only convert to Islam out of terror or in quest for power, or to avoid heavy taxation, or in fear of being taken prisoner, or because they have fallen in love with a Muslim woman.❞

SOURCE 11 Orders concerning Jews and Christians in Baghdad

❝***807/191*** *The Caliph ordered some Jewish and Christian houses to be seized and turned into mosques.*

Jews and Christians were not allowed to have jobs in the government, where they might be more important than Muslims.
849/235 *Jews and Christians were ordered to wear honey-coloured hoods.*

Jewish and Christian women were ordered to wear one red and one black shoe, and a copper bell on their necks.❞

6. Look carefully at Sources 7–11. Find as many examples as you can of Jews and Christians being treated well, and make a list. Then find as many examples as you can of Jews and Christians being treated badly, and make another list. Compare the two lists.

7. Look again at pages 118–119 of this book. Where were the Jews treated better – in medieval England or in the Muslim world?

Activity

You are the Christian artist who worked on the water bottle in Source 9. You live in the Muslim Empire. Write a letter to a friend in Britain.
a) Describe the bottle you have created.
b) Explain what it is like to be a Christian living in a Muslim city. (Use Sources 7–11 to help you.) On the whole, do you think you are treated well or badly?

Were Muslims healthy?

As THE Muslim Empire grew, the caliphs gathered a huge collection of Greek books on medicine. The Greeks had made many discoveries in medicine. Their books, although written hundreds of years earlier, were still the most advanced.

Many of these books were kept at Baghdad and were translated into Arabic. If this hadn't happened, many books would have been lost forever.

Muslim scholars studied these ancient books very carefully and wrote their own medicine textbooks. Some of those were still being used in Western Europe 800 years later.

Historians disagree about whether the Muslim religion encouraged new discoveries in medicine.

Lists A and B show some of the arguments they have put forward. Let's see if the evidence can help us find out why there are these different views.

LIST A

■ The Muslim religion taught that the sick should be looked after and hospitals should be built for them.
■ The Muslim religion taught that people should keep themselves clean.
■ Muslims improved drugs and medicines.
■ Muslim doctors made new discoveries about disease and the human body.

LIST B

■ The Muslim religion did not allow doctors to cut up human bodies, so they did not find out very much new about the human body. They believed what they read in books.
■ The Muslim religion did not allow much surgery to take place.
■ Muslim doctors copied the ideas of the Greeks, but did not have many new ideas.

SOURCE 1 Written by a ninth/third-century Jewish doctor working in the Muslim world

"The best of doctors are those who are always reading the books of the ancient experts, especially those of Galen, the prince of doctors. Life is too short to understand a single disease by practical experience, so we should learn from the wisdom of the ancients."

SOURCE 2 From a recent book about the history of medicine

"Galen, a Greek doctor from the second century AD, believed that blood passed from the right side of the heart to the left side through small holes in the septum. Galen's ideas were believed in Western Europe until the sixteenth century.

SOURCE 3 Written by Ibn Nafis, a Muslim doctor who lived in the thirteenth/seventh century

"There is no passage between the two sides of the heart. It must therefore be that blood is passed into the lung to mix with the air.

---

1. How do Galen and Ibn Nafis disagree about the movement of blood?
2. Look at Source 4. Who was right, Galen or Ibn Nafis?
3. Galen, not Ibn Nafis, was believed by most European doctors until the sixteenth century. Why do you think this was?

SOURCE 4
Simplified drawing of the circulation of the blood

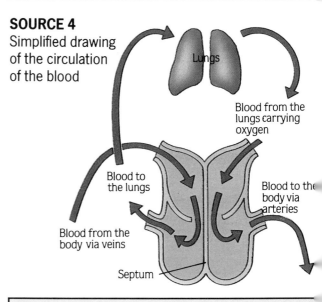

Lungs

Blood from the lungs carrying oxygen

Blood to the lungs

Blood to the body via arteries

Blood from the body via veins

Septum

SOURCE 5 Instructions from Muhammad*

"Cleanliness is half of faith.
Keep your houses clean. God does not like dirt.
Brushing the teeth cleanses the mouth and pleases God.
Every Muslim must have a bath once a week.

SOURCE 6 An eighth/second-century Islamic drawing of a baby being born by 'Caesarean section'. This way of saving a child when the mother was dead or dying had been used by the Greeks and Romans and was continued in the Islamic world

SOURCE 8 An extract from a book on medicine written by Ibn Sina, a famous Muslim doctor

❝The greatest care must be taken during surgery to prevent infection, because surgery is impossible if the wound is infected. If the blood in a wound becomes infected it must be got rid of.❞

SOURCE 7 A description of the hospital in Cairo

❝It had four great courts, each with a fountain in the centre; wards for each separate disease and a lecture room. Some patients were visited in their own homes. When patients left the hospital they were given some money so that they did not have to return to work immediately.❞

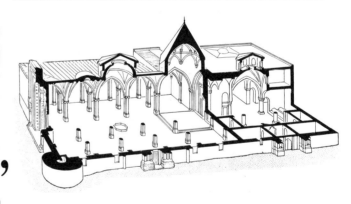

SOURCE 9 The Great Mosque and hospital at Divrigi, built in 1229/626. Most towns had hospitals, paid for out of religious funds. They gave free treatment to the poor

4. How would each of the features of the hospital in Source 7 help people to get better:
   - the fountains
   - separate wards for different diseases
   - treatment at home?
5. Are there any other things about the hospital which would help people to get better?

6. Look at Sources 1–9. Which support the arguments in List A opposite?
7. Which support the arguments in List B?
8. Can you find evidence on these pages of the Muslim religion
   a) helping developments in medicine
   b) encouraging people to be healthy?

From the Greeks, the Muslims learned about the use of drugs and herbs as painkillers. They also made important discoveries in drugs and medicines. They started to use alcohol as an antiseptic.

Activity

You are a *muhtasib* (a market inspector). The *Qadi* (a judge) has asked you to do the daily inspection of the market stalls and streets of Seville.

In Source 11 you can see some of Seville's market laws, which were intended to make sure that the food was in good condition. Your teacher will give you a longer list of these rules.

First of all divide the rules into:

- those making sure the food is good and clean
- those making sure the customers are getting a fair deal
- those about women's behaviour.

Look at Source 10. Are the rules being obeyed? Now write your report for the *Qadi*.

SOURCE 10 A reconstruction drawing of a street scene in Seville, a city in Islamic Spain

SOURCE 11 Market laws in Islamic Seville in the twelfth/sixth century

❝■ *Egg-sellers must have bowls of water in front of them, so that bad eggs may be recognized.*
■ *Cheese should only be sold in small leather bottles which can be washed and cleaned every day.*
■ *No slaughtering should take place in the market, except in the closed slaughterhouses, and the blood and refuse should be taken outside the market.*
■ *Only a skilled doctor should sell medicines and mix drugs. These things should not be bought from the grocer whose only concern is to make money.*❞

The Black Death

In 1348/748, Seville, like many other Islamic and European cities, was living under the shadow of the Black Death. Ibn Battuta, a famous Muslim traveller, was travelling the Islamic world at this time, and Source 12 shows extracts from his travel diary.

SOURCE 12 From Ibn Battuta's travel accounts

❝[Early June 1347] *We heard the Plague had broken out at Gaza. There were over 1000 deaths a day.*
[Late June 1347] *On travelling to Hims I found the Plague there. About 300 people died the day I arrived.*
[July 1347] *I then went to Damascus where the number of deaths had reached 2400 a day.*
[1347 to 1348] *When I reached Jerusalem I found that the Plague had stopped.*
We then found the greater part of Gaza deserted because of deaths from the Plague. I was told by the Qadi that over 1100 a day had died.
[Summer 1348] *We continued overland to Alexandria and here found the plague dying out. The deaths had reached 1080 a day.*
[October 1348] *I then travelled to Cairo where I was told that the number of deaths had reached 21,000 a day.*❞

1. On your own map of the Islamic world, mark the route of Ibn Battuta's journey.
2. Mark next to each city the number of deaths per day which he records.
3. Look back at all the information on pages 190–193 about health in the Islamic world. Are there any aspects of Muslims' health care or their rules about public health which might help them fight against the Black Death? Explain your answer.

Crusades or invasions?

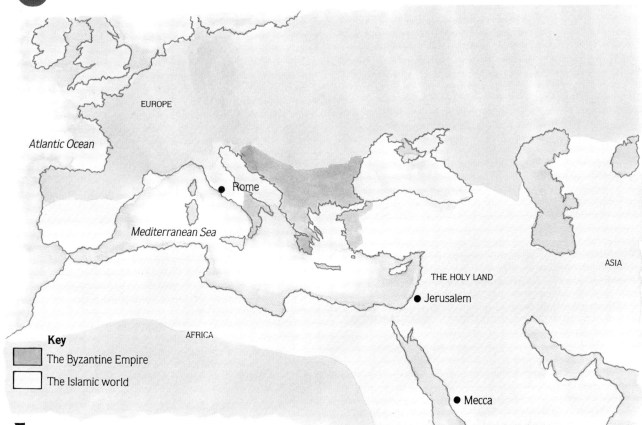

▲ **SOURCE 1** Map of Europe, the Holy Land and the Byzantine Empire

EUROPE

Atlantic Ocean

Rome

Mediterranean Sea

ASIA

THE HOLY LAND

Jerusalem

AFRICA

Key

The Byzantine Empire

The Islamic world

Mecca

FOR a period of nearly 200 years, from 1100/492, Christians and Muslims fought for control of the HOLY LAND. The two sides saw this struggle very differently. For the Christians it was a holy CRUSADE in the name of God, but the Muslims saw it as a FRANKISH invasion.

The Crusade to rescue the Holy Land

The Pope was head of the Christian Church in the West, but in the East there was the great BYZANTINE Empire, which was also Christian. This Empire was threatened by the advance of a new Muslim nation, the Seljuk Turks. In the eleventh/fifth century, the Turks conquered the Arab Muslim Empire, including the Holy Land and the city of Jerusalem. The Arab Muslims had allowed Christian pilgrims to visit Jerusalem, but in 1076/468 the Turks captured the city. They made it much more difficult for the pilgrims.

In 1095/487 the Byzantine Emperor asked the Pope for help. Five months later, at Clermont in France, Pope Urban II preached a sermon asking people to go on a Crusade. Other preachers travelled around Europe persuading people to join. The response was amazing. People from all walks of life and countries flocked to join.

Why did people volunteer so readily?

SOURCE 2 A thirteenth-century Christian map of the world with Jerusalem at the centre

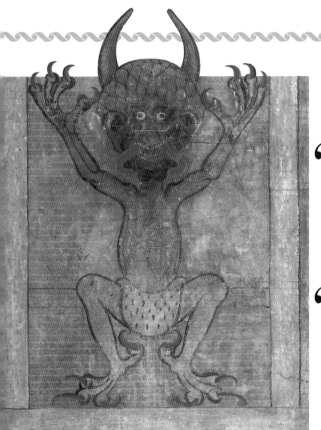

SOURCE 3 A medieval Christian view of Muslims

SOURCE 5 Part of a sermon preached by Abbot Martin of Paris in 1201/597 to persuade people to go on Crusade

❝*The land for which you are making is richer by far than this one and more fertile; and it could easily come to pass that many of you will find a more prosperous way of life there.*❞

SOURCE 6 From a letter written by St Bernard of Clairvaux in 1146/540

❝*O mighty soldier, you now have a cause for which you can fight without endangering your soul; a cause in which to win is glorious, and for which to die is gain. Or are you a shrewd businessman, a man quick to see the profits of this world? If you are, I can offer you a splendid bargain. Do not miss this opportunity. Take the sign of the cross. At once you will have forgiveness for all your sins.*❞

SOURCE 7 Written by William of Malmesbury, a monk

❝*In 1096, Robert, Duke of Normandy, decided to go to Jerusalem at the prompting of Pope Urban II. To pay for this he had to pawn his duchy to his brother.*❞

SOURCE 4 Extracts from Pope Urban's speech in 1095/487

❝*You must run as quickly as you can to help your brothers living on the eastern shores. The Turks have overrun them, slaughtering and capturing many and destroying churches. They cut open their navels, and tear out their most vital organs. They tie them to a stake, or drag them around and flog them.*

Jerusalem is the navel of the world. This royal city is now held captive by her enemies and is enslaved by a people which does not acknowledge God. She asks you to rescue her.

All men going there who die, whether on the journey or while fighting the pagans [non-Christians], will immediately be forgiven their sins.

Until now, you have fought and killed one another. Stop these hatreds among yourselves, silence the quarrels. Instead, rescue the Holy Land from that dreadful race.❞

SOURCE 8 A description by Fulcher of Chartres, a French priest, of people going off to the Crusade in 1096/488

❝*Oh what pain! What sighs! What weeping! When a husband left his dearly beloved wife, his children, whatever possessions he had.*❞

2. Why do you think Jerusalem was such an important place for Christians? Source 8 on page 115 will give you some clues.
3. How were people persuaded to go on the Crusades?
4. Imagine you are Robert, Duke of Normandy, trying to decide whether you should go on the Crusade. Write an entry in your diary which tries to consider the reasons for going and those against going.

1. What were the Pope's three aims for the Crusade?

In 1098/491, the first crusaders began to make their way from Europe to Jerusalem.

SOURCE 9 A German monk describes the actions of some crusaders as they passed through Germany on their way to Jerusalem

66*They suddenly attacked the Jews. They decapitated many and inflicted serious wounds, they destroyed their homes and synagogues, and divided a very great sum of looted money among themselves.*99

SOURCE 10 Written by Anna Comnena, daughter of the Byzantine Emperor, about the crusaders

66*Their whole race is very fond of money. They will sell even their dearest possessions for a little money.*99

The capture of Jerusalem

On 7 June 1099/492, the First Crusade reached Jerusalem. The city had strong defences, but the crusaders were short of food and water in the baking heat. They could not manage a long siege. Also, there was rivalry between the two crusader leaders, Raymond of Toulouse and Godfrey of Bouillon. They attacked opposite sides of the city, both hoping to succeed before the other.

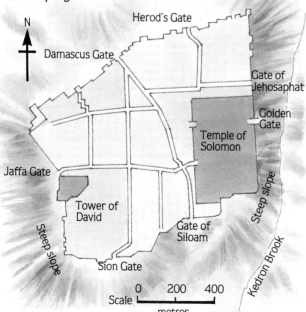

SOURCE 11 A plan of Jerusalem

SOURCE 12 An eye-witness account of the First Crusade

66*We were in daily distress, for the Saracens [Turks] used to lie in wait around the springs and would ambush our men, kill them, and cut them to pieces. They would also lead off our animals.*

Then our commanders made arrangements for Jerusalem to be captured with siege engines. They made two siege towers and many other machines. Godfrey made his own siege tower with engines in it on the northern side and so did Raymond on the southern side. The Saracens made remarkable improvements to the city's fortifications. When our leaders saw which part of the city was the weakest, they brought a wooden siege tower and a machine up to the northern side.

We attacked just east of Herod's gate but could make no headway. We were all very frightened. Then one of Godfrey's knights, Lethold by name, climbed up on to the walls of the city. All the defenders fled and our men, following Lethold, chased after them. Because of this the Egyptians defending the south side surrendered.

SOURCE 13 Extract from a letter from the crusader leaders to the Pope

66*Since the army was suffering greatly in this siege from lack of water, the bishops preached that we walk round the city with bare feet. The Lord was pleased with this act of humility, for he handed over to us the city, together with his enemies.*

SOURCE 14 Written by Ibn al-Athir, an Arab historian of the time

66*While the Franks [Christians] were conquering and settling in our territories, the rulers and armies of Islam were fighting among themselves and weakening their power to combat the enemy.*

SOURCE 15 An eye-witness account

Our pilgrims entered the city, and chased the Saracens, killing as they went, as far as the Temple of Solomon. There the enemy fought a furious battle, so that their blood flowed all over the temple. Our men captured many men and women and killed whomsoever they wished. Soon our army overran the whole city, seizing gold and silver, horses and mules, and houses full of riches of all kinds."

SOURCE 16 The attack on Jerusalem, painted in the fifteenth/ninth century

SOURCE 17 The ransacking of Jerusalem by the crusaders, painted in the fifteenth/ninth century

1. Copy Source 11, the plan of Jerusalem. Mark where the attacks took place.
2. Describe in your own words the attack and capture of Jerusalem.
3. What different reasons are given in Sources 11–17 for the crusaders' success at Jerusalem?
4. Is one of these reasons more important than the others?
5. Look at Source 4 on the previous page, which gives the Pope's aims for the Crusades. Study Sources 9, 15 and 17. Do you think the Pope would be pleased with the results of the Crusade?
6. Is there any evidence on pages 194–197 that people went on the Crusades simply to make their fortunes?

CRUSADES OR INVASIONS?

Defence against the Franks

What Christians call the Crusades, the Muslims call the FRANKISH Invasions. The invaders captured Jerusalem in 1099/492, but it was almost 50 years before the Muslims really began to resist the Invasions. By this time, the Franks had carved out four Christian states, occupying most of the Holy Land (see Source 18). Why did it take Islam so long to respond? To answer this question, we must first look at what had been happening in the Islamic Empire in the years before the invasions.

By 850/235, the Islamic Empire stretched from Spain to the borders of China. But over the next 200 years the caliphs in Baghdad became less powerful. The religion of Islam united the various Muslim countries, but Baghdad was no longer really important as a political centre. By 1000/390, the Islamic Empire had become a number of small empires, sometimes at war with each other.

In 1055/446, the Turks, a fierce warrior people from central Asia, who had only recently converted to Islam, took control of Baghdad. For the first time in two centuries the Muslim Middle East was united under a single ruler. The Turks were determined to bring back the past glory of Islam. As we have seen, they also brought with them a new, tougher attitude to Christianity, and prevented Christian pilgrims from worshipping in Jerusalem. It was this which provoked a large army of FRANKS (or Franj) from all over Europe to march on the Holy Land and capture Jerusalem.

In view of this unity, it is particularly surprising that the Muslims took so long to respond to the Frankish Invasions.

SELJUK EMPIRE

Edessa

Antioch

Aleppo

To Baghdad

Krak des Chevaliers

Tripoli

Mediterranean Sea

Sidon

Damascus

Tyre

Acre

Caesarea

Desert

Ascalon

Jerusalem

Bethlehem

Cairo

EGYPT

1. Why did it take the Muslims so long to react? Look at the following explanations. Then study Sources 19–27. Which explanations are supported best by the sources?

■ 'They were afraid of the Franks who were stronger and superior.'

■ 'The Franks were not a threat. They worshipped the same God. What's more, they were backward and uncivilised. Anyway, they were a long way from Baghdad. What happened in Jerusalem was not important.'

■ 'In the past, the Muslims had been prepared to fight *Jihad* (holy war) against any enemy. But the days of *Jihad* had long gone. The Muslims were more concerned with their own power struggles.'

◀ **SOURCE 18** The four states set up by the Christians

SOURCE 19 Written by a Muslim in the twelfth/sixth century

Jerusalem is as holy to us as it is to you; it is even more important to us, because it was there that our Prophet made his miraculous journey, and it is there that our people will be reunited on Judgement Day. It is, therefore, out of the question for us to abandon it.

SOURCE 20 An extract from the Quran (Sura 29.46)

Be polite when you argue with Christians, except those who do evil. Say 'We believe in that which is revealed to us and that which is revealed to you. Our God and your God is one.'

SOURCE 21 Written by a modern Arab historian

The Franj's main strength lay in the heavy armour with which their knights covered their entire bodies, and sometimes their horses as well. They were magnificently protected against arrows.

SOURCE 22 Frankish knights attack Muslims. This painting was done by a Christian artist

SOURCE 23 From a recent history book

The idea of the holy war had become a distant memory to the Muslims. They did not even see the Crusade as a Christian holy war but as just an attempt to conquer territory. Anyway, they were busily engaged in fighting one another. They were also not very good soldiers at this time.

SOURCE 24 Written by Usamah, an Arab prince, quoting a doctor, in the twelfth/sixth century

They took me to see a woman with consumption. I gave her a cleaning and refreshing diet. Then there appeared a Frankish doctor who said, 'This man has no idea how to cure people.' He examined the woman and said, 'She has a devil in her head. The devil has got into her brain.' He took a razor and cut a cross on her head, and removed the brain. The woman died instantly. At this moment I came away, having learnt things about medical methods that I never knew before.

SOURCE 25 Written by a Muslim who fought against the Franks

All those who were well informed about the Franj saw them as beasts, superior in courage but in nothing else, just as animals are superior in strength and aggression.

SOURCE 26 Written by a modern Arab historian

The sack of Jerusalem, although it was the starting point of 1000 years of hostility between Islam and the West, aroused no immediate sensation in Baghdad. Few Arabs were clear-sighted in weighing the scope of the threat from the West.

SOURCE 27 Written by Abul-Muzaffar al-Abiwardi, an eleventh/fifth-century poet

*Sons of Islam, behind you are battles in which heads rolled at your feet.
Dare you slumber in the blessed shade of safety, where life is as soft as an orchard flower?*

CRUSADES OR INVASIONS?

Two interpretations

Here are two timelines. One is from a British book and the other from an Arab book. As you read the timelines, you may need to look back at Source 18 on the previous page to remind yourself where the places are.

SOURCE 28 From an Arab history book

Invasion 1097–99
1097 First great Frankish expedition
1099 Fall of Jerusalem – followed by massacres and plunder

Occupation 1100–1125
1104 Muslim victory stops Frankish eastward advance
1124 The Franj take Tyre. They now occupy the entire coast except for Ascalon

Riposte 1126–1146
1144 Zangi (the ruler of Aleppo in Syria) takes Edessa, destroying one of the four Frankish states

Victory 1147–1187
1148 Debacle at Damascus for a new Frankish expedition
1187 Saladin (the ruler of Egypt) reconquers Jerusalem

Reprieve 1188–1229
1190–92 Setback for Saladin. Intervention of King Richard the Lionheart of England enables the Franj to recover several cities
1204 The Franj take Constantinople. Sack of the city

1218–21 Invasion of Egypt by the Franj. They head for Cairo, but the Sultan finally repels them

1229 Al Kamil gives up Jerusalem to the Franj, causing a storm of indignation in the Arab world

Expulsion 1230–1291
1244 Franj lose Jerusalem for the last time

1291 The Sultan Khalil takes Acre, putting an end to two centuries of Frankish presence in the Orient

---

SOURCE 29 From a British history book

1099 First Crusade. Christians recapture Jerusalem

1144 Turks recapture Edessa
1146 Second Crusade

1148 Crusaders are defeated at Damascus
1187 Saladin recaptures Jerusalem and most of the Holy Land
1189 Third Crusade
1192 King Richard of England makes peace with Saladin after failing to recapture Jerusalem

1204 Fourth Crusade, French knights plunder and burn Constantinople
1212 Children's Crusade. 30,000 children set off from France and Germany for Jerusalem. They fail to reach the Holy Land and thousands are sold into slavery
1217 Fifth Crusade. Three-year campaign fails to recapture Egypt

1228 Sixth Crusade. Emperor Frederick II regains Jerusalem by diplomacy

1243 Muslims recapture Jerusalem
1248 Seventh Crusade. Most of the French army is eventually captured

---

Opinions about events can be expressed in many ways, e.g. by what a writer decides to include or to leave out, or by the words used.

1. Find events which are included in one timeline and left out of the other. Why did one author leave these out? Why did the other author include them?
2. Find two words in each timeline which express an opinion. Explain why you have chosen those words.
3. Each timeline is divided into stages. The first is divided by headings, such as Occupation. The second is divided into numbered Crusades. Why are they divided in these different ways?

Living together

The Frankish Invasions covered a long period. In that time the Holy Land was not usually at war. In fact there were only a handful of major battles and sieges over the 200 years. In the long periods of peace, the Christians and Muslims learned to live and work together.

SOURCE 30 Written by Fulcher of Chartres in 1127/520

"We who were Westerners have become Easterners. The man who was a Frank has here become a Palestinian. We have already forgotten the places where we were born. Some have married a wife who is a Syrian, or even a Saracen who has become a Christian. He who was once a stranger here is now a native.

SOURCE 31 Written by Usamah Ibn Munqidh, a Muslim living in Syria during the Frankish Invasions

I used to enter the al-Aqsa Mosque, when it was occupied by the Christians, who were my friends. The Christians would leave the little adjoining mosque so that I could pray in it.

One day, however, a Frank rushed on me, got hold of me and turned my face eastwards, saying, 'This is the way you should pray.' The Templars returned and threw the man out and apologised, saying, 'This is a stranger who has only recently arrived from France, and he has only ever seen people praying eastward.'

SOURCE 32 Written by Ibn Jubayr, a Muslim historian, when he visited the Holy Land in 1184/579

The Christians make the Muslims pay a tax, which is applied fairly. The Christian merchants in turn pay a duty on their goods when they pass through the territory of the Muslims. There is complete understanding between the two sides.

SOURCE 34 A place of learning – the Baghdad library

If the Frankish settlers had travelled beyond the narrow coastal strip, what would they have seen? Look at Sources 34 and 35.

SOURCE 35 A place of culture – a music recital, with a working man in the background

SOURCE 33 An engraving of a Christian and a Muslim playing chess, from the 1250s/640s

Activity

You are a crusader who has settled in the Holy Land. Write a letter back to your family in Europe describing the good and bad things about living in the Holy Land. Use Sources 11–35 to say what has and has not impressed you.

Saladin 'The Merciful'? . . . Richard 'The Lionheart'?

IN THE twelfth/sixth century, the Muslims began to fight back against the Frankish invasions. By the 1180s/570s, under the leadership of Saladin, they had won back Jerusalem and most of the Holy Land. In response, the Christians launched the Third Crusade. This became a struggle between two great leaders: Saladin and King Richard I of England.

SOURCE 1 Portrait of Saladin by an Egyptian artist. Pictures of Islamic leaders are very rare

Saladin is one of the few Islamic leaders who make it regularly into our school history books. See if you can work out why by reading Sources 2–4.

SOURCE 2 A description of Saladin by one of his friends and advisers

❝Small and frail with a short neat beard, his thoughtful and sad face would light up with a comforting smile that would put anyone talking to him at ease.❞

SOURCE 3 Written by Baha al-Din, one of Saladin's officials

❝I never saw him find the enemy too powerful. He would think carefully about each aspect of the situation and take the necessary steps to deal with it, without becoming angry. At the battle for Acre, the centre of the Muslim army was broken, but he stood firm with a handful of men and led them into battle again.❞

SOURCE 4 Written by Baha al-Din

❝A scout came to us with a sobbing Frankish woman. 'Yesterday some Muslim thieves entered my tent and stole my little girl. I cried all night and our commanders told me: "The King of the Muslims is merciful".' Saladin was touched, and tears came to his eyes. He sent someone to the slave market to look for the girl. Less than an hour later a horseman arrived bearing the child on his shoulders. Thus was her daughter returned to her.❞

1. Compare the portrait of Saladin in Source 1 with the description in Source 2. Do they give a similar impression of him?
2. Read Source 4. What did the Frankish commanders think of Saladin?
3. Was their opinion justified?
4. Do you think these sources give us the whole picture of Saladin's character?

SOURCE 5 A painting of Richard entering the city of Acre in 1191/586. Richard is on horseback, nearest to the front of the picture. This picture was painted about 100 years ago

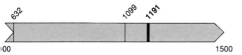

In 1191 Richard and Saladin's armies came up against each other at Acre. Sources 7, 8 and 9 are three views of what happened after the siege, which ended in victory for Richard.

SOURCE 6 A jousting match between Richard and Saladin. The picture was drawn in Western Europe. They never actually met

SOURCE 7

❝Saladin offered to surrender the city of Acre and the Christian prisoners, if Richard would let the Muslims leave the city. In return, they would give 200,000 gold pieces. As a guarantee that they would carry out these conditions, they offered as hostages all the men of noble rank in the city. The space of one month was fixed for Saladin to hand over the money and the Christian prisoners.

When the month had passed, Richard waited for three weeks to see if Saladin would keep his word. When it became clear that Saladin had not taken any steps to keep his word, Richard ordered 2700 of the Muslim hostages to be led forth from the city and hanged. His soldiers marched forward with delight to take revenge upon those who had destroyed so many Christians.❞

SOURCE 9 Richard watching the execution of the Muslim hostages. Painted in the thirteenth/seventh century in western Europe

SOURCE 8

If Saladin handed over the money, Richard was to allow the Muslim hostages to go free, but if the money was not given they were to be taken into slavery. When Saladin delayed in paying the money, Richard broke his word to the hostages. He put his secret plan into effect, even after he had received the money and the Christian prisoners.

He and his army marched to the centre of the Plain. Then they brought up the Muslim prisoners, more than 3000 men in chains. They fell on them as one man and massacred them in cold blood with sword and lance. Many reasons were given for this slaughter. One was that they had killed them as revenge for the Christians killed by Muslims. Another was that Richard had decided to march on Ascalon and did not want to leave behind him a large number of enemy soldiers.❞

5. Which figure in Source 6 do you think is meant to be Saladin?
6. What do Sources 7 and 8 disagree about?
7. Whose side do you think the writers of Sources 7 and 8 are on?
8. Which of the two accounts of the events at Acre does Source 9 support the most?
9. Do Sources 1–9 show Saladin and Richard to be similar kinds of men?

Who benefited from the Crusades?

YOU will probably agree that in the short run the Muslims won the long war against the crusaders. The Christian countries of Western Europe had to give up the idea of capturing Jerusalem and the Holy Land. Their armies returned home defeated, leaving the Muslims in control of the Middle East. But who benefited the most in the long term?

Effects on the West

Let us look first at the effects on the Christian West.

Most historians agree that after the Crusades Europe prospered. They also agree that many aspects of European life benefited from ideas from the East. Europe's trade increased, and its sailors began to discover and explore the rest of the world. Advances were made in science and medicine, and in art and architecture. European languages and eating habits also changed. The result was that 100 years after the Crusades the lives of many people had changed as a result of the influence of Islamic societies.

> **SOURCE 1** New ideas introduced to the West from the Islamic world
>
> ■ *Arabic numerals were used instead of Roman ones. You have already seen how much easier it is to use Arabic numerals.*
> ■ *Banks were introduced in Europe as a result of the Crusades. Banks lent money to businesses which helped them to grow.*
> ■ *Windmills were built from Islamic designs.*
> ■ *Stirrups were introduced, which made it easier for soldiers to fight on horseback.*
> ■ *Messages were sent by carrier pigeon.*
> ■ *Hand grenades began to be used in battle.*
> ■ *Most of the books of the Greeks and Romans had been lost in the West but as we have already seen the Arabs had large collections of them. These books contained ideas about medicine, science and mathematics. Copies of these books found their way to the West and encouraged scholars to develop all kinds of new ideas in medicine and science.*

> **SOURCE 2** Products introduced to the West from the Islamic Empire
>
> *Rice, coffee, spices (for preserving food), perfumes, cotton cloth for clothing, carpets (for walls and floors), sherbet, raisins, glass mirrors, melons, dates, paper for writing, enamel ware for plates and jugs, apricots, rhubarb, sugar, lemons, slippers.*

Western cities like Venice and Pisa became centres for trading these goods. Gradually, all over Europe, towns grew and developed. The MERCHANTS became rich from the profits from trading with the East.

SOURCE 3 The idea of chemists' shops where a wide variety of drugs could be bought was introduced to the West from the Islamic world. This is a seventeenth-century chemist's shop in Paris

SOURCE 4 The castle of Krak des Chevaliers in the Holy Land. The idea of castles with concentric walls was introduced from the East and influenced the design of castles such as Beaumaris in Anglesey

SOURCE 5 Sailors using compasses. The idea of using compasses and astrolabes for navigation came from the East

How much change did the East bring to Europe?
1. In pairs, use the following headings to organise all the changes shown in Sources 1–5 into groups:
   ■ What people looked and smelled like, and what they ate
   ■ What houses looked like inside
   ■ Fighting
   ■ Travelling and communications
   ■ Running a business
   ■ Treating sick people
   ■ Changes to the landscape.
2. In which group do you think there was the most change?
3. Is there anything important which we use today which might not have been developed without contact with the East?
4. Why might the faith of Islam not have spread much to the West after the Crusades, while its products and ideas did?

WHO BENEFITED FROM THE CRUSADES?

Effects on the East

What about the effects on the Islamic world? Look at Source 6. According to this source, what were the effects of the Frankish Invasions on the Muslims?

> ### SOURCE 6
> "The Crusades started an economic and cultural revolution in Western Europe. But the Muslim world turned in on itself. It became over-sensitive, defensive and intolerant."

We can get a good idea of what the Islamic world was like 50 years after the end of the Frankish Invasions from the writings of Ibn Battuta (see Source 7). He probably travelled further than anyone else of his time. He spent 25 years visiting every Muslim country, and travelled over 70,000 miles. Let us see whether he gives any evidence to support the statement in Source 6.

1. Read Source 7. As you are looking at these extracts from Ibn Battuta's travel writings, see if you can find any evidence of the following:
   - Islam still very worried about the Frankish Invasions
   - hatred of Christians
   - suspicion of outsiders
   - the Muslim religion becoming inward-looking and dead, not open to new influences.

Activity
You have been given the job of interviewing Ibn Battuta about his travels.
   Write out your questions and his answers.
   Try to ask questions about what he has noticed. Make sure you ask questions about the three points listed in question 1.

SOURCE 7 Written by Ibn Battuta around 1350/750

a) In Egypt

"As protection against spies from Iraq, they smooth down the sand at nightfall so that no track is left on it. In the morning, the governor comes and looks at the sand. If he finds any track he commands the Arabs to find the person who made it.

b) In Uzbeg

I have never seen people more generous or friendly to strangers.

c) In Damascus at the time of the Black Death

After the dawn prayer they all went out together on foot, holding Qurans in their hands. The procession was joined by the entire population of the town, men and women and children; the Jews came with their Book of the Law and the Christians with their Gospel. Everyone sought the favour of God. God did help them. The number of deaths in a single day did not reach 2000, while in Cairo it reached 24,000 a day.

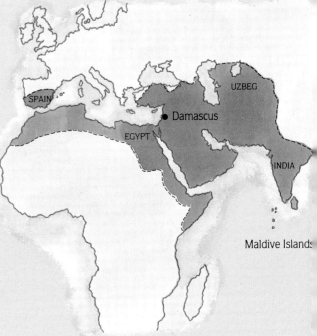

d) In India

The women of this town and all the coastal districts are beautiful and virtuous, and each wears a gold ring in her nose. Another unusual thing about them is that they all learn the Quran by heart. I saw in the town thirteen schools for girls, a thing I have never seen elsewhere.

Source 8 was written by the Muslim historian Ibn al-Athir while the battles against the crusaders were still going on.

SOURCE 8

The events I am about to describe are so horrible that for years I avoided all mention of them. It is not easy to announce that death has fallen upon Islam and the Muslims. Alas! I would have preferred my mother never to have given birth to me, or to have died without witnessing all these evils. Not until the end of time will such a disaster be seen again.

was invaded by the Mongols, a warrior tribe from central Asia. They swept across Persia and Iraq and eventually destroyed Baghdad. Ibn al-Athir writes much more about the Mongol Invasions than about the Frankish Invasions.

2. Which do you think the Muslims were more worried about, the Frankish Invasions or the Mongol Invasions?
3. What impression does Source 9 give you of the Mongols?

But Ibn al-Athir isn't describing the Crusades. He is actually describing another, more serious, invasion. While the Crusades were still going on, the Islamic world

e) In the Maldive Islands

The Qadi [judge] is held in greater respect among the people than all other officials. His orders are obeyed as though they were the ruler's. There is no prison. Criminals are kept in wooden cases, held fast by a piece of wood, as we do in Morocco with Christian prisoners.

f) In Spain

I then proposed to take part in the Jihad [holy war] and the defence of the frontier, so I crossed the sea to Spain. This was after the death of the Christian tyrant Alphonso XI and his ten-month siege of Gibraltar, when he thought that he would capture all that the Muslims still hold of Spain.

SOURCE 9 Mongol workmen building a royal palace

The Islamic Empire reborn?

LOOK at the timeline. It shows the main events in the history of Islam. You can see that at first one ruler governed much of the Islamic Empire. Then in around 800/183 the Empire began to break up, and was governed by several rulers. Many of these rulers did not survive long. They were assassinated, or deposed after civil wars.

However in about 1400/802 there was another change. The Empire came together again under the OTTOMANS. They were Muslims from Turkey, and had conquered much of the Islamic world.

The great ambition of the Ottoman Emperor, Mehmed II, was to capture Constantinople, which no Muslim ruler had ever managed to do. He wanted to make it his capital city. Constantinople was the capital of the Eastern Roman Empire (also called the Byzantine Empire). Although it was not as great as it had once been, it was still a magnificent city. It was also important because of its position (see Source 1).

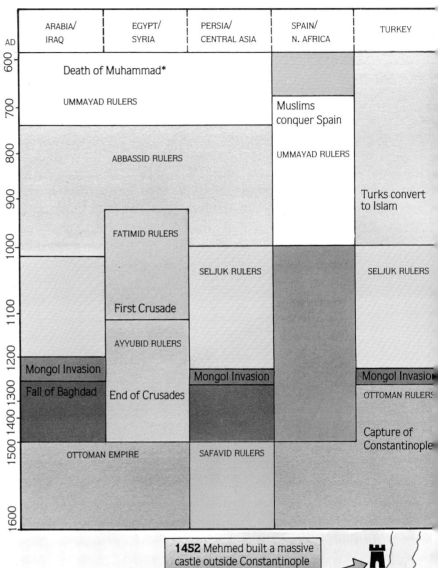

	ARABIA/ IRAQ	EGYPT/ SYRIA	PERSIA/ CENTRAL ASIA	SPAIN/ N. AFRICA	TURKEY
AD 600	Death of Muhammad*				
700	UMMAYAD RULERS			Muslims conquer Spain	
800	ABBASSID RULERS			UMMAYAD RULERS	
900					Turks convert to Islam
1000		FATIMID RULERS			
1100			SELJUK RULERS		SELJUK RULERS
		First Crusade			
1200		AYYUBID RULERS			
1300	Mongol Invasion / Fall of Baghdad	End of Crusades	Mongol Invasion		Mongol Invasion / OTTOMAN RULERS
1400					Capture of Constantinople
1500	OTTOMAN EMPIRE		SAFAVID RULERS		
1600					

---

1. Look at Source 1. Why were the Ottomans so keen to capture Constantinople?

▶ **SOURCE 2** Mehmed's campaign

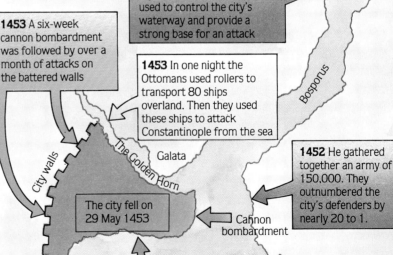

1452 Mehmed built a massive castle outside Constantinople in just three months. It was used to control the city's waterway and provide a strong base for an attack

1453 A six-week cannon bombardment was followed by over a month of attacks on the battered walls

1453 In one night the Ottomans used rollers to transport 80 ships overland. Then they used these ships to attack Constantinople from the sea

1452 He gathered together an army of 150,000. They outnumbered the city's defenders by nearly 20 to 1.

The city fell on 29 May 1453

Cannon bombardment

Bosporus

Galata

The Golden Horn

City walls

Cannon bombardment

BYZANTINE EMPIRE
Black Sea
● Constantinople
OTTOMAN EMPIRE

▶ **SOURCE 1**

Rebuilding Istanbul

> **SOURCE 3** A Turkish writer records how Mehmed rebuilt Istanbul (the new Islamic name for Constantinople)
>
> *'Whoever wishes, let him come, and let him become owner of houses and vineyards.' And they gave them to everyone who came. The Sultan then gave orders to send families, both rich and poor, from every province . . . Houses were given to them and the city began to fill up. They built mosques and private houses and the city became great again.* **"**

Within 25 years, the population of the city had risen ten times to 80,000, and Istanbul was a thriving capital city.

► **SOURCE 4** A bath-house in Istanbul

◄ **SOURCE 5** Istanbul in the sixteenth/tenth century

> **1.** Look at Sources 4 and 5. Why would each building shown be important in an Islamic city?

What did the Ottomans achieve?

The Empire thrived under the Ottomans. By 1526/
932 they had conquered the area shown in Source 8
and were threatening to capture Vienna.

> 1. Look at Sources 6 and 7. Are the defences of
>   Vienna better than the defences of Arg?
> 2. Are the Ottomans' methods of attack and
>   siege at Vienna better than in the earlier
>   siege?

SOURCE 7 The siege of Arg by the Turks in 1003/
392, painted in the fourteenth/eighth century

Despite a long siege, the Ottomans failed to
capture Vienna, and they never advanced further
into Europe. But their Empire covered much of the
Islamic world and remained powerful for another
400 years, into the twentieth/fourteenth century.
The Ottomans built many magnificent buildings all
around their Empire (see Sources 9–12).

SOURCE 8 The Ottoman Empire

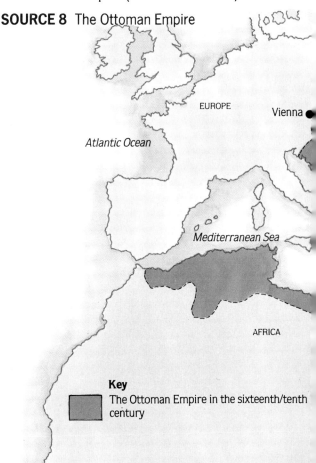

Key

The Ottoman Empire in the sixteenth/tenth
century

SOURCE 6 The siege of Vienna, 1526/932

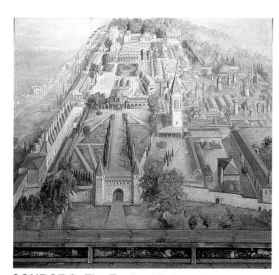

SOURCE 9 The Topkapi Palace in Istanbul

SOURCE 10 An Ottoman bridge which is still standing today

SOURCE 11 Engraving of Suleyman, one of the most successful Ottoman rulers. In the background you can see the Suleymaniye mosque, which was named after him. The Ottomans did not follow the general Muslim rule of not making pictures of rulers

> **3.** Look at Source 11. How does this engraving suggest that Suleyman was proud of his mosque?

SOURCE 12 A Turkish writer records the reactions of European visitors to the Suleymaniye mosque, which had one of the biggest domes in the world

> 66 *I once saw ten Frankish infidels who . . . when they saw the dome, tossed up their hats and cried out. One of them said that nowhere was so much beauty inside and outside to be found united. In the whole of Europe there was not a single building that could be compared to this.* 99

> **1.** Do you think the Islamic Empire changed much under the Ottomans? Working in pairs, use the following headings to compare the Arab Empire in 750/132 with the Ottoman Empire in 1500/905: the size of the Empire, art, buildings, methods of conquest.

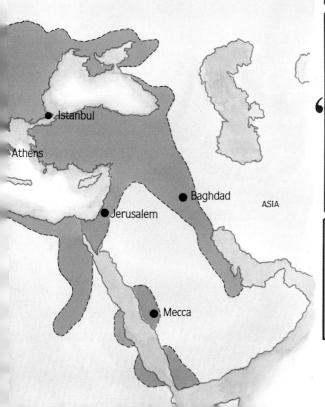

What makes a mosque?

AT THE heart of every Islamic city is a central mosque, called the Friday mosque. All Muslim men are meant to go there on Fridays for the weekly prayers and sermon.

> 1. Sources 1–3 show mosques in different places, built at different times. Using the information below, put the mosques in the correct chronological order.

SOURCE 1

Stage 1
Mosques were modelled on Muhammad's* house in Medinah — a courtyard with a covered area to one side — a typical town house of the time.

Stage 2
Mosques grew bigger as Islam grew. Domes were introduced, as decoration and as a symbol of Heaven arching over the earth.

Stage 3
The great mosque in Damascus had square towers at the corners, from which the people were called to prayer. Some new mosques, particularly in cities, copied this style and built square MINARETS on the mosque.

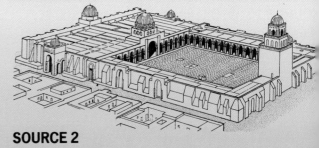

SOURCE 2

Stage 4
As Islam spread to countries with different climates, the mosque architecture changed. In rainy places, the courtyard was sometimes left out altogether.

Stage 5
Architects competed to build the biggest and finest mosques. Sinan, an Ottoman builder, said 'With the help of God, I made the dome of the Selimye mosque wider and deeper than the dome of the cathedral of St Sophia' (which had previously been the biggest dome in the world). Domes were used for the main roof, instead of just as decoration. Minarets became circular, very tall and highly decorated.

SOURCE 3

Inside a mosque

Mihrab

Minbar

Kursi

Fountain

Rack

SOURCE 4 Reconstruction of the features of a mosque

---

1. Can you match up the features shown in Source 4 with their uses?
   - Alcove to show which way to bow towards Mecca
   - Where the preacher stands to give his sermon
   - Where worshippers leave their shoes
   - For ritual washing before prayer
   - For supporting the Quran.

2. Look at Source 5. How many people are involved in the running of this mosque? Who else might be needed who isn't mentioned here?

3. What might a) the matting, b) the spices, c) earthenware jars, d) the oxen be used for?

4. How many of the things that money was set aside for in 1010/400 might not be needed today? Explain your answer.

SOURCE 5 A list of money spent on the great mosque of Cairo in 1010/400

❝For the preacher: 84 dinars
For matting: 108 dinars
For glass lamps: $12\frac{3}{4}$ dinars
For spices and the attendant in charge of them: 15 dinars
For sweeping the mosque: 5 dinars
For 200 brooms to sweep the mosque: $1\frac{1}{4}$ dinars
For earthenware water jars and the cost of moving them: 3 dinars
For the wages of 3 people who lead the prayers, 4 caretakers, 5 muezzins [men who call the people to prayer] and the superintendant: $556\frac{1}{2}$ dinars
For sweeping the cistern: 1 dinar
For straw for the oxen of the cistern: 8 dinars
For wages of the person who feeds the oxen and the water carrier: $15\frac{1}{2}$ dinars
For paying the man in charge of the washing basin: 12 dinars❞

Contrasting civilisations

What does it mean to be civilised? Does it mean different things to people of different cultures and religions?

How important do you think each of the following ideas were to:
a) people in medieval England
b) people in the Islamic world?
- to be clean
- to be strong and make conquests
- to have beautiful buildings and art
- to be good at science and medicine
- to be rich
- to be tolerant of people who were different
- to look after the poor.

Write this list out twice. First, put the ideas in order of importance to people in medieval England. Second, put them in order of importance to Muslims in the Islamic Empire. The sources and the timeline on this page will help you, but you will also need to look back through the book to remind yourself of certain subjects in the list.

Explain the order you have chosen. You can use simple drawings to explain your choice.

SOURCE 1 From records about libraries in the ninth/third century

66 *In the ninth/third century the largest library in Christian Europe had 36 books. At the same time the Islamic library in Cordoba contained half a million.* 99

1. With a partner, draw up lists of the following:
- causes of air pollution
- arguments for or against the breast-feeding of babies.

Now compare your ideas with those of Ibn Sina in Source 2. You are living 1000 years after Ibn Sina. Are your answers any better than his?

SOURCE 2 Advice from Ibn Sina's book, *The Canon of Medicine*

66 a) *Whenever possible babies should be fed on their mother's milk, because that is the food most like what they have been feeding on in the womb.*

b) *Air is good when it is not contaminated with the vapours from marshes and lakes or canals and open sewers, or the gases from chemical works, or smoke or soot.*

SOURCE 3 An Astrolabe

Using their knowledge of maths, science and geography, Muslim scientists were able to use the Astrolabe to map their position by measuring the distance of the sun and stars. It was very useful to European travellers when they discovered America and other places in t... fifteenth century.

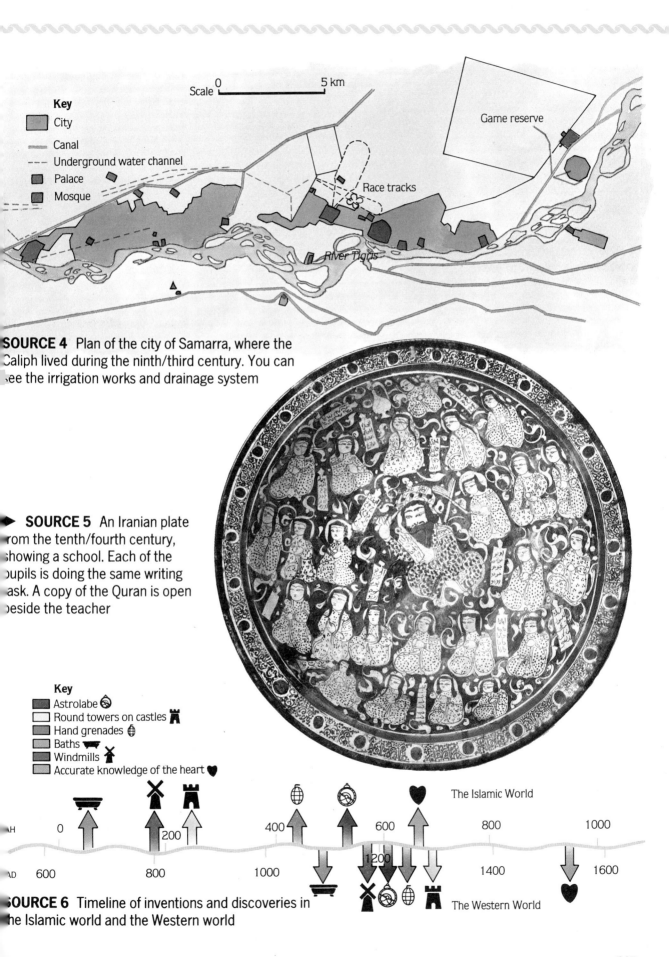

SOURCE 4 Plan of the city of Samarra, where the Caliph lived during the ninth/third century. You can see the irrigation works and drainage system

Key
- City
- Canal
- Underground water channel
- Palace
- Mosque

Game reserve

Race tracks

River Tigris

Scale 0 — 5 km

SOURCE 5 An Iranian plate from the tenth/fourth century, showing a school. Each of the pupils is doing the same writing task. A copy of the Quran is open beside the teacher

Key
- Astrolabe
- Round towers on castles
- Hand grenades
- Baths
- Windmills
- Accurate knowledge of the heart

The Islamic World

AH   0   200   400   600   800   1000

AD 600   800   1000   1200   1400   1600

The Western World

SOURCE 6 Timeline of inventions and discoveries in the Islamic world and the Western world

215

Glossary

Abbassid a family of **caliphs** who ruled the Islamic world 750–1258. Their capital was Baghdad

AD stands for *Anno Domini* which means 'in the year of the Lord'. It is used for dates after the birth of Christ. Muslims call AD dates CE, which stands for Christian Era

AH stands for After Hijra. It is used by Muslims to describe dates after AD622 (see **Hijra**)

Al Arabic for 'the'

amphitheatre a round arena in a Roman city where **gladiator** fights took place

Anglo-Saxons people from Germany who ruled England from the fifth century until 1066

aqueduct channel bringing water to Roman towns, sometimes raised on arches

Arab an inhabitant of Arabia, or native speaker of the Arabic language

archaeologist person who studies past peoples, usually by digging for remains they have left behind, such as buildings or tools. These remains are called **archaeological** evidence

barbarian the name the Romans gave to all the **tribes** on the northern frontiers of their Empire including Goths, Huns, Franks, etc.

bailiff a medieval manor official appointed by the lord (see **reeve** and **steward**)

baron a powerful lord who was granted land by the King (see **Feudal System**)

Basilica a Roman building found in every town, where business deals, official ceremonies and law courts took place

BC Before Christ. BC years are counted backwards from the birth of Christ, so 200BC comes before 100BC

bishop a man in charge of the affairs of the Christian Church over a large area called a diocese

boon-work see **week-work**

Byzantine name given to the Eastern Roman Empire after the collapse of the Western Empire

Caliph a ruler of the Islamic world, a successor of Muhammad*

Carthaginians North African people from Carthage who were Rome's main rival for control of the Mediterranean until 201BC

Celts people living in Britain and northern France before the Romans invaded the area

centurion Roman soldier in charge of a group of about 80–100 men called a century

Charter a medieval document setting out the rights of a town or a group of people

Christendom a collective word for all the countries where Christianity was the main religion, or all the Christians in the world

citizen free adult males who could vote and had special rights in the Roman state. People in **provinces** could earn Roman citizenship by, for example, serving in the army for 25 years

civitas capital town of a tribal area in the **provinces** of the Roman Empire

clergy all the people such as priests, monks, nuns who have been appointed to perform religious duties in the Christian Church

colonia (colony) Roman town in a province, lived in only by retired Roman soldiers and their families

consul highest and most powerful official in the Roman Republic. Two consuls were elected for a year at a time

Crusade a holy war to conquer the Holy Land declared by Christians during the Middle Ages

demesne the part of the **manor** farmed by the lord himself in the Middle Ages

dictator a ruler who could take decisions without consulting the Roman **Senate**. A dictator could be appointed in an extreme emergency to hold absolute power for six months

Druid Celtic priest in Roman times

Emperor the powerful ruler of the Roman Empire, from Augustus onwards. Emperors were not elected and did not have to consult the Senate

Empire the large area of territory controlled by a powerful country

Feudal System the way society was organised throughout Western Europe during the Middle Ages. The King gave land to a small number of powerful men such as barons, knights or lords. In return they supported the King and provided him with an army when he needed one. Ordinary people had to perform various duties for the barons, knights and lords

Forum open market square in a Roman town or city where all the important public buildings were found

Frank/Franj Muslim term for a Westerner

freeman a peasant who had achieved some freedom from the lord (see **villein**)

Gaul more or less the area of modern France, occupied by the Gauls

gladiators Roman warriors who fought to the death against other gladiators or animals

governor highest official in a Roman province

guild an association of merchants, or workers with a particular craft

Hadith something the Prophet Muhammad* is believed to have said or done

Haj pilgrimage to Mecca, which a Muslim is supposed to make at least once in his/her life

Hijra Muhammad*'s journey from Mecca to Medinah

Holy Land the area of the Eastern Mediterranean including many places such as Jerusalem which are holy to the Jews, the Christians and the Muslims

Ibn Arabic for 'son of'

idol an object worshipped as if it were a god

Islam the religion based on the teachings of the Prophet Muhammad*. The word Islam means 'submitting', i.e. submitting to God